LONG S...

SUMMER

THE YEAR OF THE FOUR ENGLAND CRICKET CAPTAINS 1988

NEIL ROBINSON

AMBERLEY

First published 2015

Amberley Publishing
The Hill, Stroud
Gloucestershire, GL5 4EP
www.amberley-books.com

British Library Cataloguing in Publication Data.
A catalogue record for this book is available from the British Library.

ISBN 978 1 4456 3758 7 (print)
ISBN 978 1 4456 3772 3 (ebook)

Typesetting and Origination by Amberley Publishing.
Printed in the UK.

Contents

Contents

Acknowledgements

There are several people without whose help and support the writing of this book would have been near impossible. I must thank Chris Cowdrey, John Emburey, Mike Gatting, Graham Gooch, Micky Stewart and Louise Shipman for generously giving up their time and recalling events that they might have preferred to leave buried. Don Mew, whose tireless networking and advocacy on my behalf opened so many doors, has been an invaluable help, as has Derek Prince, whose enthusiasm and interest never failed to break the ice. I am grateful too to Mrs Judy Martin-Jenkins for allowing me to quote from her late husband's notebooks, and to the late Bill Frindall whose detailed scoresheets allowed the cricket of 1988 to come to life again. The proofreading skills of Glenys Williams and Robert Curphey have been greatly appreciated, as has the support of many colleagues at MCC, notably Adam Chadwick, Colin Maynard and Clare Skinner. Andrea Quaine and Jo Davis of the Lord's Taverners also provided valuable assistance.

1

Pick Your Own England Team

There comes a time in life when the games played in childhood are played once more. In December 2013, during a lull between courses at the annual lunch of the Master's Club, which gathers at the Oval once per year to remember the great Surrey and England batsman Sir Jack Hobbs, a guest on my table passed round a piece of paper. Upon it, he asked his companions to inscribe their choice of eleven players for England's first Test match against Sri Lanka the following spring. At the time, the England team was about halfway through a catastrophic tour of Australia, which would see the surrender of the Ashes and calls for wholesale changes in English cricket. It was an appalling comedown for a team that only a few months earlier had achieved a convincing home victory over the same opposition and had embarked on their tour with some prominent pundits confidently predicting a 5-0 whitewash in their favour. Instead, there was a feeling of giants humbled, and of careers coming towards a less than glorious close.

The parlour game played at the Master's Club lunch was certainly topical, but it was also something of a novelty. An almost unprecedented decade of stability seemed to have made amateur selection debates of this kind a thing of the past. For a time, the progression of the England Test side from match to match, from series to series had been accompanied by a rare sense of continuity. Changes seemed to be planned well in advance and were managed with skill and sensitivity. Players who were an integral part of the side would, if they fell out of form, be helped to find it again through work with a backroom staff of expert coaches. Above all, they would be helped by the knowledge that their next poor display would not simply see them consigned to the outer darkness of county cricket, their Test careers written off forever by selectors, media and public alike. Young players coming into the side for the first time suddenly found themselves with several games in which to find their feet, and that their performances in that series were not judged solely in terms of runs scored or wickets taken, but as a starting point in from which their potential for future development would be assessed. They were helped too by having, in most cases, been part of a development programme aimed at identifying young cricketers with potential to play at international level from an early age. It was just what legions of former players and expert commentators had been saying for years should happen. The results were obvious. For a modern generation of cricket fans, this seemed to be the established status quo. And for all they knew it might always have been this way.

The members of the Master's Club were old enough to know how different the state of English cricket had usually been throughout its long and turbulent existence. In previous eras, the end of one Test match or series had often been followed by a protracted debate about the personnel likely to be taking part in the next. All across the land schoolboys pored over the scores and averages printed in the daily newspapers and friends argued out the permutations over a few pints down the local pub; club members in their pavilions, journalists in their press boxes and ordinary cricket fans, huddled together under blankets and umbrellas at windswept cricket grounds from Bodmin to Berwick, wondered where to turn next. Had old so-and-so had his last chance? Was young whatsit really living up to his promise? That other young lad they tried at the Oval, a talented strokeplayer certainly, but did he really have the technique for the highest level? Perhaps A was a fine player of spin, but wouldn't B be a better bet against top-class fast bowling? Was there any point playing a spinner at Headingley? And who, *who* might replace Ian Botham?

So were careers dissected, dismissed and discarded. To any fan painstakingly watching the county scores and averages from one Test disappointment to the next, it seemed the most natural thing in the world. It was a mindset everybody shared, a game everybody played. For the guests at the Master's Club lunch it was all too familiar. I had never realised quite how deeply engrained it was in the psyche of English cricket until I began researching this book, and it reached its apotheosis in the summer of 1988.

Like many of my generation, my passion for cricket was really ignited during the summer of 1981. England's Ashes triumph that year has been largely credited to a change of tack by the England selectors, not least their chairman, Alec Bedser. In relieving a beleaguered Ian Botham of the burden of captaincy following the Lord's Test, Bedser gave Botham the freedom he needed to play his natural game and also gave him, in the form of returning captain Mike Brearley, the kind of 'father confessor' figure England's wayward champion so badly needed. Was it a stroke of genius by Bedser? Or was he simply following the established pattern for England selectors? If you have even the slightest suspicion that it might be broke, for pity's sake fix it.

Brearley, of course, was a short-term solution; he was coming to the end of his cricket career and had no desire to lead England on an overseas tour. A new man would be needed for that task, and the job of selecting him would fall to a new man as well. At the end of that glorious summer, Bedser stepped down as Chairman of Selectors and handed over to his old England and Surrey colleague, Peter May. It was a golden year for May. He had spent the summer serving a one-year term as president of Marylebone Cricket Club – one of the game's greatest honours, and one which provided the theme for an interview he gave to Christopher Martin-Jenkins, then editor of *The Cricketer* in November 1981. The subject of Test selection was never far below the surface though, and the question of May's choice of man to succeed Mike Brearley was one Martin-Jenkins addressed directly. May had gone for Keith Fletcher, captain of Essex. Fletcher had had a fairly successful Test career as a batsman in the late 1960s and 1970s, but he was now thirty-seven years old and had not played a single Test since the last tour of India five years previously. Since then, however, he had turned Essex into one of the most formidable teams on the county circuit. It was his reputation as a sound captain, rather than his potential as a pivotal batsman, that had got him the job. However, as with Brearley, his age made his appointment open to question: 'Do you intend Keith Fletcher to be a long-term appointment as captain?' was the question Christopher Martin-Jenkins posed. Peter May's answer to it is central to everything that follows in these pages: 'I hope so' he said. 'There's no point in chopping and changing.'

May would bear the principal responsibility for selecting England sides for the next seven years. Over the course of his tenure it is probably fair to say that the prestige of English cricket endured something of a decline. It did not help that immediately after Fletcher's Indian tour and before May and his colleagues had the chance to sit down and choose their first team for a home Test match, several senior players embarked upon a rebel tour of South Africa and were issued with three-year bans from selection for international cricket by the Test and County Cricket Board (TCCB). Some of these players were, in any case, at the end of their careers, among them Geoff Boycott, Derek Underwood and Alan Knott. But others, such as Graham Gooch and John Emburey, were at their peak, and expected to be part of the Test side for years to come. The loss of Boycott and Gooch together meant that when May chaired the first selection meeting of the summer of 1982, he and his fellow selectors had to pick an entirely new pair of opening batsmen. They also ended up sacking Fletcher and choosing a new captain. It was hardly the start May would have dreamed of.

Other setbacks would follow: a first ever home Test defeat to New Zealand in 1983, the first against Pakistan since 1954 at Lord's in 1982. However, in between those disappointments came some notable successes. The painful 5-0 'blackwash' at the hands of Clive Lloyd's West Indies in 1984 was followed by a thrilling recovery from 1-0 down to win a difficult Test series in India. Then, in 1985, the return of the South African exiles Gooch and Emburey helped England to see off the old enemy in a 3-1 Ashes victory, which relieved the misery of one of the most sodden summers in living memory.

The promise of those two victories was soon extinguished by another blackwash in the Caribbean in the early spring of 1986; the West Indies stalked those years like a fearful spectre. Over the decade that began with their coming of age under Lloyd in 1976, England went up against them in five Test series and failed to win a single match. It seemed that any promising beginning to a young English player's career, any nascent new era for the team as a whole, would inevitably be snuffed out at the first sight of a maroon cap or the first few syllables in Clive Lloyd's Guyanese drawl of 'we'll have a bowl.'

Following the second blackwash, England's misery extended into their own summer. The scheduling of a West Indies tour did not help. By the time the final Test concluded with a 280-run defeat on 16 April, the County Championship season was just ten days away. The first Test against India began at Lord's just seven weeks later on 5 June. Tired minds warped by the West Indies' relentless assault were left with no time for recovery. A five-wicket defeat was sufficient to see a jaded Gower relieved of the captaincy. His replacement for the second Test at Headingley, Mike Gatting, could be forgiven for having somewhat mixed feelings about the appointment. Gatting's frustratingly unfulfilled Test career had finally blossomed under Gower's leadership on the tour of India in 1984/85. Granted the dual responsibilities of the vice-captaincy and the No.3 slot in the batting order, this vastly talented batsman had at last found his feet and produced, over that series and the Ashes summer that followed, four centuries of the highest quality. Perhaps the best of these was his 207 at Madras, an innings at the very heart of a nine-wicket victory – one of the finest England wins of the decade. However, Gatting's very selection for that tour had been a matter of some debate.

'David was under pressure not to pick me,' Gatting recalled in an interview for the MCC Audio Archive in 2008. 'I think there were certain people who felt that I'd had enough chances, but he [Gower] stuck his neck out and said "look, Mike's one of the best players of spin we've got in the country."' Indeed, not just certain selectors, but significant sections of the cricket press and public were of the opinion that Gatting's time had gone. His recall for the Lord's Test in 1984 had had the feeling of the 'last chance saloon' and his ignominious failure in that match, twice out lbw padding up to straight balls from Malcolm Marshall, looked to have brought down the curtain on his England career. 'When the selectors met,' wrote Gower in *On the Rack*, 'I was adamant that he should not only be included but should be my vice-captain. There was some opposition but I won the point, with well-chronicled results. We won the series and his career had at long last taken off.'

This demonstration of personal faith in Gatting had gone a long way to giving the Middlesex batsman the confidence to translate, at last, his outstanding county record into genuine achievement at Test level, and was particularly important given how the batsman had felt about the welcome he received when first chosen for England in 1977:

When I first got in the England side it wasn't very nice. It was all 'you've just come in sonny, you mind your P's and Q's, you sit over there and keep your mouth shut,' when what you really needed was to make young players feel welcome. And that was one thing I said, if I ever got be to captain of England, the first thing I would do is make sure that the young guy who comes in is well looked after, he gets right in the middle of things and is not left out on the side, and snide remarks aren't made. You've still got to prove yourself, but it's nice to know that people want you there, whereas one or two made it very obvious that they didn't think I should be there.

One of David Gower's most significant successes as England captain was in offering Gatting that kind of welcome when he returned to the side for that India tour. 'David was better at that than a few we had,' acknowledges Gatting.

The end of the Gower reign did not come as a particular surprise to Gatting: 'We'd been to the West Indies and got hammered. David was holding optional nets and people were saying "who's in charge of this side?" and there had been a little bit of unrest.' But being asked to take over from the man whose faith in him had allowed his career to blossom and brought him to the position of being the obvious successor to the captaincy caused Gatting some real discomfort; the manner of his appointment did not help.

Peter May came up to me and said 'we want you to captain the side.' I said have you told David? And he said 'no, there's no point telling David unless you say yes.' So I said well, how long have I got? And Peter said 'oh, a couple of minutes if you need them.' Well it wouldn't have taken me a couple of minutes to say yes, but you just think, crikey, it's the one bloke who has helped me to get into Test cricket and I'm being asked to take his job off him.

'It was a messy handover' recalls Gower, 'and Mike did not know what to do or say. For someone who had just been handed the biggest job in cricket, he looked remarkably miserable. For the next few weeks he still called me captain out of long habit.'

Gatting's first match in charge did not exactly go to plan. Dropping down to No.5 in the order as England went in with three opening batsmen, Gatting saw his side destroyed by the medium paced swing of Roger Binny; bowled out for 102 in the first innings and 128 in the second. England were crushed by 279 runs and had surrendered the series 2-0. They had now lost seven Tests in a row. Some face was saved in the final Test at Edgbaston, where an unbeaten 183 from Gatting helped England to a creditable draw. However, a 1-0 defeat to New Zealand in the summer's Second Test series only helped to reinforce the impression that England's cricketers had, as Martin Johnson of *The Independent* put it a few months later, only three problems: 'they can't bat, they can't bowl and they can't field.'

Johnson was swiftly proved wrong. For Mike Gatting, the 1986/87 tour of Australia would turn out to be the high point of his entire career. England retained the Ashes by a comfortable margin of 3-1. The new partnership of Mike Gatting as captain and Micky Stewart as team manager appeared to work well, and a palpable sense of team unity off the field made a significant contribution to success on it.

'My fondest memories of touring with England are of 86/87' remembered John Emburey, who claimed eighteen wickets in that series, in an interview for the England and Wales Cricket Board (ECB) website in 2010. 'The good thing was that everyone got on with each other. The camaraderie was great, the mickey-taking on the field and off the field, and there were no cliques. It is not all hunky-dory when you're off touring for so long, and it can get a bit fractious at times, but it helps enormously if you all get on most of the time.' Another senior player, Ian Botham, echoed Emburey's view in his autobiography:

> It was one of the happiest and most enjoyable tours I'd been on, and Gatt deserves a lot of credit for that. If hard work was needed, he wasn't afraid to ask for it, but for the most part he was content to let his senior pros choose their own workload in training and practice. We were all experienced professionals and Gatt reckoned that we knew better than anyone when we needed to step up the training or put in an extra session of bowling practice, and when we were in good shape and could take our foot off the gas. So he left us to keep ourselves in shape and form, and it paid off in team spirits and results.

In just a few months, Gatting had put together a team that enjoyed success on the field and each other's company off it, in which the vastly experienced likes of Botham and Gower had blended together with unproven talents like Chris Broad and Phillip DeFreitas and allowed them to blossom. It was precisely what he had vowed to do when he considered taking over the job, and in the process he had followed in the footsteps of Len Hutton, Ray Illingworth and his own mentor at Middlesex, Mike Brearley, in skippering a successful Ashes campaign down under. With plenty of young talent emerging through county cricket, the future for the national team looked set fair.

The following summer was beset by frustration and controversy. A five-Test series against a strong Pakistan side was marred by wet weather: England had batted first and set up strong positions in both the first two Tests, only for rain to prevent Pakistan from completing a single innings. Humiliating defeat followed at Headingley, with the visitors' captain, Imran Khan, making far better use of the helpful conditions than England's bowlers to claim a match winning haul of ten wickets. In the Fourth Test at Edgbaston, England made a valiant effort to chase down 124 for victory in the final session, but the run-outs of Gatting, Emburey and Edmonds saw them fall just 15 short with three wickets in hand. In the final Test at the Oval, a magnificent 260 by Javed Miandad put England under huge pressure, but following on a long way behind, England's blushes were saved by Gatting once more, who made an undefeated 150 to save the game. A 1-0 home defeat was not what England had expected after their sensational winter, but, Headingley apart, England had competed well against one of the strongest sides in the world. There was no disgrace in narrow defeat to Imran's Tigers.

However, the atmosphere between the English and Pakistani players had become increasingly toxic. At Headingley, Pakistan wicketkeeper Saleem Yousuf's attempt to claim the wicket of Botham caught behind off Wasim Akram had been exposed by TV replay as grossly dishonest, the ball slipping from his right glove and being scooped up on the bounce by his left. Pakistan's dissatisfaction with umpire David Constant, labelled 'a rude man' by Imran, led them to request that he be stood down for the final Test, a request turned down by the TCCB. Cricketing relations between the two countries had never really got over the treatment of Pakistan umpire Idris Begh on Donald Carr's MCC tour of 1955/56. Begh had a bucket of water tipped over him in what to MCC players and officials had been nothing more than a bit of university style 'ragging' brought on by high spirits, but to the Pakistanis had seemed rather less harmless. Now, personal relationships between some of the players on both sides had deteriorated to a dangerous degree, while Pakistan's long-standing campaign for neutral umpires grew ever more strident. It would have even more shocking consequences in the months to come.

The best thing for both England and Pakistan at this point would have been to spend some time apart to let tempers cool. It was not to be. The schedule for the coming winter would see England arrive in Pakistan for two separate visits. English cricket was about to experience some of the most traumatic months in its long history. For Mike Gatting, the nation's hero just a few months earlier, it would be a low point from which his playing career would never truly recover.

2

'People Have Been Murdered in This Country for Less'

For any cricket historian trying to identify the point when the once leisurely business of cricket tours became the insane merry-go-round of today, the winter of 1987/88 would be a good place to start. For the first time, the Cricket World Cup was to be held outside England, in India and Pakistan, and for England this meant trying to accommodate a World Cup campaign alongside Test tours of Pakistan and New Zealand. Worse still, they had agreed to contribute to the celebration of the Bicentenary of Captain Cook's landing in Australia by taking part in a one-off Test in Sydney. Somehow, these four separate commitments, involving seven Test matches and up to fifteen one-day internationals, had to be squeezed into one English winter.

Those chosen to face the full severity of this schedule would find themselves departing from Heathrow en route for the World Cup on 28 September, less than two weeks after the final round of County Championship matches had concluded, and returning home from New Zealand on 23 March, just three weeks before the next county season was due to begin. A three-week Christmas break between the two legs of the tour would offer the players their only refreshment. Most were expected to report to their counties by 5 April. If they were lucky, their children might have remembered who they were by then. Unsurprisingly, Peter May and his fellow selectors found that several of their senior players considered the prospect unpalatable.

Ian Botham had already signed a three-year contract to play Sheffield Shield cricket for Queensland, perhaps looking forward to an escape from his stormy relations with the British press. David Gower went one step further and decided to take a break from the game completely, enjoying instead a trip to Africa, a skiing holiday in Europe and a visit to the Winter Olympics in Calgary. Graham Gooch, with a young family to consider, chose a more domestic hiatus; he opted to join the pre-Christmas part of the tour, but withdrew from consideration for New Zealand and Australia. With players of such quality and experience unavailable, it was surprising that the selectors chose not to recall Allan Lamb to the Test side from which he had been absent since the end of Gatting's victorious Ashes trip and pick him for the World Cup alone. True, since his *annus mirabilis* of 1984 his highest Test score had been 67, but he remained a player of quality. As if to prove the point that he was not simply a one-day player, having played a key role in England's World Cup campaign, Lamb returned to his native South Africa to play for Orange Free State in the Currie Cup, and in his very first first-class match made a career best 294 over 394 minutes.

Despite these absences, England's squad for the World Cup was balanced in favour of experience. The average age of the party was thirty years, and ten of the fourteen-man squad had taken part in the two one-day tournaments England had been involved in the previous winter. Of the other four, Graham Gooch, Paul Downton, Derek Pringle and Eddie Hemmings, not one lacked experience at the highest level. Despite being in a strong group with West Indies, Pakistan and Sri Lanka, England's World Cup campaign was largely a smooth one. Although they lost both their group matches against hosts Pakistan, two wins each against the West Indies and Sri Lanka ensured England progressed to a semi-final against India in Bombay, where a shock 35-run victory over the hosts set up a final clash with the old enemy Australia.

The anticipated final between the co-hosts had failed to materialise, but the surprise matchup between two other old rivals was not to disappoint. Gatting's battle-hardened warriors went into the match full of confidence, but their opponents were a team that skipper Allan Border, following two successive Ashes defeats, was beginning to turn into a tough old gut of a fighting unit.

Australia batted first and got off to a flying start against some wayward new-ball bowling from England: 'We bowled poorly at the start, otherwise we would have been chasing less,' recalls Micky Stewart. This analysis was corroborated by Mike Gatting: 'Our one big strength in that World Cup was the guys up front with the new ball. They did brilliantly, they got us wickets and they kept it down generally to three or four an over with all the fielders in; they really did well. But unfortunately this time they actually disappeared for a few [runs].' Tight spells from Foster, Emburey and Hemmings pegged the Australians back in the middle of their innings, but an anchoring innings of 75 from 125 balls by David Boon kept wickets in hand during those tight middle overs, before some late aggression by Border and Mike Veletta (45 from 31 balls) saw Australia reach a total of 253 for 5. 'At the end they ran us ragged,' Gatting recalls, 'and they probably got about ten or fifteen too many. And you think, it was seven runs, it was just those extra ten or fifteen runs at the end which they shouldn't have got, and it would have been a different story perhaps.' It was a total that, while competitive, was by no means beyond a capable England batting line-up.

England lost Tim Robinson lbw to the second ball of the innings, but Gooch and Bill Athey put on 52, then Athey and Gatting 69. England were 135 for 2 with plenty of overs left, and well placed in terms of required run rate. Although none of his bowlers were really taking punishment, Border decided the time had come to bring himself into the attack. Border's first ball was full and looked to be heading down the leg side, but Gatting reached forward and, with a quick switch of the hands, tried to execute the reverse-sweep that had served him so well earlier in the tournament.

'With the field that Allan Border had, there was only one place he was going to bowl it. He knew that and I knew that,' remembers Gatting.

> Actually it was far too wide, if I'd let it go, it would have been a big wide, but I'd made up my mind to play it. I could play it from most places, but it was so wide. I got a bat on it, got it nicely, but what people don't realise is it caught my shoulder. Had it been a bit straighter it would have just gone down my arm and would have missed, but because it was so far over it came over the top of my arm and just clipped my shoulder and the wicketkeeper ran round and caught it. Had it not, well, who knows, we'd have won the World Cup.

For Gatting, the choice to play the reverse sweep was no sudden aberration, but part of a deliberate game plan:

> We used it [the sweep] in the semi-final to great effect against India. They had two spinners, Ravi Shastri and Maninder Singh, who had bowled well throughout the tournament; they had only been going at

about three an over. So Goochie and I were talking and saying 'we've got to get these guys going at five an over. Get them all going for five an over, we get 250 and we're in with a chance.' A lot of the sides in that tournament had only been getting about 210 because of the spinners. So Goochie for two or three days in Bombay just practised the sweep in the nets. He had these left-arm spinners and would say 'just bowl at me' and he'd be hitting it in front of square, behind square, whatever. I was practising my reverse sweep as well.

The strategy worked, for that match at least, but it would backfire badly in the final.

It was far from the end of England's challenge. Gatting was replaced at the wicket by Allan Lamb, possibly England's most capable batsman at the one-day game, and the team still had wickets and overs in hand. But something in the momentum of the game had, perceptibly, changed. Lamb's 45 from 55 balls kept the tempo up when he was on strike, but at the other end Athey's innings was becoming a painful grind. His 58 occupied 102 balls and included only two boundaries; it lasted more than two hours. Athey fell trying to scamper one run too many, then Paul Downton followed soon after. A partnership of 30 between Lamb and Emburey just kept England in touch, but first Lamb was bowled by Steve Waugh, then, two runs later, Emburey too was run out. A brief flurry of boundaries from Phil DeFreitas gave England hope, but when he fell for 18 trying to crash another boundary off Waugh, the game was up. Border's resurgent Australians claimed their first honour and demonstrated the will to win that would characterise their nation's cricket for the next two decades.

'We played well throughout the tournament,' recalls John Emburey, 'and it was hugely disappointing that we lost the final having got to it. The way we played, we were one of the best sides in the tournament. I still think now, some 27, 28 years on, of Gatt's reverse sweep, when we were in a good position. All right, he doesn't know he's going to get out to that particular ball, and it's a shot that he played well, but it's the one thing that really rankles everyone who was there.' Despite all the other factors that contributed to England's loss that day, the expensive new-ball spell from Phil DeFreitas and Gladstone Small, missed run-out chances at the end of the Australian innings, Bill Athey's momentum-killing innings, Gooch and Lamb getting out when well set,

England's defeat, the closest they have yet come to claiming the one-day crown, still seems associated most closely with Gatting's reverse sweep. And what the players themselves felt about it was certainly mirrored by administrators, press and public: 'People blamed it, well Peter May certainly did, on Gatt's reverse sweep. Well, that was part of it,' remembers Micky Stewart.

> Peter was adamantly against the reverse sweep, but Gatt used to play it pretty well. 'If you can play it well, play it' was what I used to say. It was silly to say that it was that one stroke that cost us the match. The Aussies played well, they kept their heads and we didn't do the job. It was very disappointing.

Peter May himself never made his thoughts public, but the British press were not so reticent. 'GATT: I GOOFED!' squealed *The Sun* on a back page that detailed the 'England Skipper's Day of Shame.'

Just ten days after their defeat in the World Cup Final, England found themselves in Lahore, embarking upon a wholly superfluous three-match series of one-day internationals as a preface to a Test series in Pakistan. Thanks to this curious schedule, Gatting's team did not play a single first-class match before the first Test. Local cricket fans too seemed to sense the pointlessness of the one-day series, which attracted a total of only 20,000 spectators across the three games. England improved on their World Cup form by completing a 3-0 whitewash over their hosts at Peshawar, just three days before the first Test was to get underway in Lahore. But even before the first ball of the Test series had been bowled, it was clear that things were about to get much more difficult for the England team.

Micky Stewart remembers how he received some alarming intelligence:

> We were due to fly the next day, both sides, for Lahore, and suddenly there was a rushing around and commotion in the Pakistan dressing room. I asked Ramiz Raja, whom I knew quite well, what was going on, and he said 'we've been summoned to appear in front of the President.'

When the team arrived in Lahore, Stewart received a message from a local contact requesting an urgent meeting.

I said, well we saw each other before we flew off, what's so urgent?'
Anyway, we met at lunchtime and he said, "expect anything in this
first Test match?" I said "what do you mean?" and he said "Pakistan
won't lose the Test match." Stewart was incredulous. I said "what? The
umpire's been nobbled?" He said "yes."

In its early days as an independent nation, cricket had been one of
Pakistan's first expressions of its national identity and prestige. For
many years its mere presence at cricket's top table had been sufficient
to satisfy national pride, as long as its players and officials were taken
seriously – hence the deep offence taken at the treatment of Idris
Begh by cricketers of the country's former colonial overlord. But now
that achievement had matched enthusiasm, and the team contained
world-class players like Imran Khan, Javed Miandad and Abdul Qadir,
success on the field was also demanded. Hopes had been high that the
first World Cup to be held on Pakistani soil would lead to Pakistani
triumph. The shock semi-final defeat to an Australian team whose
reputation had not yet caught up with its renaissance, followed by a
3-0 home capitulation to Gatting's England whom Pakistan had twice
defeated in the group stage of the World Cup, had been a severe blow not
just to the nation's cricket fans, but to the nation's wider sense of self-
esteem. For President Zia-ul-Haq, painfully aware of an approaching
election, another defeat could not be permitted. This was the message
the Pakistan team had been given following the one-day international in
Peshawar.

It was hardly the news to inspire the England team on the eve of an
important Test series, and Stewart was careful not to alarm the players
with it: 'I told Peter Lush, who was excellent as tour manager, and Gatt
and that was it.' There was probably little necessity to warn the squad
as a whole of the umpiring difficulties that lay ahead of them. Previous
experiences of touring in Pakistan, plus the whole history of cricketing
conflict between the two countries, made it clear that on a tour of the
subcontinent in those days umpiring controversy would never be far
from the back pages. Nevertheless, in a team meeting before the match,
Gatting warned everyone not to allow themselves to be provoked by
any umpiring decision.

In the light of what was to happen, Gatting himself might reflect how easy it is to issue such an injunction, and how difficult it is to abide by it. By the end of the first day, Pakistan were sitting comfortably on 13 for 0 having bowled England out for just 175. This marked something of a recovery for England, who had been 94 for 8 at the loss of Chris Broad. The great Pakistan leg-spinner Abdul Qadir had claimed his best ever Test figures of 9 for 56. It was the fifth best bowling performance in the history of Test cricket and remains the best innings analysis ever recorded against England in Tests. Four of his wickets were claimed lbw, including, crucially, Mike Gatting, attempting the orthodox sweep this time, for a second ball duck. A photograph by Graham Morris shows Gatting after receiving this decision, his front foot still placed well down the wicket, his bat vertical, his arms crossed across the top of the handle and his head slumped in despair into his left forearm. John Thicknesse, reporting the match for *The Cricketer*, considered that Qadir's leg-break would have missed the off-stump by inches. Modern technology has taught us that a batsman striding down the wicket can be out lbw more often than was once thought, but in 1987 such a decision was considered equivalent to a shot in the dark with a rusty blunderbuss. Footage of Gatting's dismissal can still be seen on *YouTube*: Qadir's looping leg-break lands just inside the line of off-stump and spins viciously, striking Gatting's front pad, clearly planted some distance down the pitch, around 6 inches outside off-stump, heading towards first slip. In his report for the BBC, Christopher Martin-Jenkins, ever the master of polite understatement, described the umpire's decision as 'hasty'.

In his notebook that night, Micky Stewart recorded that five out of the ten wickets to fall had seen the batsman 'sawn off' (i.e. dismissed unfairly). Out of Abdul Qadir's four lbw victims, three had, he felt, been struck outside the line. The umpire in each case was not Shakoor Rana, who would achieve notoriety in the next Test at Faisalabad, but a man standing in only his third Test, Shakeel Khan. Khan had already raised eyebrows in the England dressing room when raising his index finger in dubious circumstances during the first one-day international in Lahore. Pakistani faith in its own umpires was so great that in their home Test series against West Indies the previous year they had appointed two Indian umpires – V. K. Ramaswamy and P. D. Reporter – to stand in the Test matches at Lahore and Karachi. Yet now, despite the availability of

experienced officials, Mahboob Shah and Khizer Hiyat, who between
them had experience of standing in thirty-four Tests, the Pakistan Board
offered the Test to a thirty-four-year-old with only two Test matches
and eleven one-day internationals under his belt, and who had not been
selected to officiate during the World Cup. If Khan was hoping this
match would gain him great face with the Pakistan Board and lead to
further opportunities at Test level, he was to be disappointed. He would
stand in only three further Tests.

In Pakistan's innings of 392, England would only gain one lbw decision
– against Mudassar Nazar when the opener had already made 120. Five
of the ten wickets England claimed in that match were clean bowled.
The team's frustration would begin to boil over when they batted
again. Broad was on 13 when left-arm spinner Iqbal Qasim appealed
against him for caught behind. The tall opener was thunderstruck when
Shakeel's finger went up again: 'I was at the other end,' wrote Graham
Gooch in his book *Captaincy*, 'and there was certainly a noise of some
sort as the ball beat the bat. Chris stood there and said, "I didn't hit it,
I'm not going," and he started to exchange heated words with the close
fielders. I came down the wicket and told him he had to go – and he still
refused.' It was some time before Gooch could persuade an outraged
Broad that he must return to the pavilion. Broad's dissent – it is hard
to find another description – had been protracted enough to have been
obvious to any observer at the ground, or following the match on
television or radio. Peter Smith, writing in the *Daily Mail*, thought that
Broad – and Abdul Qadir, who had visibly expressed displeasure at one
decision – 'were each guilty of outrageous acts of dissent. Both were
distressing incidents. They have no part in cricket.'

That evening, the England management team held a disciplinary
hearing. Despite his disagreement with Broad's actions, Gooch spoke
against any formal disciplinary action, 'which in retrospect was wrong
of me. I feel we should have fined him – not only for the gravity of
the offence but also to alert the rest of our tour party that that kind
of dissent is simply not allowed, whatever the provocation.' At the
press conference that followed, tour manager Peter Lush announced
that Broad had been censured but not fined or otherwise punished.
Perhaps ill-advisedly during a Test match, Lush allowed some obvious
criticism of the umpiring to seep into his comments. None of this was
what Gatting would have had in mind when he delivered his pre-match

warning speech about reacting to provocation. Had the team managed to stick to this original line and turn the other cheek, hard as that might have been, what followed might never have happened.

'Shakoor Rana was a good umpire,' recalls John Emburey. 'All the issues we had were in the first Test match, when we had a lot of decisions go against us, but Shakoor Rana wasn't umpiring in that game. It was just something which blew up out of nothing.' England had lost the first Test by an innings. Graham Gooch had followed Chris Broad half an hour later, also given out by Shakeel Khan caught behind off Iqbal Qasim, while Abdul Qadir had claimed another three lbws. In the second Test at Faisalabad, Broad put his demons behind him with an unbeaten century on the first day. Ably supported by his captain, who made a belligerent 79, Broad had finally fallen for 116 early on day two, and although England had lost their last six wickets for just 48 that morning, they had gone on to reduce the hosts to 106 for five with only Salim Malik of the front line batsman remaining.

With the clock ticking rapidly towards the close of play and Salim Malik due to face the fifth ball of an Eddie Hemmings over, Gatting was naturally keen to get in another over before stumps, and ideally with the lesser batsman, Aamer Malik, on strike. Hoping both to aid a quick changeover and to prevent Salim taking a single, Gatting called David Capel in from deep square leg to a closer position. As Salim Malik would later confirm, Gatting had warned him that he was bringing the fielder in, but as Hemmings began his run-up – and the ball therefore came into play – Capel was still moving.

'Gatt kept looking over his shoulder to see where David Capel was,' remembers Emburey,

and as Eddie Hemmings turned to come in Gatt said [to Capel] 'no, no, you're coming in too far, just go back a little bit.' Just with hand signals. And then the umpire thought that he was moving the field while the ball was in play without the batsman's knowledge. Shakoor Rana made a bit of a fuss and said 'you can't do that, it's cheating, moving the fielder while the ball is in play and the batsman's not aware of it.' Of course there was an altercation, but then they walked away.

Shakoor turned back to his position at square leg, heading towards where David Capel was now stationed. 'He was walking towards David

Capel and mumbling something under his breath. David more or less read his lips and said to Gatt "he just called you a ... cheat" and of course it all went off again and that's when the whole episode blew up. But Gatt didn't hear it and if David Capel didn't say anything, nothing would have happened.'

TV footage does indeed show that Gatting and Shakoor Rana had two separate discussions, but it shows that the first one was already growing quite heated before they parted to return to their positions. The famous images of them face-to-face wagging fingers at each other comes from the first part of this discussion. In a statement issued to the press at the time, Gatting said 'although I was at backward square-leg, the batsman was always aware of what I was doing. I told the umpire that I didn't think it was his role to interfere like that and he replied that I was cheating.' For Gatting, the use of this word was surely what caused him to blow a fuse and turn an ill-judged discussion with the umpire into a full-blown argument. Watching the footage, Gatting first approaches Shakoor and appears to be explaining his action, his right hand extended in a passive gesture. Suddenly it changes, and the England captain visibly bristles and begins to gesture at the umpire, who responds in kind. Gatting turns and walks away, but gets no more than four steps before something off screen makes him turn around again. Is this David Capel's intervention? Whatever it is, it reignites Gatting's temper, and this time he has to be almost pulled away from the umpire by Bill Athey.

It goes without saying that England did not get their extra over in.

It was an ugly scene, and one from which neither participant emerged with any credit. For a captain to engage in a heated argument with an umpire on the field of play, let alone at Test level, was then, and is now, anathema. But Shakoor Rana must also bear responsibility for his choice of words. 'Mr Rana called Gatting a cheat in strong terms and there were half a dozen witnesses to that on the field,' said Peter Lush in a statement to the media. Shakoor Rana's public statement revealed more about what might be termed local cultural sensitivities than anything else. 'No captain has ever used such language to me. This man has insulted my mother and there is no way I will back down without an apology. People have been murdered in this country for less.'

The following day, all the action took place not on the field but off it. 'We went out on the field,' remembers Emburey, 'but the umpires didn't come out and the Pakistan batsmen didn't come out. We stayed out there for about an hour, eventually realised that they weren't going to come out and we walked off the field. I think Javed Miandad may have stirred it up a little bit with the umpires saying "you should demand an apology from the captain."'

It soon became apparent that Shakoor Rana was unwilling to take the field again unless he received an apology from Gatting, while Gatting was unwilling to make such an apology unless he received one from the umpire. The whole day was wasted in fruitless negotiations. 'At one stage' reported *Wisden* 'a settlement looked forthcoming, but Shakoor prompted, it is thought, by the Pakistan captain Javed Miandad dug his heels in again after initially agreeing to a joint apology.' In his autobiography, Javed strongly denied having influenced Shakoor for his own purposes. Instead, he claimed, the umpire had come to him for advice on how to deal with the situation, and Javed had urged him to insist on an apology from the England captain. Although not denying that he influenced the umpire's attitude, Javed's claim was that his advice was intended not as a means of delaying a resumption of the game, and therefore damaging England's hopes of levelling the series, but as a means of enhancing Pakistani honour in the light of perceived insults from the former colonial power.

Back at Lord's, the TCCB was assembled that very day for its winter meeting. Such mid-tour controversy had not visited the Home of Cricket since the dark days of Bodyline fifty-five years earlier. This time the authorities were not reacting to cabled notes of protest about events they had not seen and could not even imagine; they were in direct telephone contact with the team and its management in Faisalabad. Every one of them had seen the TV news reports showing the England captain nose to nose with an umpire in a Test match, and every one had read the newspaper reports and knew the reaction of the public and the cricket world, both at home and around the globe. The *Daily Mail* had that morning plastered across its front page the headline 'NOW GATTING COULD BE OUT'. *The Sun*, meanwhile, having run for several weeks with stories of how Pakistan were regularly 'cheating' 'our cricketers', now expressed a less sympathetic view: 'GATTING GOES RAVING MAD!'

The Board was in an uncomfortable position. Aware as it was of the team's insistence that the bad language had been started by Shakoor

Rana and not Gatting, having seen the TV reports showing some of the poor decisions made by Shakeel Khan at Lahore, and knowing that the team as a whole was fully behind Gatting's refusal to apologise unless he received one in return, it had somehow to negotiate a way through this impasse. The easiest option, on the face of it, would be to call off the tour and bring the players home. This had already been suggested by Ijaz Butt, the Secretary of the Board of Control for Cricket in Pakistan (BCCP): 'With the mood in which this series is being played, I personally feel that there is no point in carrying on.' But such a move would have led to a serious loss of revenue for the BCCP for which it might well have sought recompense from Lord's. Pakistan undoubtedly held the winning hand. If the tour were called off, they would receive financial compensation and be left with a 1-0 victory, while, whatever had actually been said on the field at Faisalabad, the abiding memory of the tour, carried into living rooms around the world, would have been of a Pakistani umpire being gesticulated at by the England captain.

It is interesting to compare the Board's response with that of MCC to the first accusations of Bodyline in 1933. 'We deplore your cable' it had written back to the Australians, in staunch defence of the England captain and his tactics. But the TCCB chose another approach, perhaps best categorised as unconditional surrender. In a private communication to the team, Gatting was ordered to write a note of apology to Shakoor Rana. In a more public media release the following morning they wrote: 'It was unanimously decided that the current Test match in Faisalabad should restart today after the rest day. The board manager in Pakistan, Peter Lush, was advised of this decision immediately and asked to take whatever action was necessary to implement it.' No conditions were placed upon this. Lush and Stewart had to get the game back on whatever the cost, whatever indignity it might involve. It was certainly a major change of tack from the statement issued twenty-four hours earlier by the TCCB chief executive A. C. Smith, to the effect that they were leaving the situation to be handled by Lush and Stewart as they saw fit.

It was widely reported at the time that the TCCB had discussed the situation with officials from the Foreign & Commonwealth Office before instructing Lush and Stewart to get the team back on the pitch. The substance of these discussions has never been made public, but it is interesting to note that in April 1987 Pakistan's Prime Minister had visited the United Kingdom and discussed with the Secretary of State for Defence, George Younger, the possible purchase of several British-built Type-23 Frigates. Pakistan was a key export market for British industry, and one of the FCO's principal remits in the country was to ensure that it remained so. With the head of the BCCP also being the Head of State, it is hard to imagine a situation less conducive to the separation of sport from politics. Peter Lush now issued his own statement:

> The Test and County Cricket Board has instructed me as manager of the England team to do everything possible to ensure this match continues today and that we honour our obligations to complete the tour of Pakistan. We have tried to resolve amicably the differences between Mike Gatting and umpire Shakoor Rana following their heated exchange of words which took place on the second day. We all hoped this could have been achieved in private and with a handshake. Umpire Shakoor Rana has stated he would continue to officiate in this match if he received a written apology from Mike Gatting. The umpire has made it clear he will not apologise for the remarks he made to the England captain. In the wider interests of the game Mike Gatting has been instructed by the Board to write an apology to Shakoor Rana, and this he has now done.

'Dear Shakoor Rana,' wrote Gatting, 'I apologise for the bad language used during the second day of the Test match.' The note's brevity says all it needs to about what he thought of being ordered to make an unreciprocated apology. Gatting now being completely hamstrung, it was down to the players to invoke the spirit of the MCC committee from five decades earlier. 'The England players deplore the fact that it was not possible to effect a compromise solution,' their statement read. It went on to directly criticise the TCCB for ordering Gatting to apologise while no effort was made to insist on an apology from Shakoor Rana, and left no doubt that the players felt that the 'wider interests of the game' cited by the board as justification for its actions were no more than the financial and political interests of the board itself. The players, it is clear from this statement, felt let down by the board. Some of the younger members of the tour party were all for refusing to take the field, but more seasoned heads cautioned them against this. 'Do you realise what it means if you do that?' asked Graham Gooch. 'You'll be breaking your tour contract and you could never play for England again.' Common sense prevailed.

A. C. Smith and TCCB chairman Raman Subba Row flew out from London to Karachi in time for the final Test. They brought with them conciliatory words for their Pakistani counterparts and the promise of a £1,000 'hardship payment' for the players. A request that in the interests of calming the mood Shakoor Rana not be appointed to stand in the final Test at Karachi was met with a simple reminder that an identical request from Pakistan regarding David Constant a few months earlier had been rejected. There could be no response to this. In the event, Pakistan's two most experienced umpires, Khizer Hayat and Mehboob Shah, were appointed for Karachi. The Pakistanis had made their point, and when the proposal that Test matches should be umpired by officials from a neutral country next came before the International Cricket Conference (ICC), the TCCB did not oppose it.

As for the England players, they viewed their hardship payment with disdain, and some even spoke of refusing to accept it. However, outside the bubble of the England camp, news of the payment had leaked to the press and in some quarters it was being made to look as if the players had bargained for this payment as a condition for continuing the tour. Of course they were already playing in the tour's final match when they first heard of it from Peter Lush. After the third day's play and the rest day at Faisalabad had been lost to negotiations, the refusal of Pakistan to allocate an extra day to make up for the time lost ensured that the match fizzled out into a draw and England's chance of squaring the series had been lost. At Karachi, a flat wicket and two teams who had seen enough of each other ensured another drawn match, which was called off at tea on the final day.

Twenty-four hours later, on 22 December, the players arrived back in England just in time to spend Christmas with their families. It is unlikely that any of them felt inspired by thoughts of peace on earth and goodwill to all men. As Micky Stewart had written to his wife a week or so earlier, 'I have never seen anything like it in all the time I have known the game.'

3

Spare the Rod and Spoil the Child

When the England squad flew out from Heathrow again after a three-week break at home, there was little enthusiasm in the party, and the shadow of events in Pakistan still hung over the team captain. Whatever conversations Mike Gatting had had with Peter May and the TCCB hierarchy over Christmas and New Year, they couldn't have done much for his confidence in his long-term hold on the captaincy. In a pre-departure press conference at Heathrow's Sheraton Skyline hotel, he commented: 'I will do the captaincy job as I see it, but, if people are not happy with the way I perform, then I will stand down. I will give 100 per cent as I always do but, if I cannot be captain, then I would love to continue playing for England.' Were these the thoughts uppermost in the England captain's mind as he set off on an overseas tour? Or were they simply an attempt to play a straight bat to questions from a press pack that would not let the affair of Shakoor Rana lie? Either way, it proved that however much Gatting might want to put the whole sorry business behind him he would not be allowed to. Nor, it seemed, would Peter Lush, England's tour manager, obliged to promise better behaviour from his team: 'We must put Pakistan behind us and get on with it. We are aware what is expected in behaviour on the field. We will take the rough with the smooth and will not query the umpires' decisions or publicly discuss them.' Lush too, it seems, was being held to account for his ill-judged press conference comments in Lahore.

There were three changes to the party which had left Pakistan with such relief. Graham Gooch had opted out of the second half of the winter schedule and Yorkshire's Martyn Moxon came in to replace him. A straightforward tactical swap of Worcestershire seamer Neal Radford for the left-arm spin of Nick Cook was the second change. The third was hard to fathom. Jack Russell had had little chance either to impress or to disappoint on the field in Pakistan. Almost universally considered to be the finest gloveman in England at the time, the twenty-four-year-old Russell was clearly the coming man, and his replacement by Surrey's Jack Richards seemed a retrograde step. Richards had been first choice under Gatting on the Australian tour in 1986/87 and had made a fine 100 at Perth, but he had only made one Test appearance since the end of that tour, in the sole defeat against Pakistan at Headingley the previous summer, where innings of six and two had done nothing for his future prospects. Richards was one of Gatting's trusted men, but to send him to New Zealand as No.2 to Bruce French suggested that the selectors did not yet have much faith in Russell's abilities as a batsman should French's bad luck with injuries continue.

Even the dropping of Cook was the product of questionable logic. That a third spinner on a tour of New Zealand would be a luxury was undeniable, but replacing Cook meant that England would be choosing between the two off-spinners, Emburey and Hemmings, in New Zealand and might end up playing both on the spin-friendly Sydney Cricket Ground against Australia. Cook, of course, was nowhere near as reliable as the other two with the bat; Hemmings' last appearance at Sydney in 1982/83 had very nearly resulted in a Test century. It all added up to the conclusion that England's selectors, in the absence of Gooch, Gower, Botham and Lamb, had little faith in their batsmen and were doing whatever they could to generate runs from further down the order.

After a short warm-up in New Zealand, England flew to Sydney for the Bicentenary Test, beginning on 27 January. Allan Border's Australians, fresh from their World Cup triumph and a narrow Test series win over New Zealand, were very much on the up, but it was a match England would dominate. If the huge crowd hoped for entertainment to match the fireworks and celebrations of 200 years since the first fleet sailed into Botany Bay, however, they were to be disappointed. Without its core of experienced players, England's batting revealed itself to be decidedly one paced. Chris Broad's 139 anchored the innings, but it was a dour affair coming from 361 balls. With Gatting out for only 13, England lacked the ability to force the pace, and their 425 took them until 5.10 p.m. on the second day.

A good all-round bowling performance saw Australia bowled out for just 214 by lunch on day four; they might have been dismissed even more cheaply had it not been for the loss of almost two hours play to bad light at the end of day three when they were reeling on 164 for 7. With Dilley and Foster having bowled just 19 overs each, and his third seamer, Capel, just six, Gatting can have had little thought of not enforcing the follow on. England had five sessions to bowl out Australia and seal their first Test win in twelve months. David Boon's sixth Test century, a marathon 431-ball 184 not out, ensured that they would not.

It was a disappointing end to a solid performance from Gatting's men. His two off-spinners had only been able to take one wicket between them on a fifth day pitch at Sydney, and his batsmen had lacked the enterprise that might have given him more time to bowl out Australia twice, but Gatting's team had still had much the better of the match against their oldest adversary. England's supremacy over Australia, perhaps the most important yardstick for judging the fortunes of the team, remained intact. Gatting had been forced to rely on his spinners (who together shared a burden of 90 overs) due to Dilley and Foster both aggravating knee injuries. In Foster's case, it was bad enough to rule him out of the rest of the tour. A specialist in Melbourne confirmed a tear in the cartilage of his right knee; he returned home for surgery and his lack of full fitness would cast a shadow over England's bowling for the remainder of the year.

If that was not enough, the last thing Gatting's team needed was a further case of public controversy. Chris Broad looked to be well set for a double century an hour before lunch on the second day when, having seen off a morning spell from Australia's spearhead, Craig McDermott, he received a shortish ball from medium pacer Steve Waugh. Not quite trusting himself to pull the ball as it moved back into him, Broad turned his back on it. The ball crashed into his forearm and ricocheted into his stumps. Stunned and disappointed, Broad turned and swatted his leg-stump out of the ground with a savage swipe of the bat, which might have been better aimed at the ball he had just tried to leave. As his actions were replayed on the main screen, instead of leaving the field of play to gracious applause from an appreciative Sydney crowd, Broad left to a chorus of boos, like a man ejected from a house party for breaking the furniture.

Broad's moment of madness remains the act most remembered from this celebratory match. It was an isolated incident in a match played largely in good spirits, but in the light of the events of Pakistan it was all the press needed to create new headlines about English indiscipline. This time the management team was swift to act, fining Broad £500 almost as soon as he arrived back in the dressing room. 'He had no excuses. It was a stupid thing to do and he knew that he had done wrong,' said Peter Lush during a hastily convened press conference held at lunch. 'All the players were warned about their behaviour before this tour. He knows the form. It was a sad end to a great innings.'

'I don't know why he did it,' Gatting told the MCC Audio Archive, 'but we fined him immediately and there was no problem.'

'Broad is a dignified and charming man,' wrote Bill Frindall in the *Mail on Sunday*, 'but his recent displays of outrageous petulance reveal a childish streak which he must control.' 'BOTHER BOY BROAD TOLD: YOU'LL BE SENT HOME' declared the *News of the World*, quoting Raman Subba Row: 'anyone who cannot behave properly should not be playing cricket. This was a dreadful incident.'

England would dearly have loved to have a single match pass by without any taint of controversy, but this was clearly not the winter when the fractious atmosphere surrounding the team would be left to dissipate. The draw in Sydney was followed by three more in New Zealand. In the first Test at Christchurch another Broad century was accompanied by no controversy, but unfavourable umpiring decisions once more ate away at English morale. In the first innings, Graham Dilley produced one of the most effective spells of his Test career to take 6 for 38, but with New Zealand set an unlikely 304 to win with almost a full day's play having been lost to rain, frustration got the better of England's premier bowler. Having claimed the first two New Zealand wickets lbw, a swift succession of appeals going against him saw Dilley stride back to his mark, his arms rigid by his side, directing a torrent of foul language at his feet. Not at the batsman, nor at the umpire, it should be noted, but at his feet and, symbolically at least, at his own foul luck.

The fact that Dilley had not sworn directly at the umpire or taken his frustrations out on the stumps probably helped to commute his sentence to half the fine imposed upon Broad at Sydney; TV coverage and the fairly new innovation of stump microphones would also have impacted the severity of the fine. In light of the last few months, the footage would be seen not just in cricket highlights but in news bulletins too. The need for action was clear. Dilley's 'lamentable outburst,' wrote Bill Frindall, 'was the behaviour of a spoilt child, at least equal in "criminal" magnitude to Broad's stump-chopping act at Sydney.' *The Sun* devoted the best part of three pages to its coverage, complaining that 'Graham Dilley brought new shame to English cricket yesterday with a disgraceful, foul-mouthed outburst.' The paper accused Dilley of 'making a mockery' of Peter Lush's assurances of good behaviour. In Colin Milburn's column, the former England batsman called for the board to 'kick out the persistent offenders and, if necessary, send them home in disgrace.' Dilley's teammates, captain and manager were more sympathetic. 'Dilley had Martin Crowe out three times,' recalls Micky Stewart.

> He was lbw, he was caught bat-pad at short leg, he was caught at cover by DeFreitas. It was one of those where it had scraped his pad and it had gone over there [to cover] and it had carried. All three were given not out, and after the third one Dilley let it all out. Of course it was picked up by the stump microphones and all across New Zealand housewives doing the ironing heard it clearly.

New Zealand Television had muted the sound on the stump microphones before his outburst, but it made little difference. Dilley's loss of temper was clearly audible across Lancaster Park, and anyone who saw but didn't hear it would have had little need of subtitles. 'Dilley shouted so loudly his words were picked up by sound microphones in the stand roof' said television producer Gavin Service. Micky Stewart, a man who played his cricket in an era when television coverage was not so intrusive with regard to the subtleties of on-field language and gesture, was inclined to be understanding of a player's instinct to let out his frustrations. 'I asked the controller of ITV about it later,' he told me. 'I asked him, "why, when you've got a batsman on at a low point and he gets out, why do you show his disappointment and not the bowler?" He simply told me "it makes better television, Micky."' There's no news like bad news.

What made it worse, no doubt, was the fact that the next two Test pitches in New Zealand were certain to be low, slow, draw-makers. Chances against any half-decent batsman would be at a premium then; if either side wanted to force a win in the series, it would need to be here at Christchurch. So to have three chances in quick succession to take the wicket of Martin Crowe, one of the world's top middle-order batsmen, and have all of them denied would have tested the patience of a saint. For a competitive cricketer, and a fast bowler at that, it was a situation bound to end in blue air. Fred Trueman would probably have sparked off a thunderstorm. Bill Frindall pointed out that each of the three decisions that went against Dilley contained sufficient measure of doubt to justify umpire Brian Aldridge's verdict, but since Dilley's outburst was not personally directed at Aldridge this is only partly to the point. In giving vent to his frustration, Dilley suffered the consequences where a player of an earlier generation would have got away without any penalty whatsoever.

What caused many of the journalists as much concern as Dilley's outburst was the rest of the England team's reaction to the catch claimed at cover. Frindall described how 'the entire England team remained frozen like a Madame Tussaud's tableau. It was sad to see Gatting joining in rather than exerting his authority and ordering them back on duty immediately.' But if there is a line to be drawn between showing disappointment and dissent, does this example really cross it? According to *Wisden's* report of the tour, 'it would be impossible to pretend that the series was well umpired.' Yet because of what had happened in Pakistan and Australia, the England team was now expected even to withhold the slightest visible sign of disappointment when things did not go their way. It was asking a lot of professional sportsmen.

'If you want a team of robots,' commented Gatting later, 'then pick a team of robots and see how you like it. But if you want to pick a team of human beings, then you have to expect them to react like human beings in the situations they are put in.' For the England party, the usual close of play press conference was beginning to feel like a visit to the local magistrate's court. An unusually packed crowd of twenty journalists attended that evening for news of the fine handed out to Graham Dilley. They were not amused by a thirty minute delay before Peter Lush and Micky Stewart entered the room, nor by a 'tense and irritable' refusal by Lush to make any statement or answer any questions until the captain arrived, nor by Stewart having to go and locate Gatting in the dressing room after ten more minutes. Gatting's chirpy quip of 'Sorreee' when he did finally make an appearance did not help matters either. Lush's complaints about the stump microphones would simply give the press more material for their growing thesis on the subjects of the England team's insularity, petulance and indiscipline.

It was not simply the news media, anxious to keep alive the story which had been running since Faisalabad, who made hay in the Christchurch sun. Senior cricket writers across all the daily newspapers were near unanimous in their condemnation. Writing in *The Observer*, Scyld Berry, who had travelled with most recent England sides overseas, expressed deep concern at the solidarity with Dilley he had found the England players privately expressing:

> They think his reactions to the umpiring decisions of Brian Aldridge were permissible, even justified. And since they are unable to see the line, there is every danger they will overstep it again until they do. Their vision is even more blinkered on the issue of the team's dissent. As far as they are concerned, England's behaviour this winter has not deteriorated to an unprecedentedly and intolerably low level. I would say that no international team, except Pakistan when Imran Khan is not in control, so consistently question umpiring decisions, or rather cast doubt and contempt upon them, as England do now.

This behaviour, thought Berry, had its origin in the unique circumstances of Faisalabad and Lahore, 'but they have since failed to understand the distinction between that umpiring and the manifestly fair-minded incompetence of one of the New Zealand umpires in the first Test.'

Perhaps it was just as well that the final two Tests were as bereft of interest for the media as they were for the spectators. After John Wright edged the first ball of the match between a motionless Bruce French and John Emburey at first-slip, by far the most entertaining part of the second Test at Auckland was a fight between two magpies on the outfield. Whether they had disagreed over an umpiring decision is not known, but if they had done it might have been over the mistaken signal of leg-byes which cost Martyn Moxon three runs that would have given him his first, and as it turned out, only, Test century. He was caught at slip off Ewen Chatfield for 99. Matters were not helped by the absence after Christchurch of New Zealand's spearhead Richard Hadlee. Without him, the hosts appeared content to settle for a draw and, when they won the toss at Wellington, they batted first and ambled their leisurely way to 512 for 6 just over an hour into the third day. England were able to progress to 183 for 2 by the close, but Moxon's hopes of making that elusive Test 100 – he was 81 not out overnight – were ruined by rain which washed out the last two days. He was probably the only man alive not to have been glad it was all over.

England's tour fizzled out with a series of four one-day internationals in which honours were shared 2-2. The second match was notable, *Wisden* recorded, for 'some appalling cricket from both sides.' In the third match England 'let themselves down with fielding of a deplorable standard.' It was evidence of two tired sides with little interest in the cricket they were playing. In an end-of-tour press briefing at Napier, Micky Stewart remarked on the toll the winter programme had taken on the team captain: 'Mentally and emotionally Gatt is completely and utterly drained.'

'It's more mental tiredness than a physical thing,' Gatting himself confirmed, 'and the cricket which has been played over the last six months hasn't helped too much either.'

Gatting's mental state would have been helped little by the press coverage of the tour and by the reaction of the TCCB to it. One day before the Wellington Test began on 2 March, the TCCB convened again at Lord's for its spring meeting. 'It will be a meeting of some significance,' said chief executive A. C. Smith, 'where the ramifications of the tour will be discussed by the delegates. But it will be an informal meeting and will not be minuted.' Those ramifications would, according to Paul Fitzpatrick in *The Guardian,* include the 'breakdown of players' self-discipline that has been all too apparent this winter, manifesting itself in blatant questioning of umpires' decisions, bad language, "sledging" on a scale that would have impressed Ian Chappell and the smashing of stumps.'

When the delegates emerged from their two days' non-minuted purdah, the official statements did not disappoint those hoping for a crackdown on indiscipline. 'If a player steps out of line he will be dropped,' said A. C. Smith, 'and no cricketer should suppose there is going to be anything of the soft touch about this.' Smith reported that the delegates had been greatly concerned by the damage to the game's reputation caused by the events of the last few months, and were particularly worried about the example being set to schoolchildren. There were commercial considerations too, with many worrying that the erosion of cricket's reputation for well-mannered competition might drive away sponsors. Not only the board of the TCCB would be responsible for enforcing this new line on discipline; the England selectors themselves would be expected to take a player's behaviour into account when selecting a side. 'They must exert the greatest influence and maintain the highest possible standards. There must be no dropping from accepted standards of image or behaviour.' The slate would be wiped clean from the winter, Smith said, but clearly from this point on there was to be a zero tolerance attitude to anything which might besmirch English cricket's reputation.

Although the England team was still playing a Test series in New Zealand, the meeting confirmed the reappointment of the Test selectors, Peter May, Fred Titmus and Phil Sharpe, for the forthcoming summer. Nothing was said about reappointing or replacing the England captain.

Smith's statement was widely welcomed in the media, but the TCCB had acted hastily and offered itself as a hostage to fortune. The meeting had been held while a tour was still in progress, and without any of the tour party having had any opportunity to defend themselves or their colleagues. No end of tour report had been submitted; the tour was not yet over. If Gatting, Stewart, Lush, or anyone else from the England party were subsequently to return to London with arguments refuting the case put against them, it would now be impossible for the board to back down without looking intolerably foolish. The TCCB had relied upon reports from the media to justify its call for a crackdown on indiscipline. How long would it be before the media would test the board's commitment to that line, and their own power to influence it?

Could the case possibly be refuted? According to Mike Gatting it certainly could:

Bob Vance was the Chairman of the New Zealand Cricket Board, and one of his sons was in England at the time and was reading everything the press wrote about us, so he wrote back to Bob saying, 'Jesus, this must be one of the worst teams you've ever had over there.' Well, Bob spoke to the umpires who had stood in the series and they told him 'no, these are good boys, probably better than our own boys if anything.' And so Bob Vance wrote a letter to the TCCB to explain that as far as the New Zealanders were concerned we were not the undisciplined bunch we were made out to be.

That letter, along with another apparently written by the New Zealand umpires, is presumably lurking somewhere in the TCCB archives, now held by its successor, the England & Wales Cricket Board. It does not feature in the copies of board minutes deposited in the MCC Archive, but then neither does anything between the autumn of 1987 and the spring of 1989. The New Zealand tour came in the middle of an eighteen month period which, it seems, English cricket's then administrators preferred to forget. Neither did the letter have much effect upon the attitude taken by its recipients: 'I was called before the TCCB management board when I got back,' said Gatting, 'and they asked me what had gone on and why there had been so much on-field dissent and so on. Well I asked what they made of Bob Vance's letter saying that things hadn't been as bad as they were made out to be. But they just dismissed it out of hand. "You have been warned, don't let it happen again" they said.'

Looking back on the antipodean tour as a whole, Chris Broad's inexplicable stump smashing at Sydney and Graham Dilley's frustrated outburst at Christchurch stand out as examples of poor self-control. That the incidents themselves were embarrassing is not in doubt, but were they really evidence of endemic poor behaviour in the ranks? Scyld Berry's meticulous dissection of England's behaviour and one or two other examples that made it into print suggests that the team's experiences in Pakistan had left them prone to frustration and even a little paranoid about umpiring decisions. However, against this must be balanced the case offered by the players themselves, by the Vance letter, and by other pieces of reporting such as this by the *Daily Telegraph's* Peter Deeley at the Wellington Test:

> There was admirable restraint shown by the fielding side [England] at the number of leg-before appeals that went unheeded. One counted a dozen, of which perhaps three might have produced affirmative results in other quarters.

However thoroughly investigated, the picture remains a complex one. The evidence of the press can be read both ways, and so can that of the players. While those present on the antipodean leg of the tour were keen to defend the standard of their behaviour, one who took part in the first half of the winter programme did later voice concerns about those same standards. In *Captaincy*, Graham Gooch contrasted the English reaction to poor umpiring decisions in Pakistan with that on a tour much earlier in his career: 'I don't recall England complaining officially about bad umpiring on our tour to Australia in 1978/79, even though Geoffrey Boycott felt hard done by on occasions and so did I. The difference between that tour and Pakistan in 1987 was that we were winning in Australia and could therefore take the umpiring in our stride.' For Gooch, the habit of complaining when things were going against you was a canker which ate into discipline and morale: 'It's the captain's job to stamp out dissent. I was worried in Pakistan about the way that cricket was heading.'

As English cricket approached the summer of 1988, the accusation of indiscipline hung threateningly in the air, waiting to fall on its next victim. The first two it would claim in the event were both senior players – one man about to bring out an ill-timed autobiography, and another who, for once, seemed to have lost control of his own script.

4

Fallen Hero

For Ian Botham, the winter of 1987/88 had promised much. The start of a potentially lucrative three-year contract with Queensland, who had turned to this brilliant, mercurial cricketer in search of a first Sheffield Shield triumph in their sixty-one-year history, to be followed by an ambitious trek across the Alps in the footsteps of the great Carthaginian general, Hannibal, the most spectacular yet in Botham's series of charity walks in aid of Leukaemia Research. Botham had visited Australia on many previous occasions. Among its cricketers were some of his closest friends, and some of his bitterest enemies, but in Brisbane Botham would play alongside Allan Border, who was one of the rivals of recent Ashes campaigns who had, up to now, managed to maintain cordial relations with his English opponents.

'I was not the only one of the England players who had forged a reasonably close friendship with AB over the years and it was his approach to me that led me to sign up for his state Queensland during the winter of 1988,' recalled Botham. Botham's performances for Queensland that winter were solid, but not spectacular. He recorded neither a single first-class century with the bat nor a five-wicket haul with the ball, but 646 runs at 34 and twenty-nine wickets at under 28 indicated a cricketer who was still performing a useful role. The life of Ian Terence Botham, however, has rarely remained headline free for long, and while his performances on the field for Queensland did not inspire them, certain aspects of his off-field antics surely did.

It started rather well for both player and state. On Botham's home debut in Brisbane a crowd of 19,000 turned up – more the sort of attendance the 'Gabba' would expect for a day of Test cricket and almost as many as the total attendance for all five of Queensland's home matches during the previous Shield season. Botham was punctual, trained hard, wore his team blazer when required and was mixing well with his teammates, and if his performances hadn't yet pulled up any trees, his bowling was a long way from the English pie-chucking derided by so many Australians around this time. 'You might think it looks like poop from the Grandstand. Let me assure you it's not,' was the verdict of South Australian captain David Hookes. Even the terms of Botham's deal with Queensland suggested an unexpected humility, the same £30 per day plus expenses received by the rest of the Queensland squad. It was only the prospect of commercial opportunities arranged by his agent Tom Byron that would make Botham's winter Down Under a profitable endeavour.

In an otherwise complimentary piece in *The Guardian*, Matthew Engel sounded a cautionary note:

> All that may not last. The admiring crowds will doubtless drift away as the initial thrill wears off. Botham himself may get bored when the gaps between Shield matches get longer later in the season, unless Byron can keep him busy with personal appearances. Queensland's interest in the Shield may disappear until the sixty-second year if they have too many more pointless draws like this one. The Australian press, who have so far drooled over him, may yet turn as nasty as Fleet Street.

Perhaps the first indication that Botham's boredom threshold had been breached came in January, when the England team arrived in Sydney for the Bicentenary Test. Botham publicly offered to play, but was immediately rebuffed. Mike Gatting made his commitment to the selected squad very clear in his response: 'We pick from the chosen sixteen, and if one person is injured we pick from the other fifteen. If another one gets injured we pick from the other fourteen. There is no question of anyone being brought in.'

Botham returned to play out his season with Queensland. Having got off to a tremendous start, winning five and drawing one of their first six Shield matches, the state had just suffered its first defeat, by three wickets, to Western Australia in Perth. A draw against South Australia in Adelaide followed, and then came a shock defeat in Tasmania, Queensland bowled out for 314 in the final innings despite the home side having lost its new ball pair of Dennis Lillee and Peter Faulkner to injury. Hoping to arrest the decline before the team's final scheduled Shield game in Melbourne, skipper Allan Border instituted an alcohol ban for his players. It was not a policy designed to please his overseas star, who had declared shortly after his debut that 'I play my best cricket after a severe night on the ale.'

Whether the policy was aimed at him or not, Botham affected unconcern in an interview before the game and maintained an affable relationship with the Australian press. 'Apart from the pink elephants and the spiders on the walls I'm all right,' he said. 'But it doesn't worry me. The lads don't seem bothered at all by it. I think perhaps that it's just a little bit of discipline that we need for a few days before the game ... hopefully if I bowl 25 or 30 overs and it's hot the skipper will let me have a beer.' Another quip in the same interview indicates Botham's doubts about the policy's likely effectiveness: 'At Scunthorpe we couldn't have a drink the night before and we won bugger all.'

It *was* hot and if he didn't quite manage the full 25 overs as Queensland reduced Victoria to 234 for 7 on day one, he did charge in for 17, claiming the wicket of Jamie Siddons, caught in the hook trap, and took a sharp catch at slip to get rid of Victoria's captain, Dean Jones. But as the day ebbed towards its close, the heat, the frustrations of trying to force the win that would secure Queensland home advantage in the Shield Final, and perhaps the thirst too took their toll. Fielding at slip during the penultimate over of the day and suffering that most historic of ailments which affect English cricketers in Australia – a spot of not so friendly banter from the bleachers – Botham finally cracked. 'Half a dozen morons in the Melbourne crowd went well beyond the norm' he recalled. 'I like a bit of banter from the crowd – it gees me up – but this was just mindless, vicious, foul-mouthed personal abuse.' Botham had complained to the umpires and the ground authorities earlier in the day, but ended up marching off to the boundary to give the locals a taste of their own medicine. He was cited by both umpires for 'abusive language' and 'conduct detrimental to the spirit of the game.' Admitting both charges at a disciplinary hearing the following day – while nursing a strained muscle in his back that would prevent him from bowling in the rest of the match – Botham was fined £200.

It was Thursday 3 March, the very day that the TCCB concluded its spring meeting with public warnings about the consequences of players' bad behaviour. Relatively minor though Botham's offence had been, its timing could not possibly have been worse; his honeymoon period in Australia was about to turn very sour indeed.

Without their most mercurial bowler, Queensland were unable to prevent Victoria running up a total of 328 in their second innings, giving them an overall lead of 375 in the match. Moreover, Dean Jones' insistence on batting on into the final day left Queensland with too little time to make a measured run-chase. They came out for a blast anyway reaching 83 for 1 from the first 11 overs before a rapid collapse saw them lose by a disheartening margin of 203 runs. Queensland still qualified for the final, but their loss of form in their last four matches meant that they faced a tough journey to Perth to face the reigning champions, Western Australia – a repeat of the match which had brought their successful run to an end two months before.

Two days before the match, Allan Border's Queensland team boarded an Ansett Airlines jet at Brisbane Airport. By the time they disembarked in Perth, Ian Botham was facing two charges of assault and another of disorderly conduct. Botham, it was alleged, had grabbed a fellow passenger in a headlock and again used abusive language. Border had been sitting just two seats away at the time and initially tried to play the incident down saying, 'I'm very surprised it has gone this far' and insisting that Botham would still play in the final. This resolution was helped by the intervention of Botham's old adversary, Dennis Lillee, who posted the England star's bail of £2,000.

Botham began the match as scheduled, but under a distinct cloud. As well as the formal charges awaiting him, the Queensland Cricket Association had indicated it would set up its own inquiry into the airline incident, suggesting it might consider disciplinary action including cancelling the remainder of Botham's contract. The Australian Flight Attendants Association had also announced that it was considering banning him from domestic flights. Botham might have been forgiven for already feeling stranded in Perth as he spent an hour nudging his way to 9 during Queensland's less than imposing first innings total of 289. He then failed to take a wicket as Western Australia built a first innings lead of 55, and when Terry Alderman reduced the Queenslanders to 49 for 4 it was clear that Border's men would have to wait at least another year to break their Shield duck. Botham's obdurate, three-hour 54 helped save some face for them. It came to an end shortly after lunch on day four, a lunch break which had seen federal police enter the dressing room and interview several players, not including Botham, about further possible charges relating to the disorder on board the flight from Brisbane. 'The investigations and subsequent police action certainly didn't help our preparation,' Border said after the game.

Earlier that day the news had broken that Botham and Lillee were being charged by the Australian Cricket Board for causing damage estimated at £800 to a dressing room in Launceston during a one-day match between Tasmania and Queensland on 28 February. The damage was said to have been caused by the throwing of beer bottles and glasses. 'It was fairly substantial,' said ACB general manager Graham Halbish, 'there was a fair amount of broken glass, honour boards were damaged and it appears light fittings were shattered in the process.' One more wicket and one more catch as Western Australia eased to a five-wicket victory, more comfortably than the margin suggests, would be Botham's final acts as a Queensland player. Ominously, the TCCB had asked for a report from the ACB on all the incidents involving Botham that season, while following his team's defeat Queensland skipper Allan Border had cast doubt both on his own future as captain and Botham's future as a player for the state; it looked like Botham might soon be a cricketer without a team. If the AFAA carried out its threat of a domestic flight ban, Botham's only way out of Perth might be via an intercontinental flight back to London.

First he had to face his day in court. The day after Queensland's defeat in the final, the Perth Court of Petty Sessions was told that the altercation on the flight had started with an argument between Botham and Border. According to Prosecutor Jeff Scholz, Botham had used 'abusive language' throughout the flight and this had become worse once the argument had started. A passenger sitting in front of Botham, Adrian Winter, had asked Botham to moderate his language, using the words 'come on, it's becoming a bit common in here!' at which Botham had told him to mind his own business. Then, according to Scholz, 'he grabbed him by the scalp and hair around the temples and shook his head from side to side forcefully.' Another passenger had been threatened 'eyes front, or you'll be next!' Botham had apologised to Mr Winter and the other passengers when the plane landed, but the damage had been done. Botham pleaded guilty to the charges and was fined £320.

Botham's own account of the affair, revealed in his autobiography, does not attempt to refute his guilt of the technical charge of assault: 'I

shouldn't have laid hands on him, and as we got off the plane in Perth
I sought out the man and apologised for my behaviour.' His account
presents a far less menacing version of what happened. The argument
had started between Allan Border and batsman Greg Ritchie, who was
upset at being dropped from the Australian Test team, also captained
by Border, for being overweight. As the argument dragged on and
became increasingly heated, Botham 'left them to it, and went off to
have a drink with "the bowlers' club" at the back of the plane.' The
row lasted beyond a change of planes in Melbourne and the language
used began to annoy their fellow passengers. Botham attempted to
calm things down, but found Border's ill-temper now directed at him
instead of Ritchie:

> There was a bit of 'serve and volley' between us, and then someone
> in the row of seats in front of us turned round to complain about our
> language. My own temper was thoroughly up by now and, annoyed
> at the interruption, I said, 'Oh, mind your own business', placed my
> hands on his shoulders, and turned him round to face the front again.

The case for the prosecution shows an out-of-control drunken lout who
is a danger to all around him, and the case for the defence shows a
man who likes a drink and doesn't shirk an argument but occasionally
allows a situation to get out of hand. Botham was clearly involved in a
heated discussion, and clearly did lay hands on Mr Winter, but grabbing
him by the scalp and shaking his head from side to side? Only those
who were there will know just how far it went. Unsurprisingly, it was
the hostile case put by the prosecution which made all the headlines.

At first, Botham had found the attentions of the Australian press
flattering and engaging. After his Shield debut, which brought him a
rapid innings of 58, three wickets and five catches, he said, 'I've enjoyed
the media over here a lot more than I have in England.' But when Botham
arrived back in Brisbane it was clear that the attitude had changed. 'If
that man had kept his nose out of an argument that had nothing to do
with him, between Allan Border and myself, then none of this would
have happened' he told reporters waiting at the airport. 'I'm fed up with
all you people. You all read what the prosecutor said, you don't give
a stuff what the defence people say. You all jump to conclusions and
you're very quick to criticise.'

Of course it was not just the Australian media that had plundered the easy half-volleys offered up by Botham's behaviour. In fact, some of the Australian reaction to it all had been humorous and indulgent, like the allusion of one TV newsreader to Botham providing 'in-flight entertainment'. It was as if part of the Australian psyche welcomed this sign of larrikinism in their guest, which played up to his larger-than-life, bad-boy image and gave them what they had expected of Botham all along. But the reaction of the British press was quite different, from the measured disapproval of the broadsheets to the gleeful hysteria of the tabloids, there was no sign of indulgence there. On 1 April, with Botham safely out of range on the third day of his Alpine trek, *The Sun* ran a banner across the top of one page, allowing readers to revisit some of their old favourite Botham headlines: 'BOTHAM COCAINE AND SEX SCANDAL', 'AUSSIE FURY OVER BAD BOY BOTH!', 'BOTHAM HEAD BUTTS WAITER', 'DRUNK BOTH DRAGGED ME OVER THE BAR' and, perhaps most in need of calm explanation, 'BOTH TRIED TO SLIT MY THROAT'. All this came above its latest missive, headed 'BOTHAM MAKES ME SICK, SAYS GREG CHAPPELL', reinforced by a picture of Botham, unfortunately blinking as the paparazzo's shutter clicks, in mid-discourse with drink in hand.

The Chappell article, penned by Ray Fletcher, is an interesting example of the tabloid journalism of its time. The headline itself is a cunning realignment of what Chappell said in a radio interview after Botham had had his contract terminated following a hearing with the Queensland Cricket Board. Chappell's actual words, quoted in the piece, were 'what Ian has done is outside the laws of common decency and outside the legal framework in which we are all expected to live. To tell the truth, it sickened me, yet he has got nothing but flippant comments to make about it.' By this slight twist of Chappell's comments, *The Sun* made them appear a much more visceral, personal condemnation of Botham's character, rather than a comment on the morality of his particular actions. Having done this, and artfully juxtaposed a photograph of a clean-cut, smiling Chappell next to that of Botham, the paper then proceeded to attack Chappell himself by pointing out his own indiscretions, such as the notorious under-arm bowling incident in 1981 and his previous admissions to 'being in bars as late as anybody.' Reading it is rather like watching a prosecuting counsel discrediting his own witness, and yet to the casual reader, it is the accusation against

Botham rather than the flaws of the accuser which really hit home.

None of this will have come as a surprise to Botham, who left Australia claiming that the reports of his misbehaviour there had been wildly exaggerated and stating that he treated such reports and the reporters who made them 'with the contempt they deserve.' Botham had spent much of the decade being hounded by the press. Having signed a contract for a ghosted column with *The Sun* in late 1982, he soon found himself targeted by that paper's rivals. 'Bizarrely,' he recalled, 'after this had been going on for a while, *The Sun* felt impelled to join in as well, trying to outdo the sensational stories of their rivals.' Allegations of drug taking and womanising had dogged Botham and his teammates throughout the 1983/84 tour of New Zealand, and he had been fined £1,000 later that winter for comments to the effect that Pakistan was not a country fit to receive even his mother-in-law. Then, in 1986, came the admission of cannabis smoking, which brought a two-month ban followed by a triumphant return as he broke Dennis Lillee's Test wickets record at The Oval. Through it all there was the constant nagging attention of the press, stories of drink, drugs and women, even, according to one tale in Botham's autobiography, spiked drinks at public events, all helping to keep Botham's name in the headlines for all the wrong reasons.

The extent to which Botham's private life had become a well-traded tabloid currency was revealed in a study conducted by the Department of Sociology at the University of Lancaster. Attempting to assess the popularity of a variety of sports through the frequency with which they featured in the news pages rather than the sports pages, the study surveyed the contents of sixteen local and national newspapers published during 1985. This required the detailed analysis of no fewer than 3,015 editions. It was a mixed year for Botham, beginning with a *Sun* exclusive revealing that a police raid had discovered a small amount of marijuana at the cricketer's home, and ending with plaudits as he completed his first major charity walk from John O'Groats to Land's End. Cricket stories featured in 778 editions during that year, approximately once every four days. It was the second most featured sport in the entire list, a long way behind football. Remarkably, the study's authors noted in *The Cricketer*, stories about Ian Botham had accounted for no less than 40 per cent of all content related to cricket during the year, which meant more than 300 stories about Botham alone. Many would have involved the same material being published across a variety of titles, but the quantity is astonishing nevertheless. Take all Botham stories out of the statistics, and cricket dropped from second place in the list down to ninth, behind rugby, boxing and even yachting.

Botham, then, was no stranger to scandal, but this latest one had cost him dear. The three incidents in themselves had produced fines of more than £2,500; the cancellation of his Queensland contract would deprive him of two more lucrative seasons in Australia, while he also found his principal commercial backers, Carphone Group, withdrawing from part of their £150,000 deal. 'His behaviour has made it very difficult for us,' said Carphone chairman Ted Marwick. 'I don't expect him to be a saint, but there are lads and lads. We don't feel we can go on using him in advertisements out there because of his image, although we have no complaints in the UK.' And there might be worse to follow too, if the TCCB's new zero tolerance policy was to be applied to him.

As spring approached, and Botham led his elephant train over the Alps, the news continued to be mixed. His charity walk attracted the ire of the French actress Brigitte Bardot, who complained that by forcing elephants to follow him over the mountains he was engaging in cruelty to the animals. It was probably not what a generation of tabloid editors had dreamed of when they imagined a story featuring Botham and Bardot, but it would have to do. On the plus side for Botham, he had just been elected Pipe Smoker of the Year. In his editorial for the May issue of *Wisden Cricket Monthly*, David Frith mourned the decline of a 'fallen hero': 'He knows not the meaning of contrition and has no knack of reconsideration. Ian Botham knows precisely where each charity walk will end, but the path of his life seems less clear-cut, more threatening.' Frith, with long years of research behind him into cricket's tragic characters – gamblers, drinkers, depressives and suicides – perhaps saw in Botham a long-term potential to slide down the same path. But there was equal and more immediate concern for his future as an international cricketer:

Where stand the Test selectors in all this? If public demand, while not necessarily unanimous, comes into account – and it has occasionally affected selectors' thinking – then Botham will play for England this summer, unless his early-season form is wretched. If the selectors, on the other hand, feel that the new statute on discipline has to be implemented, they will be influenced heavily against Botham.

A. C. Smith had promised players a clean slate after the winter. Would Botham benefit from that? Or would the fact that the case of 'in-flight entertainment' had come some weeks after the new line on discipline had been announced count against him? Would England really choose to go into the toughest of all possible Test series' without their most brilliant attacking cricketer?

5

Champagne and Brickbats

Three weeks after arriving back from New Zealand, England's cricketers eased their way back into another county season. The physical and mental fatigue they must have been feeling would be familiar to their modern counterparts, but some other factors would be rather more of a novelty. No current Test cricketer would return from an overseas tour knowing he would have to plunge straight back into the pre-season routine, obliged to play a full part in his county's itinerary as soon as the season begins. Nor would quite so many of them begin the season unsure of their places when the selectors sat down to pick their first team of the summer. With senior players such as Gooch, Gower, Botham and perhaps Lamb likely to return, even those who could look back on reasonably successful winters, Martyn Moxon and Paul Jarvis for example, would begin the season looking anxiously over their shoulders.

Even the captain himself could not be entirely certain of his position. As Mike Gatting began the 1988 season he was, technically speaking, no longer England captain since nobody had formally been appointed to the role for the Texaco Trophy one-day series against the West Indies. Despite all the difficulties of the last few months, Gatting himself was keen to continue, but not everyone greeted his declaration of intent with enthusiasm. Writing in the *Daily Mirror*, Mike Bowen ('The column that gives it to you straight') presented himself as one of Gatting's biggest fans: 'He is the person I most like to see at the crease when I walk through the gates of any county ground,' – a neat way of persuading the reader that no one else is quite so well qualified to condemn. Bowen dismissed Gatting's 'increasingly disjointed leadership' in an article itself disjointed to the point of dismemberment.

Bowen sounded optimistic about the series ahead: 'We are licking our lips at the prospect of beating the West Indies in a Test series for the first time in almost twenty years.' It was a curious position to take with the West Indies remaining the most consistently formidable team in world cricket and England not having won a Test match in more than a year. But a glance at England's potential batting line-up did offer grounds for hope: 'England, should they select purely on form, can field a front six of Graham Gooch, Chris Broad, David Gower, Allan Lamb, Gatting and Ian Botham this summer.' Bowen felt that all this potential might be for nothing if Gatting remained in charge. The substance of his case was that Gatting had taken certain expressions of sympathy following the Shakoor Rana affair as an indication that he had the entire English nation behind him whenever he tried to 'stick it up the colonials', and that ever since his command of team discipline had been lacking. This, thought Bowen, was reason enough to remove Gatting as captain and return him to the role of 'sergeant major' he had performed so well under Mike Brearley at Middlesex. 'I believe that Gatting at the helm could prove our biggest handicap,' wrote Bowen. As it turned out, Gatting's absence from the helm would see England founder on the rocks.

In the *Daily Express* the following day, Colin Bateman was no more enthusiastic about Gatting continuing in the role, but his argument was at least based upon sounder foundations. England had gone thirteen Tests without a win, the worst sequence under any England captain, and were about to face 'an awesome five-Test confrontation with the West Indies.' Bateman felt that the selectors would probably not yet be ready to ditch the hero of the 1986/87 Ashes campaign and would reappoint him for half the summer, but 'there are almost as many people eyeing-up the England captain's job as there are people queueing up to take a pot shot at Gatting.' Bateman's preferred candidate was the thirty-two-year-old Somerset captain Peter Roebuck, a Cambridge law graduate 'in the deep-thinking intellectual mould of the highly successful Mike Brearley.' But Roebuck, despite a first-class average comparable to those of rivals for an opening spot like Chris Broad, Tim Robinson or Martyn Moxon, had yet to play a Test. And if Brearley's greatest achievement was the reinvigoration of a woebegone Ian Botham halfway through the 1981 Ashes series, Roebuck would struggle to achieve similar miracles of motivation – his relationship with the all-rounder had become impossibly strained following the departures of Viv Richards and Joel Garner from the Somerset dressing room. Botham felt that the two West Indian legends had been treated poorly by the club, and by Roebuck personally; his strength of feeling on the matter had led him to sever his career-long connection with Somerset and sign for Worcestershire the previous year. Appointing Roebuck, Bateman conceded, 'would be a revolutionary move at Lord's'.

Bateman, along with most of the cricket press, found the weakness of the rest of the field the most convincing argument for Gatting's likely retention. Neither John Emburey nor Graham Gooch were thought likely to want to tour the following winter. Gooch, furthermore, 'found the pressures of captaincy so great that he has stepped down at Essex to concentrate on his batting.' Other candidates, like Hampshire's Mark Nicholas and Kent's Chris Cowdrey, would 'struggle to justify their place in the international team'. Derbyshire's Kim Barnett had a 'carefree approach', which would suit him more to a role in the team as a batsman than a captain. None of these really fitted the bill. If Gatting was to be axed, the likeliest scenario would be a return to the man he had replaced, David Gower, returning from a winter off refreshed and hungry for more success.

Gower still had plenty of fans for his captaincy efforts – those who remembered his twin triumphs against India and Australia and thought him unfortunate to have twice come up against the West Indies at their most indomitable either side of those two wins. But if Gower was truly refreshed and eager for runs, would it be prudent to throw him straight back in as captain against the very team that had haunted his previous tenure? His old opposite number, Clive Lloyd, who had captained the West Indies in Gower's first official series as captain in 1984 and had signed up to write a column in the *Daily Express* in 1988, thought not. Gower, thought Lloyd, was not a natural captain:

He is too laidback, perhaps too self-centred. Gower lacks the authority to impose his will when senior players are questioning his tactics. And he cannot whip his men into renewed effort when their spirits are flagging. That was only too evident when England were in the West Indies in 1986. They just gave up. They thought: our opponents are better than we are and if we lose it's no big deal.

But the West Indies were now a team in transition. They still had plenty of fast bowlers to choose from, but just how formidable an opposition would they be?

Since the 5-0 drubbing of England in 1986, the West Indies had failed to win any of the four Test series they had played in. On the other hand they had not lost any of them either. Tough tours to Pakistan and India had tested the side severely, and the Indian series might well have been won had it not been for the loss of almost two days' play to rain in Bombay. A flat, slow pitch in Calcutta, which saw only seventeen wickets fall during the entire match, and another pitch, 'deplorably under-prepared' according to *Wisden*, for the final Test in Madras, which was tailor made for the home team and gave the nineteen-year-old leg-spinner Narendra Hirwani sixteen wickets on Test debut also added to the difficult circumstances. Perhaps most disappointing was the drawn series in New Zealand in the spring of 1987, which had seen the West Indies take a 1-0 lead into the final Test at Christchurch only for a spectacular first-innings collapse against Richard Hadlee and Ewen Chatfield to allow New Zealand to draw level. It was a tour that had seen an end to the distinguished Test careers of Larry Gomes and Joel Garner.

If the tour of India in 1987/88 was a case of opportunities missed by the tourists and opportunities cunningly manufactured by the hosts, the visit of Pakistan to the Caribbean in the early spring was a case of pride damaged and only falteringly restored. A Pakistan side greatly augmented by the return from premature retirement of the talismanic Imran Khan had recovered from a 5-0 defeat in the one-day series and inflicted upon West Indies their first defeat in a home Test for a decade. Centuries from Vivian Richards and Jeffrey Dujon and some fine all-round bowling had come close to giving West Indies a win in the second Test, but Pakistan's last man, Abdul Qadir, had survived the last five balls of the match to earn Pakistan a thrilling draw. The final Test was just as gripping; Pakistan took a narrow three-run lead into the second innings and then set the hosts a target of 266 for victory. West Indies slumped to 207 for 8, with only Dujon of the senior batsmen remaining, but Winston Benjamin stayed with him in an unbeaten ninth wicket stand to seal victory for the home side and retain their record of not having lost a home series since 1973.

It was widely considered to have been one of the most exciting Test series ever, and left many regretting that only three Tests had been played and not five. But there were signs that the West Indies were no longer the formidable machine they once had been. Viv Richards was now thirty-six, and while a century in the second Test at Trinidad had earned him yet another man of the match award, the runs were not coming with quite the same frequency as of old. Richards had missed the first Test after having an operation for haemorrhoids; the team's most experienced fast bowler, Malcolm Marshall, had missed it with a knee injury. Marshall, with 255 Test wickets to his credit, was now the sole survivor of the great fast bowling quartets of the past ten years, but he was now thirty and it was essential for the future success of the team that a supporting cast of bowlers emerge quickly. Richards and Marshall were not the only members of the team on the wrong side of thirty: Gordon Greenidge was now thirty-seven; Desmond Haynes was thirty-two; and Jeff Dujon would reach the same age before the Test series in England got underway.

There were talented young players coming through, but quickly enough and in sufficient numbers to replace the old guard when the time came? Richie Richardson's spectacular start to his Test career had come to a shuddering halt. At twenty-six he should have been approaching his peak as a batsman and taking some of the pressure off of his more experienced colleagues in the batting order. But since the England series two years earlier he had failed to register a single Test century and his record of 748 runs from thirteen Tests at an average of 35.62 was not what the world's leading side needed from the pivotal No.3 position. Only just twenty-one, Carl Hooper had more time on his side than Richardson, but while a fine maiden Test century in his debut series in India had marked him out as a player of genuine class and remarkable style, this promising beginning had been followed up by a disappointing home series against Pakistan, which brought a highest score of just 54 and an average of only 26. Even the experienced Desmond Haynes was going through something of a slump: only two Test centuries since the last tour of England and a record from his last ten Tests of 425 runs at 25.

Nor did the bowling attack have quite the terrifying look of a few years before. Michael Holding and Wayne Daniel had gone in 1984, Joel Garner in 1987. Winston Davis had never quite convinced at the highest level and Tony Gray had been ditched after just five Tests despite taking twenty-two wickets at 17.13. Of the current attack, Patrick Patterson was capable of fearsome pace and could be devastating in his day, but when his rhythm wasn't right or the conditions were not conducive he could be expensive. Nor was he quite as subtle a bowler as some of his predecessors, but forty-three Test wickets at an average of 25.21 would have earned greater adulation in some less fussy Test playing countries, and he was surely looking forward to striking terror into England's batsmen just as he had done in his debut series two years before.

Then there was Courtney Walsh, whose Test debut had come three years earlier in Australia, but who had yet to convince some commentators that he had the requisite belly full of fire to be a top-class fast bowler. On the tour of India he had bowled for long spells with great discipline and stamina and had claimed two five-wicket hauls, but during the Pakistan series he had been used very much as back-up to the front line attack and had claimed only four wickets in the entire series. Perhaps there was some sense in this tactic, as his county captain at Gloucestershire, David Graveney, considered him to be 'the best old ball bowler in the world'. While Walsh's control, stamina and experience of English conditions made him an obvious selection for the tour, there remained a feeling that after three years Courtney Walsh had yet to really establish himself at the top level and that, perhaps, he was just too nice to ever do so.

When the West Indies named their squad for the England tour, few in the host country would have realised the significance of the inclusion of one C. E. L. Ambrose. But in the absence of Malcolm Marshall against Pakistan, Curtly Ambrose had been given the new ball alongside Patrick Patterson ahead of Courtney Walsh. It was a clear demonstration of faith in the twenty-four-year-old who, in his first full season, had just set a new record of thirty-five wickets in the inter-island Red Stripe Cup. Ambrose's maiden Test series had brought him only seven wickets at over 50, but he had kept his place when Marshall returned to the side and taken the new ball at the start of each innings throughout the series. Little was known about Ambrose in England, outside of the Central Lancashire League where he had taken 115 wickets for Heywood the previous summer, including a devastating spell of 8 for 8 against Rochdale. This, combined with his efforts for Trinidad and his elevation to international cricket, had convinced Northamptonshire to offer him a contract for the remainder of the 1988 season, once international duties were concluded.

Curtly Ambrose was not the only young fast bowler hoping to make an impression on his first tour of England. Antiguan Winston Benjamin had played in four Tests the previous winter and had enjoyed a productive series against Pakistan, taking twelve wickets at 24.41. Completing the fast bowling options was a twenty-year-old from Trinidad and Tobago, Ian Bishop, who had earned his place with nineteen wickets at 13.61 in his first season of Red Stripe Cup cricket. Bishop was one of three players in the party who had yet to make their Test debuts – Keith Arthurton, a twenty-three-year-old left-handed batsman from Nevis, and twenty-four-year-old reserve wicketkeeper David Williams from Trinidad being the others. With Trinidadian opener Phil Simmons also making the squad after two Test appearances, which had come in West Indies' two Test defeats the previous winter, the tourists' squad contained eight players who had no more than eleven Test caps. It was a blend of youth and experience right enough, but perhaps too much at either end and too little in the middle for real comfort. The West Indies were indeed a side 'in a fidgety state of transition' as *Wisden Cricket Monthly's* David Foot put it.

Comments from the West Indies camp suggested a new modesty of expectation. As the team warmed up in the nets at Lord's, manager Jackie Hendriks paid tribute to a generation of heroes now departed from the scene and attempted to lessen the weight of history upon the shoulders of their replacements:

> We have lost Clive Lloyd, Larry Gomes, Michael Holding and Joel Garner and you don't replace greats overnight. We are bringing in younger people such as Courtney Walsh, Carl Hooper and Richie Richardson but they take time to mesh in. I still think our lads will give a good account of themselves and it should be a very good series between two reasonable teams.

One of those departed greats, Clive Lloyd, went even further in his column for the *Daily Express*. 'England have their best chance for ten years to beat the West Indies this summer because we are a side in transition,' he wrote. According to Lloyd, the team had fallen into an old habit which he, during his time as captain, had fought long and hard to rid them of – the curse of not fighting their way out of difficult situations. This, he said, was compounded by a young and inexperienced bowling attack which lacked the fearsome and intimidating aspect of old. Whereas, in the Lloyd era, the prospect of facing Holding, Garner, Roberts and others would have sown seeds of doubt in the minds of even the most accomplished of opposition batsmen before the first ball had been bowled, that was no longer the case. West Indies' new breed of fast bowlers were, said Lloyd, 'very raw' and in need of guidance from their senior colleagues. 'We have a tradition that knowledge is passed on. I would expect Courtney Walsh and Malcolm Marshall to be doing that with Ambrose. The series could turn on how quickly the youngsters adapt to conditions.'

Part of Lloyd's concern came from his respect for the likely composition of England's batting line-up. Lloyd predicted the return of Gooch and Gower, with runs to come as well from Broad and Gatting: 'A battler as well as a talented batsman. He's not savage, he's lovely to watch.' Of the younger breed, Lloyd liked the look of the 'gutsy' Matthew Maynard, and in a previous piece he had already recorded his expectation that Ian Botham would return to make runs again. The lack of a mention for Allan Lamb, who had taken three centuries off Lloyd's more seasoned attack four years earlier, is strange, but there was no mistaking Lloyd's admiration for the abilities of Graham Gooch: 'If Gooch gets loose he'll make a stack of runs and I'm concerned at what he might do to our inexperienced bowling attack.' Despite all this, Lloyd still did not think it would be easy for England's batsmen; they would still need to fight to make their runs. 'Let me make this clear ... it's the gutsy ones who will make runs. They are the ones who are going to stand up to the fast bowlers.'

England, thought Lloyd, would have players with the right amount of guts to take on those fast bowlers, and would West Indies themselves have enough guts and enough confidence to cope with a resurgent and more assertive England? 'Before a series we used to think "by how many Tests will we win?" The players still think we are good enough not to *lose* Test matches, but that's not the same thing at all.' Between them, Lloyd and Hendriks presented a picture of a changed West Indies team, a side now uncertain and perhaps vulnerable, needing great leadership from its remaining senior players as well as its captain, a man, according to Lloyd, 'facing his greatest Test.'

On Monday 9 May, ten days before the Texaco Trophy series would begin at Edgbaston, Peter May and his colleagues finally took the plunge and reappointed Mike Gatting as England captain. Just as Colin Bateman had predicted, it was a vote of limited confidence. The appointment was for just the first half of the summer – the Texaco Trophy and the first two Tests. The exact length of that tenure would have significant consequences later in the summer. Gatting had been appointed for the entire series the year before, but despite this apparent diminution of his tenure, he stated that he saw no significance in this limited reappointment: 'I am very happy to be doing the job again and don't see it as being on trial' he said. 'The selectors have seen the way I do the job for nearly two years and my trial period came at the beginning of that. I was given all five Tests last summer because we had an exceptional winter in Australia. This year the arrangement is no different from the normal one.'

His claim cut little ice with the press. 'May and Co. wanted Gatting to know they were unhappy with the poor discipline of the winter tours,' wrote Colin Bateman. 'He also has to halt a depressing sequence of thirteen Tests without a win. Against the West Indies, it will be the biggest challenge of his career.' Gatting's statement was also undermined rather by the Chairman of Selectors himself. 'Everyone who plays for England is on trial' he said, 'and even selectors are on trial as we are only appointed for a year at a time.' In the light of Gatting's temporary reappointment and the time normally allotted for a new player to prove himself in international cricket, an entire year seemed like rather a generous period of grace for the selectors to enjoy.

May had made clear earlier in the summer that selection this year would be dependent upon both form and behaviour; reputation would count for nothing. This hinted at the prospect of a side that had come agonisingly close to winning the World Cup just a few months before being consigned to history on the basis of a couple of Benson & Hedges Cup matches. It also meant worrying times for David Gower, finding early season form elusive, and Ian Botham, also struggling with form and finding that the legend of 'Bad Boy Botham' just would not go away.

On the very day that Peter May reappointed Gatting as England captain, he would have read that Botham had been accused of flicking a 'V' sign at spectators during an ill-tempered Sunday League game against Somerset at Taunton. The allegations were strenuously denied by Botham, who dismissed the story as 'another case of cheap sensationalism at my expense'. Botham could have done without the extra headlines and the rumbling on of his feud with Somerset captain Peter Roebuck. Roebuck had fallen victim to a one-handed return catch by Botham for 18, after which he was seen to gesticulate towards the bowler with his bat. Roebuck claimed he had simply been indicating that he ought to have hit the ball harder. In the circumstances, it is tempting not to believe the denials of either player.

Somerset *v.* Worcestershire at Taunton in May 1988 is more readily recalled now as the match when Graeme Hick suggested the potential to become one of the game's great batsmen by hitting 405 not out. The fact that so many influential journalists were there to witness it was as much down to Botham's poor form, and his feud with Roebuck, as it was to Hick's precocious talent and his race to complete 1,000 runs before the end of May. Botham had come into the match with first-class scores of only 3 and 4 to his credit, and no wickets claimed with the ball. Dismissed for just 7 as his colleagues ran up their huge total, Botham seemed to be clinging to hope, rather than expectation, that he would receive one more chance to take on the West Indies. 'The selectors know I'm around, and it's up to me to play well. It's as simple as that' he told journalists. 'I don't expect to walk into an England side. I expect to have to perform. But I do think the selectors will go for experience.'

Except when unavailable through injury, suspension or personal choice, Botham had never been dropped by England since making his Test debut in 1977. For all Peter May's statements about players needing to show form before being chosen for England, it seemed inconceivable that Botham, with his long record of achievement and ability to turn a match through sheer force of personality, might be overlooked. Botham tried to remain upbeat: 'Never felt better old son,' he replied to Frank Keating when quizzed about his form. However, Keating sensed time was running out for the old warrior, who had just three innings left before the selectors would choose their Texaco Trophy squad.

The tricky choice facing the selectors had been well summed up already by Christopher Martin-Jenkins in his editorial for *The Cricketer* in May: 'They will have to weigh up on one hand Botham's prodigious record, 5,057 runs, 343 wickets and 109 catches in 94 Tests, and on the other hand his increasingly less effective performances for England, especially with the ball. Last season against Pakistan in five Tests he took just seven wickets at 61.' Martin-Jenkins compared this with David Capel's recent performances in New Zealand 'on even more unhelpful pitches and with slip catches being dropped for a pastime.' Capel's five wickets at 54 did not look much better on the face of it, but the trend of effectiveness was much in the Northamptonshire all-rounder's favour. 'Capel is improving as fast as Botham is declining, and although a strong case could still be made for Botham as a specialist batsman who bowls, he would have to displace either Lamb or Gower at No.5.' It seemed an unlikely scenario, however much Gatting might want Botham back in his team. If the England skipper did want the veteran match winner in the team, it would be more down to faith in the old Botham magic as to any serious belief that his powers remained undimmed. 'Who can forget how Botham returned at the end of the 1986 season after his ban for drug taking to galvanise not just a listless England team but the entire cricketing scene? So much of his cricket has been a joy, but life would be so much more tranquil without him.'

The weekend after Mike Gatting was reappointed as England captain, he sat down with Peter May, Fred Titmus, Phil Sharpe and Micky Stewart to select the first side of the summer. In choosing their men, the selectors had to contend with not just the scratchy form of Botham and Gower but a finger injury to first choice wicketkeeper Bruce French, a groin strain carried by Yorkshire fast bowler Paul Jarvis and of course the knee injury that had kept Neil Foster out of any cricket so far this summer.

When the squad was announced it did not include Botham or Gower, but there were two surprises. The first was that it contained fourteen players, rather than the thirteen the selectors' had suggested it would. The second was the inclusion of Surrey's twenty-nine-year-old West Indian-born batsman Monte Lynch, who had never been called up to the England side at all and had only just completed an international ban imposed by the TCCB for touring South Africa with a rebel West Indies XI in 1983/84. The tour had earned Lynch a lifetime ban from the West Indies Cricket Board. Lynch could be a destructive one-day batsman, but his elevation to the England side caused some raised eyebrows. Writing in *The Guardian*, Gatting's old teammate Mike Selvey thought he had an explanation that covered both surprises: 'There can be no quibbles about the choices of Broad, Gooch, Lamb, Emburey, Dilley, Small or DeFreitas, nor even with Lynch, despite a theory that it was lunch Gatting wanted. That would explain the extra man.'

Lynch too was surprised to be called up at this stage of his career. Even a summons to act as a substitute fielder for the Lord's Test the previous summer had, he thought, been more down to his reputation as a first-class fielder than his potential as an international batsman. The call up had hastily been rescinded when it was realised he was still under his ban for touring South Africa. There were other choices that bemused Selvey and other judges. Why pick Derek Pringle when his performances in the group stages of the World Cup had brought him just 20 runs and a bowling record of one wicket for 148 from 24 overs? According to Peter May, Pringle was 'starting to hit the ball over the top' – a skill Selvey suspected Pringle would have little opportunity of demonstrating against Malcolm Marshall. David Capel, it was said, had been left out due to concerns over his recovery from knee surgery, yet he had returned to action on 5 May in a four-day Championship match against Gloucestershire, in the middle of which he also played a 40-over Sunday League game. Having come through that ordeal unscathed he had then gone into Benson & Hedges Cup matches against Minor Counties and Worcestershire, during the second of which, said Selvey, 'Phil Sharpe, a selector, watched Capel bowl to Botham the quickest ball of the season seen at Northampton, bat for two hours and take three catches, one of them after a 30-yard sprint.' To leave out Capel on the grounds of fitness seemed, after this, disingenuous, especially since Pringle had already missed matches through injury twice this season.

The inclusion of Bill Athey ahead of young talents like Fairbrother and Maynard was also questioned by Mike Selvey. Athey, he said, 'tends to dominate the strike without scoring' in one-day internationals. His inclusion could only be down to his appearance and behaviour meeting the standards expected by May and Co. The omission of Fairbrother, Maynard and Sussex's Paul Parker was probably due to more parochial reasons: 'The first two have not played against Middlesex this year, and Parker's single effort at Lord's brought his lowest score of the season.' No doubt it would help a player then to impress on the field against the England captain, but perhaps Selvey also had in mind the reluctance of some selectors to venture beyond the M25. The choice of Paul Downton over Jack Russell too, he thought, was probably due to the Middlesex wicketkeeper's close relationship with his county captain.

Lastly, Selvey asked how the selectors could justify omitting Jonathan

Agnew on the grounds that his figures flattered his performances on friendly Leicester pitches, while picking Neal Radford on the strength of his record at the notoriously green-topped New Road Worcester. It was, he summed up, 'a typical messy compromise between captain's demands and selectorial whim'. John Thicknesse, writing in the *Evening Standard*, offered an even more direct condemnation: 'Not by a long chalk for the first time in May's six years as chairman, selection of the squad was pitiful.' Such deprecation of the selectors' general abilities was to be found throughout the British press' response to this particular choice of personnel. It was perhaps the most widely condemned selection of an England team for many years, as *The Times'* veteran correspondent John Woodcock wrote: 'I have not for some years known an England selection cause such a public debate, in which the competing factors have been curiosity, hilarity and plain outrage.'

There was probably more logic to some of the selectors' choices than the critics gave credit for. Behind it all, no doubt, was a measure of justifiable respect for their upcoming opponents. Why throw in youngsters like Maynard and Russell to such a fray, with potentially damaging consequences? They surely remembered Downton's plucky performances with the bat in the summer of 1984 when the opposition had been even more formidable. In picking Pringle they may too have remembered his form exactly four years before when he was one of the stars of that Texaco Trophy series against Lloyd's men. Monte Lynch was, perhaps, a horses for courses choice, a one-day specialist who might come off, but otherwise, if he failed, would not affect future options too badly. 'Lynch has always been in the minds of the selectors' commented Peter May. 'He is a very brave batsman and a top-class fielder.' It was not, however, a selection that suggested that May's committee had much of a plan for the future.

If the choices of the England selectors had been predictably conservative, their results were unexpectedly positive. While the West Indies took some promising form into the Texaco Trophy matches, they were also carrying a few injuries. Desmond Haynes was ruled out with a knee injury, meaning a rare outing as Greenidge's opening partner for Phil Simmons, while their fast bowling options were reduced by a shoulder injury to Winston Benjamin and another knee problem affecting Patrick Patterson. Senior fast bowler Malcolm Marshall, while declared fit, was nursing a rib injury that would see him operating at reduced pace over the next few weeks. The tourists were not yet firing on all cylinders and their English hosts took full advantage. Not only was the margin of the 3-0 clean sweep convincing, each of the three matches was itself won comfortably.

England won the first match at Edgbaston by six wickets. For Derek Pringle in particular it was a triumph; having bowled with exceptional control, he restored calm to the crease after Lynch's panicky debut and partnered Gatting in the stand of 66 that saw England to victory. 'A dangerous thing is a Pringle,' wrote Mike Selvey. 'Helpings of humble pie here, although laced with proviso – there are two games to go.' Selvey was not the only cricket writer choking down a portion of humble pie that day, and no doubt many other unpalatable slices were being uncomfortably, if rather less publicly, digested up and down the land. However, as Selvey said, there were still two games to go in the series, and plenty of opportunity for this initial victory to be proven as ephemeral and insignificant as a mayfly. But before that could be put to the test, another event was to shake English cricket, and place even more significance on the sound performance at Edgbaston of Derek Pringle.

On the day after the Edgbaston match, in a County Championship game at New Road, Worcester, Ian Botham at last took his first first-class wicket of the season. Perhaps not surprisingly, it turned out to be that of the man with whom he had so publicly feuded in recent weeks – Somerset's captain Peter Roebuck. Later that day, he dived to try and field the ball and when he got up he felt a twinge in his back. This was nothing new for the thirty-two-year-old all-rounder; he had first suffered an injury to his back playing for Somerset at the Parks on a cold April day in 1980 and had suffered periodic pain ever since. At first, Botham thought that his latest twinge was no more than another bout of sciatica; he was soon having other thoughts. At 3.30 p.m. he left the field. 'There goes Beefy,' remarked an old Somerset teammate, 'just in time for the 4.40 race on the telly.' Botham would have plenty of time to watch televised racing over the coming months.

'Within half an hour of coming off I was almost totally immobilised' he said. Botham was immediately taken to hospital, where a series of x-rays revealed the bad news. His long-standing spinal injury, spondylolisthesis, where vertebrae in the back slip out of alignment causing excruciating pain, had undergone a rapid and marked deterioration. Two vertebrae had become displaced and Botham would require an operation to fuse the two together. Recovery would involve a stay in hospital of up to four weeks and at least three months of intensive physiotherapy to get the muscles supporting his spine functioning properly again. Following the operation, Botham would have to lie flat in bed for two weeks before he was even able to sit up. For three months afterwards he would wear a plaster surgical jacket to support his back while the bones fused. There was no possibility of him playing any more cricket that season. The long-term prognosis suggested that the Botham who would emerge at the end of the recovery period would be one with greatly diminished flexibility. It was, wrote Scyld Berry, 'highly improbable that Botham will ever be able to bowl again at medium pace or above at international level.'

What Christopher Martin-Jenkins wrote in his notebook that day read like an obituary for Botham's career:

The West Indies manager Jackie Hendriks summed up the reaction of cricketing folk yesterday when he described the news of Botham's injury as 'terrible, man'. Everyone is sorry when serious injury threatens the career of any professional cricketer and although the specialist apparently gives Botham an excellent chance of playing again next season there must obviously be some doubt about his ever being so effective a player again. Indeed, there was doubt already. His recent figures ... suggest very strongly that the best was past.

Both Berry and Martin-Jenkins suggested that Botham would have to concentrate in future on developing as a specialist batsman.

The man himself refused to be beaten. 'You fellows have written me off often enough in the past, but I'll bounce back from this one as well' he told journalists. The good wishes of an entire nation it seemed were with him once again; all thoughts of Bad Boy Botham were banished, for the time being at least. He received reassurance from the England selectors, with Micky Stewart saying, 'the news of Ian's injury is a great disappointment. I hope he comes through it and continues his career with Worcester and England.' Peter May too chipped in saying, 'I just hope the operation is a success and he gets fit again as soon as possible.' Even Peter Roebuck paid tribute to his most implacable enemy: 'Ian has always been brave about playing through injuries. He is a very brave cricketer.'

Of course it was inevitable that the injury to Ian Botham would lead to a frantic discussion of how to replace him. Inevitable but mistaken, as Scyld Berry calmly pointed out: 'this sort of botching-up should be resisted. Botham is irreplaceable.' Far better that the England selectors should ditch the idea of playing with five front-line bowlers and instead pick a side solidly founded on six specialist batsmen, which might also have an unexpected benefit, 'they can then afford to pick the best wicketkeeper available in Russell, whether or not his batting turns out to be uncertain against fast, short-pitched bowling.' If Berry's prescription had been followed, the next decade of English cricket might well have been very different. Instead, Derek Pringle suddenly found himself the most discussed, if not celebrated, cricketer in the kingdom.

Pringle's fine performance at Edgbaston had placed him in pole position to become England's all-rounder of choice in Botham's absence, but it also meant he became the focus for the hopes of a cricketing nation which had been seeking an answer to the question of how to replace Botham since short-term injuries first began affecting him in the early 1980s. Pringle's first elevation to the England team in 1982 had been, in part, an attempt to plan for the post-Botham period; the pressure to find such a player, and maintain the balance of the side, was immense. Derek Pringle, however, certainly wasn't showing any sign of it. 'Don't expect any Beefy-style v-signs to the press box from me' he told journalists before the second Texaco Trophy match at Headingley, 'I'm not sensitive to criticism. I was pleasantly surprised to be picked and I'll do my best, as always, to ensure I keep my place. Unless I do well there's a chance the selectors will do what they did in the winter – pick me for the World Cup and David Capel for the Tests.' Headingley was to be his next chance to prove the critics wrong. He could not have hoped for a more suitable venue, or more conducive conditions. 'You could not leave Pringle out now anyway,' wrote Mike Selvey, his tongue still worrying at a morsel of humble pie stuck in his cheek, 'there would be an outcry.'

England were unchanged, but the West Indies brought in young fast bowler Ian Bishop to replace the struggling Roger Harper. It had an immediate effect; England, put in by Richards on a typically lively Headingley wicket, struggled their way to 186 for 8, Bishop taking 2 for 32 to complement Ambrose's miserly 1 for 19. It was no easier for the West Indies when they batted, Pringle and Small again the stars, claiming 3 for 30 and 2 for 11, respectively. The West Indies were bowled out for 139, England winning by 47 runs, to take an unassailable 2-0 lead in the series. 'Any total above 180 was going to take some getting at Headingley' commented Clive Lloyd. 'It seemed the West Indies relaxed a little when they had England struggling.' Richards' decision to keep himself and Phil Simmons in the attack, leaving Ambrose and Marshall short of their full allocation of overs, brought severe criticism after the game, but Richards countered, 'I thought Simmons and myself were doing a good containing job, and if you get a side out for 186 you expect to win. But we didn't bat well enough.'

The West Indies' batting appeared especially vulnerable without the established opening partnership of Greenidge and Haynes, while Richardson was looking like a wicket waiting to happen – and not waiting very long – at No. 3. However, they could reflect on one positive aspect to this game: a noticeable improvement in their ability to put pressure on England's batsmen, not least due to the impressive debut performance of Ian Bishop. 'He already has a fine rhythm,' wrote Robin Marlar in the *Sunday Times*, 'lies back in his action like Colin Croft and, by dragging his hand across the ball, he was able to bowl fast leg-breaks to beat anybody.' With Bishop in the attack, the West Indies' bowling was beginning to look more like the relentlessly successful pace machine of old, especially since the man he replaced, Roger Harper, was struggling so badly. Harper's bowling action, thought Bill Frindall, 'resembled a badly programmed robot attempting to climb a rope ladder.'

England had delivered another hard fought, professional display. The plaudits, naturally, went to the bowlers, but Paul Downton's four important catches, part of a display with the gloves widely commended as 'immaculate' also found widespread favour. With the bat, his partnership with Derek Pringle had turned the game England's way after an uncertain start. Ah, Pringle. 'Cometh the hour, Cometh the Pringle' declared *The Guardian's* headline writers. His outstanding performances with bat and ball won him the man of the match award and served much of the press pack with another slice of humble pie. The man himself was typically content to keep his size 13 boots on the ground. 'Everything is going in my favour at the moment, but there's a long way to go before I feel I'm established in the side. I've only done well in a couple of one-day games.' Pringle was determined not to be flattered by coverage that had turned from derisive to laudatory overnight, and revealed a tender spot about one aspect of it: 'Why should it be so surprising? Do people think I came back from my winter trip to South America paraplegic or something?'

The third match at Lord's produced another dominant performance from England. Having restricted the West Indies to 178, England kept wickets in hand and then Lamb and Gatting smashed 55 from just 6 overs to see England home with 5 overs to spare. Much of the praise was for Gatting – England's man of the series for his return with the bat (140 runs and out just once), and also for his captaincy. His leadership of his side had been 'far more impressive than that of Viv Richards,' said Colin Bateman in the *Express*. 'Gatting must already have secured his job for the summer.'

Might the selectors have brought an end to Gatting's trial period now and extended his tenure beyond the second Test? This they did not do, despite the evidence of a well-disciplined side playing just as their captain would want them to. Perhaps they would have had little thanks if they had. Before the series began, all the criticism was directed at the selectors for their choice of personnel, but afterwards all the praise went to the players. 'We have had some unpleasant criticism,' said Peter May before the series. He got it in the neck for picking Derek Pringle, but when Pringle turned out to be an inspired choice, humble pie and apologies galore went to Pringle himself; May had to gloat in private and wait for the next time one of his choices misfired. He would not have to wait too long. Such is the life of an England selector.

Mike Gatting too had little time to bask in the glow of success. If he sought respite from West Indian fast bowlers after three matches against them in a week, he got none. No sooner had he unbuckled his pads, collected the series trophy and his man of the series award and answered, in perhaps slightly more forthcoming style than of late, the questions of the assembled press, than he was dashing up the motorway to Derby where a Benson & Hedges Cup quarter-final tussle against Michael Holding and Devon Malcolm awaited him the next day. Holding trapped him lbw for just 5. Such is the life of an England captain.

Amid the rejoicing over England's clean sweep of the series, thoughts immediately turned to the Test series ahead. Colin Bateman thought that the evidence of the one-day matches showed that England at least should not fear another 'Blackwash', but avoiding a 5-0 defeat was a long way from actually winning the series and the West Indies remained, player for player, the better team. 'They will take some beating' said Gatting. 'The Tests are completely different matches, but these victories must have given us confidence and we've had the chance to have a good look at their bowlers.'

The West Indians themselves had taken a good look at their bowlers, and as the series went on they increasingly liked what they saw. With no limitation on the number of overs bowled by an individual bowler, England would have Marshall, Walsh, Ambrose, Bishop, Benjamin or Patterson coming at them over after over, day after day, match after match. It was not an enticing prospect. The West Indies batting, however, continued to look vulnerable, prone to bouts of strokeless passivity and outbreaks of reckless, panicky running. If they couldn't develop some confidence and form over their two remaining county games, the odds would have to be on the Test series being as bowler dominated as the one-day series had been.

There was a limit, however, to the amount of confidence England could take from their Texaco Trophy victory. For the West Indies, the one-day series had been no more than preparation for the more serious business ahead – five Test matches. 'These one-day games are always a lottery, and I'm sure it will be easier for Viv in the Test matches' Clive Lloyd told the *Daily Express*. His successor as West Indies captain was also looking to the future. 'There's a lot of cricket left and we want to get the team right for the more important Test matches' he said. 'I remain very confident in my side. Now it's extremely important that I instil that belief in the rest of the team. The belief that we will win will never leave Viv Richards. All the other players must think the same way as me.' The message from captains past and present was consistent and clear: these one-day matches had been just a sideshow; the real contest was yet to begin.

England's selectors would have no choice but to gamble one way or another when it came to the overall balance of their team. Would they keep faith with the players who had served them so well during the one-day series? Or would they pick solely on the basis of Test cricket? The simple assumption that form and confidence would be transferred over from a one-day series to Test cricket had been challenged recently by the experience of Pakistan in the West Indies. Soundly thumped 5-0 in the one-dayers, they had come back to very nearly win the Test series. The attitude of England's selectors to this question might be judged by the choice between Derek Pringle and David Capel. Pringle had played superbly during the Texaco Trophy, but he had not played Test cricket for almost two years. David Capel, on the other hand, had played in each of England's last seven Tests, showing a gradual improvement all the while. Either way, the selectors could end up being accused of inconsistency. The choice between the two all-rounders (and nobody bar Scyld Berry seemed to be suggesting that England might go in to the match with just four specialist bowlers and pick six front-line batsmen) was complicated by the fact that both offered slightly different strengths. Pringle was the superior bowler, but was in few people's estimation a batsman capable of holding down the No. 6 position in Test cricket. According to Micky Stewart, Pringle at No. 6 was 'two or three places too high.' Capel was considered the better batsman, though not yet proven at No. 6, and a bowler who had so far lacked penetration at Test level. Choose Capel, and might England be better off picking a sixth batsman and relying upon a few overs from Graham Gooch to back-up the front line attack? Choose Pringle, and might England risk collapsing quickly once the fourth wicket had fallen?

This had a knock-on effect on the choice of wicketkeeper too. Paul Downton had kept admirably during the Texaco Trophy, but despite this was generally considered to be an inferior gloveman to Gloucestershire's Jack Russell. Russell, almost everyone now agreed, was the finest 'keeper in the country, but he was yet to make a first-class 100 with the bat. Would England really risk batting with Pringle at six and Russell at seven? Mike Selvey was one of many who thought not: 'Although Pringle, incidentally, implies Downton, the Middlesex man does not preclude Capel.' Russell had, of course, been understudy to the now injured Bruce French during the Pakistan tour. It was another case where the selectors would be unable to defend themselves against a charge of inconsistency whatever they did.

Injuries also restricted the bowling options available. Neil Foster had recently returned to action for Essex, but was a long way from having proved his fitness for five-day cricket. A few days before the match the news came through that Gladstone Small, such a crucial part of the Texaco Trophy success, had badly strained a thigh muscle and would be out of consideration for this match at least. Loyalty to the one-day squad would also mean a place for Phillip DeFreitas – a promising cricketer, but another who had struggled to take wickets in the longer form of the game. In nine Test matches up to this point, he had taken only twenty wickets, at an average in excess of 40. Clive Lloyd, however, was one who saw potential beyond the mere statistics: 'He is a terrific cricketer, who received a raw deal from the England selectors when they left him out of the side last summer. The West Indies would certainly have persevered with such a talented prospect through the bad times.'

Graham Dilley, now recovered from his virus, and John Emburey were certain to be included, probably DeFreitas too, and one from Pringle or Capel. That left just the replacement for Small to complete the likely starting eleven. Neal Radford, who had stepped in to Dilley's boots very competently at Lord's, seemed to have little support – a fact perhaps explained by his record from three Test matches of just four wickets at an average of 87.75. Jonathan Agnew, with thirty-three wickets so far that season, and Middlesex's Norman Cowans and Neil Williams all had their backers, but most felt the deserving candidate to be Yorkshire's Paul Jarvis, who had improved and impressed on the New Zealand leg of the winter tour. Jarvis was by no means a direct replacement for Small. Small was a rhythmical, metronomic sort of bowler, who hit the deck on a strict length and controlled line ball after ball, moving it either way off the seam. Jarvis was faster but skiddier, swinging the ball away from a slightly fuller length. Jarvis might bowl more wicket-taking deliveries, but he would probably be driven for more runs too.

Peter May's selection committee came up with a thirteen-man party for Trent Bridge: Gatting (c), Gooch, Broad, Gower, Lamb, Pringle, Downton, DeFreitas, Emburey, Dilley, Jarvis, Hemmings and Thomas. Of the last two names, Glamorgan's fast bowler Greg Thomas – frequently referred to as 'the fastest white bowler in England', despite playing his cricket in Cardiff – was included more as cover in case Graham Dilley suffered a relapse of his virus, while Eddie Hemmings was presumably included on the basis of continuity to act as drinks waiter; as a Nottinghamshire man, he had the local knowledge for the job after all. It was difficult to imagine England going in to the first Test at Trent Bridge, usually known as a seam-friendly pitch where the likes of Richard Hadlee and Clive Rice had been prospering for years, with two off-spinners in the side.

Mindful of how their strong words about the Texaco Trophy selections had come back to bite them, some observers were muted in their response to this team. 'This time I'm keeping Mum' said Mike Selvey. In the run up to the selectors' meeting, Selvey had suggested that a compromise line between one-day and Test 'specialists' might be the outcome, 'while one should never take one-day games as a litmus for Test cricket, only a crackpot would totally ignore it.' Now he thought the balance had gone too far the other way. 'This is not a criticism so much as an observation, but it is possible to be blinded by one-day success.' Others were less restrained. The squad was 'predictable and unimaginative', according to Colin Bateman.

'We have gone for experience' said Peter May. 'It is vital we get a good start in what will be a very hard series.' For most, this meant only one thing: England were going to start this series trying to play it safe. Where the selection of the Texaco Trophy squad had produced howls of incredulity, this one echoed to groans of resignation. There was little outrage to be heard, except from one bowler who felt he had been passed over too often. The reason for excluding Leicestershire's Jonathan Agnew had been explained by Peter May when he said 'A lot of people have been taking wickets, which is encouraging, but we have to analyse what the pitches are like and in many cases they have been helpful to the bowlers.' The suggestion was clear: Agnew's wicket-taking success had been unfairly skewed by the helpful pitches at Grace Road. True, Agnew had so far taken only two wickets away from Grace Road in the Championship this season, but Leicestershire had played four of their six matches so far at home and one of those away matches, at Derby, had been on a flat pitch where most bowlers toiled and Agnew had bowled only 6 overs in the second innings due to injury.

For Agnew, the accusation felt deeply unfair. 'I find the suggestion that I am getting easy wickets the most amazing' he said. 'Only the first two pitches at Grace Road this season were that helpful to seam bowling, the rest have been good batting tracks. Anyway, I took 101 wickets last year all around the country and most of my match-winning performances came away from Grace Road.' Agnew felt that time was running out for him, and that once Neil Foster and Gladstone Small returned from injury, his chance would have gone. 'I have had phone calls from Mike Gatting and Micky Stewart to tell me I'm close to selection and must keep plugging away. I suppose that's all I can do.'

The choice of Greg Thomas instead raised more than a few eyebrows. A total of five Tests spread across the 1985/86 tour of West Indies, and the following summer had brought him just ten wickets at an average of 50. But one penetrative spell of 4-14 at Barbados had hinted at the potential beneath the raw pace and the England management liked his bristling attitude. Compared with Jonathan Agnew's haul of 101 first-class wickets in 1987, Thomas' own bag of just 30 was hardly inspiring. Much had been made of a winter in South Africa playing Currie Cup cricket for Eastern Province, during which he had curtailed his famously long run-up, with positive results. 'My line is better' he said, 'I have greater control and I've been getting vital early wickets.' The result in South Africa was twenty-three wickets at an average of 29, more or less the same as his record the previous summer. Thus far in 1988, he had claimed just twelve wickets. Was this selection according to form, as the selectors had promised at the start of the season? Was it, yet, selecting experience, as Peter May claimed now?

They had certainly gone for experience in the choice of David Gower, who had begun the season painfully out of form. 'If I'm honest, I'm not quite back to my best,' said Gower after learning of his selection. 'I have played better, but in the last few weeks I have felt more settled. The 74 I got against Middlesex ten days ago has made me feel happier.' Nevertheless, Gower conceded that in this case at least, the selectors had chosen on the basis of reputation rather than current form. His selection, he thought, 'could be called a gamble'.

In the West Indies camp meanwhile, concerns were being voiced by the management itself. The vital warm-up matches at Bristol and Worcester had both been badly affected by the weather: the bowlers had not got enough overs under their belts and the batsmen were still struggling to adjust to the conditions. 'It is very worrying that the top order is not clicking as we would have hoped' said Jackie Hendriks. 'The players are physically fit but they are still coming to terms with the English conditions with the ball moving about, particularly the younger ones. We have some sorting out to do before Thursday.'

Even the team captain was hedging his bets: 'We've had a few hiccups and I'm worried about the performance of one of two players. But I'm hoping that on the big day the guys will relish the occasion. I'm very optimistic' said Viv Richards. Richards was keen to emphasise his team's proud record in Test cricket – not having lost a Test series in the last eight years – and his determination to maintain it. He was also keen to write off the loss of the one-day series as a hiccup which would have no bearing on the Tests. 'Test cricket is the real thing, because over five days the better team should win. It would have been nice to win the one-dayers for the sake of confidence, but those matches are a lottery. The Tests are what we are here for.' This was fair enough as a statement of intent, but as a report on the state of his team it was less than convincing.

As the first Test approached, it was tempting to reflect that with England about to take on an opponent that they had lost their last ten Test matches to, and West Indies about to take on an opponent they had lost their last five international matches to, neither team was exactly full to the brim with confidence.

6

Queering the Pitch

There remains a tradition in England of preparing the best possible wicket for cricket, irrespective of whether it might favour the England team or not. The first Test of the 1988 series at Trent Bridge was an exception to this rule. In normal circumstances a hard, true surface with even bounce and good 'carry' is favoured by both batsmen and bowlers, but how many England batsmen in 1976, 1980 or 1984 might have wished that the pace were just a little less rapid and the bounce just a shade less lively? Perhaps they might have dreamed of a pitch that would have encouraged a West Indies team of old, led by the spin of Lance Gibbs. They were usually disappointed, and if there was any departure from the fast, true bounce it was usually in the form of unevenness, which might result in their ducking into a short one that 'didn't get up' or playing forward to one that suddenly reared up towards the throat. How tempting it must have been to sidle quietly up to the groundsman and suggest that what the doctor really had in mind on this occasion was something slow and flat where if anything were to bounce above waist height it would do so like a back-spun tennis ball, with a plaintive appeal of 'hit me'. At Trent Bridge in 1988, England did just that.

Through the 1980s, Trent Bridge was usually known as a bit of a 'greentop'. Nottinghamshire twice won the County Championship during the decade, largely thanks to a top-class seam attack led by Richard Hadlee and Clive Rice, backed up by English bowlers such as Mike Hendrick and Kevin Cooper. That the pitches at Trent Bridge were prepared to favour the home bowlers was an open secret on the county circuit. In an interview with *The Independent* in 1992, head groundsman Ron Allsopp revealed how, under Rice's captaincy, Nottinghamshire had sought the aid of the groundsman to guarantee success. 'We went out to inspect pitches we planned to use. One day I pointed to a suitable one for a match against Warwickshire and Clive looked around and said "No, I want that one" looking at a pale green surface. I said "someone might get killed" and Clive replied "what's up Ron? Are you getting religious?" He meant it too.' On that occasion, Allsopp's better instincts prevailed. Home advantage was one thing, outright danger another. The 'greentop' was very much part of Trent Bridge, while Notts had the bowling attack to make the most of it.

> With Clive Rice and Richard Hadlee in our team, why not exploit their talent?' asked Allsopp. 'I hated producing dull pitches, so I gave the square rolling, rolling and more rolling pre-season. It quickened the surface and I left some grass on, nothing more. It seemed a revolutionary step, I suppose, but Surrey had played to their own strengths when preparing pitches in the 1950s.

In 1988, England's demands were rather different. The last thing they wanted to see with the prospect of Marshall, Ambrose, Walsh and Patterson steaming in at them was a little extra grass on the pitch. What they got instead was a surface that looked brown, mottled and shaved within a couple of millimetres of its life.

Clive Lloyd declared himself amazed to see Carl Hooper bowling before lunch on the first day and getting some turn; Jackie Hendriks offered a similar view from the West Indies' dressing room: 'It is not a surface I thought we would have seen for a Test match at Trent Bridge. I'm disappointed by the inconsistency of the bounce. There is not too much pace, it is a little slow and there is not a lot in it for the batsmen. A few balls behaved as one would not have expected.' Not a lot in it for the batsmen, nor, more pertinently, for the West Indies pace attack. It was, almost everyone agreed with the word, 'unresponsive', and just what England had hoped for.

There was an explanation for this, as John Emburey explains:

> About a week before the game we asked the groundsman to water the centre of the pitch to stop the bounce and pace in the wicket. And the groundsman did it, and of course the centre of the pitch was like plasticine. We drew that match. They couldn't get us out because the batsmen were just getting back and you had plenty of time to play

on the back foot. It's probably one of the only times in a match that I played in that a pitch was prepared to nullify the opposition bowlers.

It was not, it has to be said, a terribly positive strategy. A slow pitch that neutralised the West Indies fast bowlers would neutralise England's too. Perhaps Dilley and Jarvis relied more on swing than outright pace, but Marshall could swing the ball as well as either of them, and was Phillip DeFreitas really possessed of greater control than Ambrose and Walsh? Perhaps the pitch might offer more turn, a possible advantage in the likely absence of a front line spinner in the West Indies XI, but was John Emburey really bowling well enough to take advantage of such conditions?

Nevertheless, after Mike Gatting won the toss and elected to bat first, for the first couple of hours it looked as though the plan had worked. Batting was not easy as such. There was no racing start with drives skidding through the covers or cuts and pulls flashing away to the boundaries square of the wicket, but England had fewer scares against the new ball in the hands of West Indian pacemen than had been the case in many a long year. The ball was largely kept up to the bat and when, after more than half an hour, the first short ball of the day from Patterson struck Broad on the helmet, it was only because he had ducked out of instinct and the ball had bounced barely higher than the stumps. By lunchtime, all four fast bowlers had been tried and Richards had even brought on Carl Hooper for a short spell of gentle spin. England were 80 without loss and, with the ground unusually silent due to new security regulations having barred spectators from bringing in banners, flags, drums and all the other paraphernalia, which on previous tours had made English Test match grounds seem like a home from home for the West Indies, it had all been curiously soporific in the cool early summer sunlight.

For a few overs after lunch, it looked as though it had not all been a mirage. Gooch, having passed 4,000 Test runs, reached his half-century with his sixth boundary. Then he broke his bat, and suddenly everything seemed to change. The tourists came back to the fray with new vigour. Marshall, still clearly troubled by his rib injury, cut down his pace and, with clouds rolling in over Nottingham, began to make the ball swing and cut both ways alarmingly. It seemed impossible to predict what any ball bowled by him might do. Gooch, from driving and pulling with all the authority of his thirty-four years just a few minutes earlier, was suddenly a passive, uncertain, strokeless figure; Broad, never quite as fluent, looked a man on borrowed time. Gooch was dropped at slip by Greenidge on 69, but four runs later he drove firm-footed at a Marshall in-swinger and deflected it on to his wicket. Gatting lasted just fifteen balls before prodding forward at another ball that seemed to curve back at him late through paranormal interference and edging the ball via his thigh pad to short leg. Then, on the stroke of tea, Broad, already reprieved once when Patterson had bowled him with a no-ball, tried to cut a wider delivery, which only bounced enough to catch his bottom edge and, just as Gooch had done, dragged it onto his stumps.

England went into the interval at 161 for 3. Two balls after it they were 161 for 4, Lamb's return to the Test side after a twelve-month absence having lasted no longer than that, lbw shuffling across the crease to Marshall. All England's early momentum had been lost, blown away by Marshall in a brilliant unchanged spell of 19 overs. The innings had reached its crucial point: England's last specialist batsman at the crease was the experienced but out of form David Gower; with him was Derek Pringle, the country's new number one all-rounder who had an immediate opportunity to prove to the doubters that he could bat at no 6 in a Test match against the best bowlers in the world. In the event, it was Pringle who looked the more secure of the two as they battled out the final session of the day. Gower had one of those inexplicable days when he looked to be doing everything right, but the runs simply wouldn't come. Never looking hurried and possessing a graceful, almost balletic, poise at the crease is all very well, but it just makes the game all the more stupefying when you're out of touch. All of Gower's balance and ease of movement were there, but the ball came off his bat with the dull thud of a watermelon falling off the back of a farmer's cart.

Gower too was the beneficiary of Greenidge's bad case of butterfingers at slip, but he only made two more runs after that, having misfired his way to 18 over the course of more than an hour and a half. An ill-judged slash at a wider ball from Ambrose did for him, safely caught by Dujon. It was now the task of England's Texaco Trophy heroes, Pringle and Downton, to see the side through the last 20 overs before the close. There was no more of Marshall to be faced, but Ambrose and Walsh were still in full cry and, with Pringle taking most of the strike, there was no vigorous counter-attacking on view for the Trent Bridge crowd until a smooth cover drive off Carl Hooper in the final over of the day took Pringle to a well-played 39 and England to the relative security of 220 for 5, and the absolute safety of the Pavilion.

At lunch on day one, England might have entertained hopes of a total in excess of 400 – something they had failed to register against the West Indies since 1976. They began day two with the more modest hope of reaching 300. Despite the continued placid character of the pitch, the heavy, humid conditions made it a better morning for bowlers than batsmen, and the force was still with Malcolm Marshall. His first ball was wide, but he soon found his range and with the second ball of his next over, the first Pringle had faced from him that day, he produced another in-swinging Yorker, which ducked in late and cleaned up the Essex man's stumps. Marshall then switched his line of attack to around the wicket, and with the final ball of his over slanted one across Emburey who could only get a thin edge through to Dujon. In the space of 4 overs, England had garnered just 3 runs and managed to lose two crucial wickets. Downton was still there, but, in the space of just eighteen balls, Ambrose cleaned up the tail with bowling that was fast, full and straight at the stumps. Despite their best efforts to manage the conditions in their favour, England had been bowled out for 245 by high quality fast bowling. It was 1984 all over again. Well, not quite. For a start, there had been very little of the short-pitched bowling that had crushed the English will to survive in the last two series. Marshall in particular had deliberately reduced his pace a touch to obtain greater control over his many and minute variations of swerve and cut. He had done it brilliantly, and had been well backed up by the accuracy of his colleagues. Shrewdly, Vivian Richards had declined to take the new ball when it had become available early that morning, since Marshall and Ambrose had been using the old one so well.

Not that this was a case of a new, morally reformed West Indies team pitching it up and inviting the drive in the finest traditions of the game. This had been a simple tactical response to England's strategy of producing a lifeless pitch. Whatever England might have asked Ron Allsopp to do to the pitch, he could in no way influence the overhead conditions, and if Curtly Ambrose could direct the ball at pace to a point on the pitch around 8 inches in front of off-stump then the nature of the surface would have little to do with the outcome. 'Why would we need to bowl bouncers on a pitch like this?' grinned Richards. 'When the ball is lifting from a length as it sometimes did you can get an even better effect by pitching it up.'

Clive Lloyd too was delighted that the West Indies had refuted all the old charges 'that they get wickets by cracking bones'. But Lloyd also thought it likely that the uneven bounce already apparent would get worse as the game went on, and that with West Indies having to bat last, a lead of at least 100 on the first innings would be essential. 'As long as Desmond Haynes stays there, you can build a whole innings around him. Richards is, of course, the destroyer, and although the wicket is taking spin, John Emburey turns the ball into him and he likes that. In fact, he is fearsomely strong there.'

If the West Indies were hoping to get their reply off to a racketing start they were foiled by one stalwart English adversary: rain delayed the start of their innings and only 6 more overs were possible before lunch. After lunch, more rain came, washing out the entire session, and it was only fifteen minutes after the end of the scheduled tea interval that play was able to resume. England's new ball attack of Graham Dilley and Phil DeFreitas looked innocuous at first. Dilley seemed out of rhythm following his viral infection and was struggling with his run-up, overstepping as badly as the West Indians had. DeFreitas was, if anything, bowling the faster of the two, but his line was awry. Balls pitched outside off-stump, which might have induced a risky slash in the one-day matches, were simply let go. When he tried to adjust and bowl at the stumps the ball simply arrowed straight towards leg stump, where the batsmen clipped it away off their pads.

Things began to change when, after Jarvis had replaced Dilley at the Radcliffe Road end for a single over, Pringle came on at that end and bowled such a nagging line that the scoreboard operators were stopped in their tracks. Only two scoring strokes were played off Pringle during his initial seven-over spell. When Jarvis then replaced DeFreitas at the Pavilion end, he found Greenidge's outside edge with only his second ball, which flew knee-high to first slip where Emburey could not hold on to it. Greenidge was not to profit from his escape; just three balls later he drove at another full ball and got a thin edge again. This time Paul Downton took the catch comfortably behind the stumps.

Richie Richardson struck his third ball from Jarvis for four, but soon found himself bogged down and strokeless against the accurate Pringle. That Gatting now removed Pringle from the attack and brought the out-of-sorts Dilley back instead raised a few eyebrows in the press box, but just a few minutes later another bowling change by England's captain produced an immediate dividend for the third time in the innings. With the last ball of his first over, John Emburey, who had not taken a Test wicket in England since 1986, produced turn and bounce and Richardson's inside edge rebounded via pad to Gatting at short-leg. At 84 for 2, honours stood more or less even, but with Viv Richards striding to the crease that would not last long.

Richards saw off his first five balls with circumspection, and then took two off Dilley from his sixth. He would only make five more scoring shots before the end of that day's play, but each one of them went to the boundary as he and Desmond Haynes took 43 runs from the final 6 overs. Pitching short to try and unsettle the West Indies captain, Dilley found himself hooked away to the boundary with vicious power twice in one over. With the light rapidly deteriorating, Dilley's short stuff could have only one other effect and, despite Gatting's attempt to reduce the danger by replacing Dilley with Pringle, after just one ball of the medium pacer's over the umpires offered the light to the batsmen, who walked off perfectly satisfied with their afternoon's work. The West Indies were well placed on 126 for 2.

Rain wiped out most of the third morning, and when play resumed at 2 p.m. Haynes could not get going again with quite the same fluency. After almost playing on to Pringle he fell to a catch behind the wicket off Jarvis. For a while everything was quiet as Richards and Hooper rotated the strike, but when a tiring Jarvis was twice driven beautifully straight for boundaries by Hooper in the eighth over of his spell, Gatting called on John Emburey to replace him. Even on the second evening there had been some evidence of a deliberate policy by the West Indies to hit Emburey out of the attack. There had been delaying tactics towards the end of the session: Richards pulled away unsighted, adjusting his kit or simply not being ready when Emburey wanted to bowl. This could have been an effort to reduce the number of overs England could bowl at them before the light inevitably closed in, or it might also have been part of a plan to upset the experienced off-spinner's rhythm and ensure he could never settle in to the long, probing spell which might bring a return of form and potency. Brought back into the attack an hour into the third day's play, Emburey's first over brought 16 runs. There was an element of luck with the first stroke: pumped audaciously towards long-off by Richards, Allan Lamb's desperate effort almost snared the Antiguan at the first attempt. But the next ball saw the swift-footed Richards make room for himself and cut for three. Hooper stepped out to the next two balls and drove them both through cover for boundaries and then completed the rout with a single from the last ball.

Emburey's next over saw Richards biff him through cover three more times, taking eleven from the over and bringing up the 50 partnership from just 52 balls in the process. When Richards came down the wicket and swiped the first ball of his next over past wide mid-on for six, Emburey was probably grateful to get away with only another four from the next five balls. But still, the assault on him had brought 37 runs from just 3 overs. In 21 overs so far, the West Indies had advanced their score by 102 to 228 for 3; Richards poised menacingly on 80 and Hooper looking very nearly as dangerous on 30. They were just 17 runs behind England with seven wickets in hand. The home side badly needed a break, and in the next over they got it from Richards himself when he accepted an offer of bad light from the umpires. Although only five minutes remained before the tea interval, it seemed an astonishing decision. Runs were coming as unstoppably as lava flowing down a volcano, and with Emburey and DeFreitas bowling the batsmen were hardly in danger. Neither of them, come to that, had seen fit to wear a helmet. Now England had the chance to retreat to the pavilion, regroup and reconsider how on earth they were going to get rid of the most destructive batsman in the world.

Soon after play resumed thirty minutes later, Richards strode forward to drive DeFreitas through the covers, but only managed to edge head-high to second slip. Graham Gooch was knocked backwards by the impact, but came up again with the ball clasped between his hands. England had claimed the prize scalp, but if they thought they might be in for a respite they were soon disabused of the idea. Gus Logie came to the wicket in a positive mood and opened his account with three crisp offside boundaries. Runs continued to flow in an alarming manner – 27 from the first 5 overs after Richards' dismissal. Carl Hooper was reminding Clive Lloyd of the time he had first seen him bat in the nets at Georgetown as a fourteen-year-old: 'He was composed, he was completely at his ease and I saw again that lovely straight bat, those lovely clean strokes.'

In fading light, Gatting brought back his fastest bowler, Graham Dilley. His first three balls produced another 6 runs, but their short length nevertheless induced the umpires to offer the light to the batsmen again. Bafflingly, after a brief discussion and a look to the pavilion balcony for guidance, they accepted once more. 'I was surprised when we came off,' admitted Jackie Hendriks, 'but apparently the batsmen found it difficult because Dilley's arm was coming from above the sight screen.'

The West Indies were already ahead with six wickets still in hand. Despite missing out on a hundred, Viv Richards ended the day in a positive mood. 'It's a pity we've had so many interruptions,' he said, 'but everything is going to plan. If we can get a 150-run lead and have two clear days on this wicket we will have something to work at.' The West Indies said nothing about the alleged policy of targeting John Emburey, but the bowler himself was happy enough to comment on it. Sunday, after the manner of those more easeful days, was a rest day and many of the England players spent it striking smaller and less lethal balls around in a charity golf event. Emburey took time out to tell the *Daily Express* about the experience:

> I've never been hit like that before, but when Viv is in that sort of mood anyone can disappear for plenty of runs. There was a deliberate policy to get after me and when Carl Hooper started to play the same way as Viv it became very difficult. But I take it as a back-handed compliment. They may have thought the wicket may turn in the next two days and I could cause problems, so they tried to upset my rhythm.

It was an approach confirmed by Richards himself in an interview with *The Sun's* Chris Lander: 'We saw John as the man to worry about on this pitch. He'd got Richie Richardson the previous evening.' There was one other motive as well, the West Indies' captain acknowledged – the need for quick runs to set up a winning position in a match that had lost significant time to the weather. By attacking Emburey, the West Indies may have been trying to insure against the danger of batting last on a deteriorating pitch against a world-class finger spinner who had found his way back into form, but in doing so they were also creating a problem for England that would take even more damaging effect later in the series.

Monday 6 June was a brighter day, with only intermittent cloud cover. England started well; Dilley and Pringle bowled with great control and stamina for an hour and three quarters until shortly before lunch. Pringle found some extra lift in his second over to clip Logie's glove and send a catch to second slip where Gooch, after a nervy juggle, managed to hold it. Dujon then managed to dominate the strike without ever quite finding his timing, leaving the more fluent Hooper somewhat becalmed at the non-striker's end. Dujon seemed to play and miss at least once for every over he faced and had nudged his way to 16 from 60 balls when a badly mistimed pull sent the gentlest of return catches back to bowler Dilley. Pringle was by now coming towards the end of a spell of 11 overs, which cost just 15 runs. Had he been able to, Gatting would probably have kept him on all day, but Jarvis and DeFreitas managed to restrict the rate of West Indies' progress before the tourists went in to lunch on 334 for 6.

It was DeFreitas who got the breakthrough with his second ball after the interval, Hooper gloving a lifting ball towards first slip where Downton dived across to take a well-judged catch. Hooper had never quite managed to recapture the fluency of the third day's play. His 52 runs on the Saturday had come from 78 balls, but his last 32 on the Monday had taken him another 7, and he had survived a difficult chance low to Gooch's right at second slip off Dilley that morning. Perhaps he had fed a little off the sense of intimidation that his captain had brought to the wicket, in the same way that a lesser bowler can sometimes take advantage of the doubts sown in a batsman's mind by a more taxing spell at the other end, but Hooper's effortless style and stroke-playing freedom would linger in the memory long after the impact of win, lose or draw would be forgotten. His departure for 84 was disappointing to more than just the West Indies diehards.

With just three wickets yet to claim, and the West Indies still less than 100 ahead, England might have felt they had a sniff of winding up the innings before the gulf became too great. That sniff was swiftly and violently suffocated as Malcolm Marshall and Curtly Ambrose put together a partnership of 91 in just 22 overs. That Marshall could play a bit surprised no one; he had four first-class hundreds to his name and four years earlier had smashed England all round Headingley with just one hand, but Ambrose was a complete revelation. The giant, willowy fast bowler had a very simple technique, planting his front foot down the middle of the pitch and addressing the ball with a full swing of the bat. When it came off he could look for a moment like Frank Woolley, and on this day he would have several such moments.

Gatting tried to break the partnership by replacing DeFreitas with Emburey. After the slaughter of Saturday it was a brave move with the West Indies clearly looking for quick runs again, but at first it looked to have worked as the off-spinner, bowling over the wicket to the right-handed Marshall and round to the left-handed Ambrose, began his spell by conceding only one scoring stroke from his first 4 overs. It could not last. With Pringle replacing Dilley at the Pavilion end, the batsmen seemed to find new determination not to get bogged down against England's two most disciplined bowlers. After Ambrose had nudged the ball just over a leaping Gower at forward square leg, Marshall struck Emburey's next two balls for six, first over mid-wicket, then over long-on. The first ball of Pringle's next over also disappeared over long-on for six as the Essex seamer was hit for an uncharacteristic 14 runs. It was a memorable assault, but a short one. Emburey tightened things up with another maiden, then Pringle managed to restrict the batsmen to just three from his next over. Marshall then managed to take two from each of Emburey's next two balls, but stepping away from the fourth ball to hit through the off side, he missed it and was bowled.

With Courtney Walsh joining Ambrose at the crease, the West Indies added another 23 runs either side of the tea interval, Ambrose striking another impressive six straight back over Emburey's head, before declaring on 448 for 8 after Ambrose was run out by Gooch's direct hit from mid-on. John Emburey finished with the bruising figures of 16-4-95-2 – the result of two deliberate, brutal assaults on his bowling. 'It was all rather bizarre,' remarked Mike Selvey, 'for at no stage did he bowl particularly badly.' Indeed, Emburey's spell was in some measure a triumph; his four maidens came in the space of 5 overs when the batsmen were eager for quick runs. Marshall had hit him for 18 runs in the space of six balls, but the spinner had held his nerve and taken Marshall's wicket. A lesser bowler, and a weaker character, might have crumbled under such pressure, and the weight of runs England were faced with might have been even greater, the time they would need to struggle under that weight longer still.

As it was they faced a deficit of 203 runs and a long session of two and a quarter hours to bat out before the close of play. The final day still loomed ominously ahead. It was a situation gloomily familiar for those who had witnessed England's last ten attempts to stave off defeat against the West Indies, but despite the huge deficit, the deteriorating pitch and the four dangerous fast bowlers they faced, Gooch and Broad began England's rearguard solidly enough. It was not spectacular stuff; runs came along at roughly two per over. There were some nervy moments too, including Gooch surviving a fierce early shout for lbw from Marshall who, bowling around the wicket, had managed to straighten one almost enough to convince the umpire. When Ambrose replaced Marshall after a short burst of 4 overs, the bouncer rate increased noticeably. The batsmen sensibly opted to leave them alone, but Broad did misjudge one that kept low and struck him in the ribs as he tried to duck under it.

Except when batsmen were rash enough to take them on, the West Indies had rarely seen the outright bouncer as a wicket-taking delivery. It was more a tactic used to force the batsman into a particular state of mind, in which he was nervous about getting forward, and his instinct told him to hang on the back foot and prepare for evasive action. It interfered with a batsman's decision making, forcing him into the wrong position to deal with other balls, and for that matter helped to keep the scoring rate down. Perhaps it was this that led to Broad's eventual dismissal for 18.

Prior to being struck in the ribs, Broad had only received one bouncer that evening – the same number as Gooch. After it, he became the prime target, receiving one in most overs and six in total. The final two came from Ambrose in the last over he faced, separated only by a straight drive, which unluckily scored a direct hit on the stumps at the non-striker's end. For the final ball of the over Ambrose went slightly wider on the crease and angled the ball across Broad. It was of that indeterminate length that leaves batsmen in two minds whether to play forward or go back. Broad's feet went nowhere and his bat was drawn away from his body, nibbling at the line of the ball; a simple edge flew easily to Dujon in front of first slip.

For Broad it was a huge disappointment, as he no doubt could have predicted the response of the press to his failure to make a crucial big innings. 'Broad,' wrote Mike Selvey, 'just does not seem able to go on to the big scores at home that he makes away.' In fact this was only the fifth home Test match he had played in since his debut summer of 1984, the four others having been against an impressive Pakistan attack the previous summer. And while Selvey's comments acknowledged Broad's fine record in overseas Tests (six hundreds in just twelve matches), they and others like them helped to create a degree of pressure on the Nottinghamshire opener that a player of his class might better have been spared. The implication was clear: make a big score soon in this series or your record overseas will count for nothing.

When the England captain came to the crease the West Indies did not bother to bounce him at all. Gooch received a couple from Marshall before the close, hooking one down to backward square leg for two, but he was more troubled by a straight one from Walsh that kept low and nearly crept under the late downward jab of his bat. Gatting crawled his way to 8 from 36 balls, but he and Gooch stood firm until the close, which England reached still 136 behind on 67 for 1.

'England face a long and difficult journey today to save the first Test at Nottingham' Clive Lloyd told *Daily Express* readers the next morning. The prospect of spending a long day at the crease facing Marshall, Ambrose, Walsh and Patterson with no hope of victory was not an attractive one. With nine wickets in hand, England were not beaten yet, but they knew that, after ten consecutive defeats against the same opposition, defeat here would be what Colin Bateman called 'a knee in the groin to English morale.' As Mike Gatting celebrated his thirty-first birthday with his teammates that night, Peter Deeley wrote in the *Daily Telegraph* that England's greatest hope might again be outside their own control: 'The local forecast that there may be rain is the sweetest music likely to be heard in the England dressing room.'

It would not be the rain that would save England. Instead, determined resistance, led by Graham Gooch at his most indefatigable, saw England through 78 overs with the loss of just two wickets, the second so late in the day as to create no real alarms in the home dressing room, where the sweetest music no doubt was the silence of players rooted to their seats, neither buckling on their pads to go out to bat nor unbuckling them after a premature return from the middle. When I spoke to him in preparation for this book, Gooch was unable to recall any particular detail about this, one of his finest innings. Perhaps it had all blurred into the general memory of a productive early summer which brought him 902 runs from nine completed first-class knocks. In truth it was not an innings filled with spectacular strokes. At one point he remained marooned on 64 for 36 balls, and for the man himself perhaps it lost some of its savour of heroism through the fairly lifeless pitch, and the absence for much of the day of the West Indies' greatest threat.

Malcolm Marshall's rib injury had worsened overnight, despite Richards having restricted him to two four-over spells the previous evening. Only when Gooch and Gatting had batted on into the second hour of the day did Richards risk bringing him into the attack at all. Progress for England's batsmen had not been entirely serene up to this point. After keeping out two low, scudding balls in the same over, Gatting had been dropped in front of slip by Dujon off an under-edged hook. A few overs later, Gooch had edged Patterson between second and third slip – a rare misjudgement that earned him a boundary. Marshall's advent brought new challenges. Bowling at little above medium pace, his first eleven balls brought only a leg bye. His twelfth drew Gatting forward, pitched middle and hit the top of off, leaving a perplexed England captain in a textbook pose for the forward defensive as his bails tumbled to the ground.

Marshall would only manage another 3 overs during the entire day, and when Gower pulled him sweetly just wide of square leg, England were in sight of lunch with eight wickets still in hand and greater hope than they had had since the early overs of the game. The final over before lunch was Marshall's last in the game. Did his side stiffen up further during the interval? Or did his captain sense that his team's long run of victories was coming to an end and that, on this ever slower pitch, it was better to save his most experienced bowler for the rest of the series than to break him for all of it in a futile attempt to force a win here? Marshall helped save the match for England as much as Gooch's determined resistence. 'The gap between him and the other fast bowlers on the West Indies team was almost embarrassing,' wrote Tony Cozier in the *Daily Telegraph*.

Without Marshall, the West Indies attack lacked the command of swing and seam movement which could make the difference on such a slow pitch. They had pace, discipline and intelligence, but against England's two most experienced batsmen, who were looking simply to bat out time, it was not enough. Both played and missed from time to time, and many of Gower's runs came from the edge rather than the middle of his bat. But runs came steadily, clipped off the pads or guided carefully into gaps in the field. Just three boundaries came in the last

20 overs before tea, but neither batsman gave a chance. Only after tea, when Richards, with one last throw of the dice, gave the new ball to Walsh and Patterson, did the West Indies begin to create opportunities. The very first ball with it found Gower's inside edge and raced away to the fine leg boundary. A loose drive from Gooch was then put down by Haynes at mid-off and Gower was nearly caught and bowled by Patterson. By the time Gooch fended at a lifter from Patterson and edged to Dujon, it was 4.45 p.m. and England were 277 for 3 – 74 ahead with seven wickets in hand.

The last assault was seen off by Gower and Lamb, Gower surviving a blow on the shoulder from Ambrose which almost saw his helmet (worn without the chinstrap) fall onto his wicket, and Lamb missed by a diving Hooper at gully. Richards called a halt to proceedings at 5.30 p. m., and England's long, grim procession of Test defeats against the West Indies was finally over.

Graham Gooch's heroic innings of 146 naturally won all the plaudits. 'It was a wonderful and responsible knock' said Viv Richards. Micky Stewart was less keen to single out an individual player: 'It was the perfect stage for people with experience to cope with the situation.' In truth, Gooch alone might not have pulled it off. Chris Broad had helped him lay a foundation and occupied the crease for most of the fourth evening. Mike Gatting had held the West Indies at bay until thirty minutes before lunch on the final day. David Gower, although clearly not back to his best, had made his highest first-class score of the season in the most difficult of circumstances. Before the series, many judges had said that England had the batting line-up to cope with a West Indies attack that was going through a process of regeneration. Here was the proof. Perhaps England now could build on this. They had proved they could survive, now if their bowlers could rediscover the threat they had posed in the Texaco Trophy series – and news that a fit again Gladstone Small had just taken 7 for 15 at Edgbaston offered hope of this – might England even match the tourists in this series?

After long years of misery against the West Indies, fans of English cricket at last had hope, but that hope was about to be dashed in the most sudden and sorry of ways.

7

A Scandal in East Mercia

Ever since the ill-judged argument with Shakoor Rana there had been a sense that Mike Gatting was on borrowed time as England captain; only the manner of his departure came as a surprise. There might have been an argument for it on pure cricketing grounds – 'two wins in 23 matches is not the kind of performance that keeps captains in office' wrote Mike Selvey – but by breaking the West Indies' run of consecutive Test victories over England, and by an immaculate performance in the Texaco Trophy, Gatting looked to have dodged that particular bullet for a while. And yet on the morning of Tuesday 7 June, the final day at Trent Bridge, with the outcome of the match still very much in the balance, the back pages of the press were filled with predictions of Gatting's imminent demise.

'GATT FOR THE CHOP' trumpeted the back page of *The Sun*. However, the story that followed had nothing to do with the 'TEST STARS IN SEX ORGY' story which would grace the front page the following morning. It was instead a combination of the uphill battle faced by England's batsman and the rumbling row over the publication later that month of Gatting's autobiography *Leading from the Front*. The book, due for publication by Queen Anne Press on 30 June, had long been known about, but the more recent revelation that its final chapter would offer Gatting's version of the Shakoor Rana affair had raised eyebrows. Under the terms of Gatting's tour contract with the TCCB, he was restricted for a two-year period from publishing anything without prior approval of the board. Board executives, keen to tidy the issue away as swiftly and silently as possible, made it clear that no such approval had been given. This apparent breach of contract, *The Sun* claimed, might cost Gatting his job.

A quote *The Sun* obtained from A. C. Smith seemed to back up their prognosis: 'If it does go ahead, it could undermine his position as England captain' Smith told the paper. 'We may not be able to get a court injunction stopping publication, but we can certainly take action against Gatting for being in breach of his tour contract.' Smith's reference to a court injunction was a response to comments the previous day by the publishing director at Queen Anne Press, Alan Sampson, who had claimed that no less a step would be required to stop publication at this late stage. 'The book is already printed. It will be published on June 30 as planned – and we have Mike's full backing.' These words from Alan Sampson were printed in *The Sun* under the headline 'GATTING: I'LL FIGHT 'EM IN COURT.' Gatting himself, busy with other matters at the time, had made no comment on the matter.

The row over Gatting's book had been bubbling under since *The Sun* first ran the story of the Shakoor Rana chapter a few weeks earlier. There had been a late attempt to outmanoeuvre the terms of Gatting's contract by attributing the offending chapter directly to Gatting's ghostwriter Angela Patmore. But the TCCB had made it clear that the presence of this chapter at all in a book published under Gatting's name was unacceptable, whoever might be claimed as its author. They were, they said, seeking legal advice on the matter.

Queen Anne Press' nimble footwork over the authorship of the chapter was almost certainly a response to some hastily sought legal advice of their own and they probably realised that this action had muddied the legal waters sufficiently to protect them from any major consequences. A. C. Smith's reluctance to threaten legal action against the publishers suggested they were right. From the publishers' point of view, to go ahead with the book with all mention of the Shakoor Rana affair excised would have been a catastrophe. Without it, where would the book's dramatic finale be? Would it end on the anti-climax of the World Cup defeat? Or with the damp squib of the Test series against Pakistan the previous summer? To finish the story on a high note would mean closing with the Ashes triumph in Australia eighteen months previously, which would leave it looking hopelessly out of date, but to publish with the chapter intact, with headlines all over the tabloid press and the England captain's job on the line was a dream come true. From a business point of view, publication was the simplest of decisions. It meant the difference between an embarrassing and costly flop and a bestseller that would outstrip their wildest dreams for an everyday sporting autobiography.

For Mike Gatting, the headlines were an unwelcome distraction. The 'I'LL FIGHT 'EM IN COURT' headline had greeted him at breakfast on his birthday. The next morning, facing a full day's batting to steer his team out of danger, it was 'GATT FOR THE CHOP' that may have caught his eye as he headed for the breakfast buffet. Perhaps an irreverent thought of pork or lamb crossed his mind. He must have realised by this stage how ill-advised he had been to treat his tour contract in such a cavalier fashion and may have been wishing the whole business would just go away so that he could get on with playing cricket.

The great pity about the row over the book is that the controversial chapter itself was such a banal affair. Christopher Martin-Jenkins, reviewing the book for *The Cricketer* wrote, 'even the contentious part of this somewhat premature "autobiography" makes mundane reading. It is debatable whether there was much point in the Board's objecting to the Angela Patmore chapter; it contains little either new or surprising.' Writing in *The Guardian*, Matthew Engel thought it 'infinitely less interesting than authority's reaction to it'. There was nothing in the text that interested readers had not already encountered in hundreds of newspaper and magazine reports over the previous seven months, but, unenlightening though it was, it came directly from the captain of the England team and that at least was new. For the TCCB, keen to patch up relations with Pakistan, that, rather than any revelation in the content, was the embarrassment. 'We prefer the diplomatic approach,' said A. C. Smith, 'and this will not help.'

Mike Gatting, summoned to Lord's to discuss the book's publication with TCCB officials on Wednesday 8 June, must have felt the noose tightening around his neck. He may have felt slightly more comfortable as Gooch and Gower batted out the final day at Trent Bridge. His batsmen had played their hearts out for him, now according to *The Sun's* Ian Todd, they were prepared to lay down their kit and careers to save him. Under a headline that declared 'SACK GATT AND WE STRIKE' – the very same headline *The Sun* ran on 10 December 1987 when reporting the deadlock in Faisalabad – Todd quoted 'a team insider' as saying 'the players are spitting mad at the way Gatt is being treated. I'm sure they won't sit back and see him pilloried just because he wants to give his version of the Pakistan tour in his new book.'

It is probable that offering any version of the Pakistan tour was the very last thing Gatting now wanted to do. The use of 'they' by Todd's source suggests that the team insider was not *very* far inside the team, nevertheless, there can be little doubt that the England team as a whole would have been disappointed to see Gatting sacked at this stage. Within hours, however, a new revelation had moved the story into completely new territory and from the back pages of the tabloid press to the front.

When Wednesday's *Sun* first went to press it did so carrying the front page headline 'TAXMAN'S FRAUD PROBE INTO KEN'. While the financial affairs of comedian Ken Dodd had top billing, page seven revealed a sportsman involved in a sex scandal: 'NELSON GETS TWO LOVERS IN THE CLUB', accompanied by a photograph of an attractive young lady giving 'randy racing champ' Nelson Piquet 'a cuddle'. Perhaps to call it a scandal is to overstate the case; the procreational activities of a Brazilian racing driver on an Australian Formula One team would have few implications beyond the lives of those personally involved. It may have been this which spared Piquet the indignity of relegating Ken Dodd to a less prominent position inside the paper, but a major sex scandal will always trump a money scandal, and by the time the late edition had been put to bed *Sun* editor Kelvin McKenzie had been through one of those evenings which most tabloid editors only dream of: you think you've got the story of the year, and then suddenly something even better comes along. It was a story that would stop English cricket dead in its tracks and put Mike Gatting through what he would always regard as the worst period of his career. 'TEST STARS IN SEX ORGY' the headline cheered. Late one night during the Test match at Trent Bridge, 'up to five Test players' had 'frolicked' with several blondes by a lake in the grounds of the Rothley Court Hotel, near Leicester, where the players were staying. These romps had later continued in the players' rooms, so the paper claimed.

Like all of the England team and management, Micky Stewart had no warning of the news before it broke:

After the Test I drove straight down from Nottingham to Swansea to watch Kim Barnett playing for Derbyshire against Glamorgan. I got to the hotel quite late, and it wasn't until I came down to breakfast the next morning that one of the press boys who was staying there came up to me and said 'have you seen the papers?' I said 'no, I've only just got here.' Well straight away he showed me the front page of *The Sun* and *Today* who both had the story.

The England manager's breakfast was delayed for more than an hour that day. Within minutes, Stewart was speaking on the phone with a distraught Peter May. 'It was so completely out of the blue,' remembers Stewart. 'Peter May was a great Mike Gatting fan even before I got there. His family too, his daughters ... they still are, all very fond of Gatt. I told Peter I'd stay where I was for the time being. I'd come all this way down, and nothing much was going to happen in twenty-four hours. To just dash off straight away would only have been to satisfy the media.'

Micky Stewart didn't have to dash off anywhere. As England manager in a hotel full of journalists, the story was bound to follow him. By the end of the day, Stewart had already started to look into the truth of the allegations on behalf of the TCCB. It was to be a lightning fast enquiry. 'I shall make my report to Lord's first thing in the morning' he told *The Guardian*. 'I am a lot closer to establishing the facts. If I see anything in the newspapers which does not hold the England cricket side up in the best possible light, I think it is serious enough to establish what the facts are. It makes me angry to see England's name dragged into this sort of thing.' Stewart had spoken to the staff at the team hotel, as well as all but four of the squad. Neither *The Sun* nor *Today* had named the players involved, but that was about to change.

'GATTING MADE LOVE TO ME' ran the headline across the front page of the late edition of Thursday's *Sun*, alleging that Gatting had 'romped' by the lakeside and in his hotel room with twenty-year-old Louise Shipman, a barmaid at the nearby Red Lion hotel, where he and some of his team mates had been drinking earlier in the evening. 'I spoke to Gatt on the phone,' remembers Micky Stewart, 'and at first he denied anything. I said "now come on Gatt, did you or didn't you?" And he said "I promise you, nothing actually happened."' Gatting intimated to Stewart that he had been the victim of a set-up by the newspapers. 'Well, then I appreciated this huge tabloid war that was going on. It got worse, but that was the start of it.'

It was during the Australia tour in 1986/87 that Micky Stewart had first learned to appreciate the potential for a scandal involving the England players:

I had a phone call from a guy I'd known for years in the press cricket correspondent ranks, he rang me up out of the blue and said 'Micky, I'm just warning you, there will be three girls in the bar of the hotel', this was in Queensland before the first Test match, he said 'they're there for a purpose, and they've all been paid for.' These girls had been sent out from the UK on paid holiday, just to get the players into compromising positions. So I said to the guys, 'nobody goes down to the bar until I go down there.'

Stewart duly went down to the bar and found three British girls waiting, who told him they were all on holiday for three weeks. Thinking to himself 'what affluent young ladies', he made sure the hotel bar was a player-free environment that evening. With the experience in Brisbane still very much in mind, it was natural that Stewart should consider this latest story as just another attempt to set up his players.

While *The Sun* ran with 'GATTING MADE LOVE TO ME' on Thursday 9 June, *Today* featured a two-page spread that offered its own edited version of an eight-page long affidavit sworn by Louise Shipman. Ms Shipman recalled how several of the England players had been drinking in the Red Lion on Sunday evening and had engaged in conversation with her and three other female members of staff. Later, Gatting had driven her back from the pub to the Rothley Court Hotel, with two more cars following behind. As well as Gatting and Ms Shipman, three other players and two other girls from the pub staff made up the party. When they arrived, she joined Gatting in his suite for a drink before sitting on his bed 'feeling woozy and very drunk.' What was alleged to have happened next is, happily, not related in detail. Ms Shipman went home by taxi soon afterwards.

This was not their final meeting. In the words of *Today* journalists Wayne Francis and Nick Constable, 'the next day, Gatting's 31st birthday, she visited his suite for a celebration drink with wicketkeeper Paul Downton, Jarvis and Sarah [Swan, the assistant head-waitress at the Red Lion]. They all left when Gatting said he was tired.' The second evening would quickly become confused with the first, with several papers later reporting that Gatting had admitted having been alone in his hotel room with Ms Shipman on the night of his birthday, but the original stories run in *The Sun* and *Today* make clear that it was only the events of the Sunday night that had led to the scandalous allegations.

It is not difficult to find inconsistencies in the two papers' reporting of the affair. *Today's* front page on Thursday 9 June said that 'all but two of the team had been interviewed last night as England manager Micky Stewart led an inquiry.' On page five, Wayne Francis and Nick Constable named those two as Graham Gooch and Derek Pringle. Yet the following day, on page forty-three, the same paper claimed that Stewart's investigation 'was not yet over – four more players, Paul Jarvis, Phil DeFreitas, Allan Lamb and Paul Downton, will be interviewed later today.' Lamb had already denied even being in the same county when questioned by *The Sun*: 'I went home to Northampton with the flu – so I missed all the fun!' The fact that these four players were to be questioned by Stewart was widely misinterpreted as meaning that they were under suspicion, whereas in fact Stewart had simply not been able to speak to them yet.

There was another, far more serious factual error in the reporting of this story, however. On Friday 10 June, the front page of *The Sun* again made reference to the alleged lakeside 'romp', saying that one of Ms Shipman's friends 'said she saw Louise and Gatting – married with two sons – have sex on the grass in the hotel grounds.' This part of the story is entirely absent from Ms Shipman's affidavit, being once more the evidence of an unnamed third party, 'one of her friends.' The headlines 'GATTING MADE LOVE TO ME' and the later 'I'M 48 NOT OUT' might suggest to most readers that they are direct quotes from Ms Shipman herself. In fact, what the paper wrote about Ms Shipman is based entirely upon what it called 'boasts' made to 'friends', a host of Rothley Court insiders, perhaps. There is no evidence of her having spoken directly to *The Sun* at all.

There are several factors which call into question the eyewitness accounts of the lakeside 'romp'. The grounds themselves were not extensively floodlit, and according to weather reports the night of 5–6 June was overcast with a temperature of around 5°c further chilled by a brisk north-westerly breeze. The effects of alcohol notwithstanding, these do not sound like ideal conditions for alfresco frolics. Even had such frolics taken place, it must be questionable how visible they would have been. But the story of the lakeside 'romp' falls down over an even more fundamental point:

There is no lake at the Rothley Court Hotel.

Louise Shipman today is understandably dismissive of this part of the story. She also casts serious doubt on the version of events that was attributed to her at the time. When I spoke with her, she told me that she and some colleagues had indeed come back to the Rothley Court Hotel for drinks late on Sunday night, but neither she nor Mike Gatting had had any intention of being alone together – there was supposed to be a drinks party in Gatting's suite, but after Gatting and Ms Shipman arrived, the other members of the party failed to turn up. 'Mike telephoned to one of the other rooms to find out where everybody had got to' she says. While she waited, Ms Shipman had a drink and leafed through a magazine. Eventually, it became clear that the others would not be turning up after all. 'I remember there being some embarrassment' she recalls. A brief, rather awkward conversation followed before Ms Shipman went home by taxi. Ms Shipman told me that she did not engage in any sexual act with the England captain.

So what are we to make of the Rothley Court Affair? On the one hand there is the story of outdoor frolics by the side of a non-existent lake, based on the testimony of unnamed third parties. On the other hand there is the allegation of sexual activity in the England captain's room, denied by both of the people present. This is the substance of the scandal that cost the England captain his job.

On the same day – Thursday 9 June – that the allegations against him were made public, Mike Gatting appeared at Lord's before the England selectors Peter May, Fred Titmus, Phil Sharpe and Micky Stewart. He denied any sexual misconduct with Ms Shipman, but conceded that he had invited her to his room for a drink on the night in question. Gatting spent an hour giving his version of events before retiring to another office. After waiting for an agonising and lonely hour, he was joined by Peter May and Micky Stewart. Alone in that room, he must have known his time as captain was at an end.

Afterwards, Gatting left Lord's without speaking to the press, leaving his views to be represented by May and Stewart. They announced that they believed without question Gatting's account – Stewart had not spoken to Louise Shipman to check her version of events – but that they felt Gatting 'had behaved irresponsibly during a Test match by inviting female company to his room for a drink in the late evening.' The England captain's behaviour was especially worthy of condemnation for having occurred in the light of all the statements on player behaviour issued at the start of the season. 'Warnings had previously been issued to all England players concerning the standard of behaviour expected of them at all times both on and off the field, and these had been ignored.'

Curiously, neither May nor Stewart made any reference to Gatting actually being sacked. May stated that Gatting was 'obviously very sad about the affair and agreed that he was not in the right frame of mind to play next week', and further, that 'Mike Gatting has lost the highest honour in cricket – to be captain of England. He has lost it for the next match. It does not rule Gatting out from being captain again.' By a strict interpretation of those words, Gatting had been removed from the England captaincy for one match only. Might he then have the opportunity of returning to the job for the third Test at Old Trafford? Here is where the fine detail of Gatting's tenure as captain becomes relevant. At the start of the summer Gatting had been reappointed as captain for the Texaco Trophy and the first two Test matches. His term would have expired at the end of the second Test at Lord's. His suspension for that match meant that by the time he was once again available for selection as an England player, he would no longer be captain of England anyway. They did not have to sack him at all.

As May and Stewart parried away as best they could the barrage of questions from a hungry press horde, one fact became abundantly clear: Mike Gatting's fate had been sealed long before he stood in front of the selectors to offer his version of events. The selectors had believed him, but dethroned him anyway. And when Peter May took exception to the use of the word 'dishonourable' in one question – 'the statement doesn't say that. It says "irresponsible". There is a difference' – his reaction suggested that more time and consideration had gone into the official statement than would have been realistic in the time between Gatting's deposition and the press conference that followed.

'The actual decision was a TCCB Management Board one' Micky Stewart recalls. 'Peter May was a member of the Board, but I was not. Prior to that, Peter May and Peter Lush – I think Lushy was there – had a meeting with Raman Subba Row and Ossie Wheatley, so that they could get our slant on it.' Stewart is no longer certain of the exact timing of these meetings, but he does recall discussing the likely suspension in advance of Gatting's appearance. Stewart and May agreed on the correct course of action: 'we said "he's out of order, so he pays the penalty of being suspended and losing the captaincy."' Stewart states that both he and May were keen for Gatting to continue after a brief suspension in order to try and retrieve some of the momentum lost after the 1986/87 tour of Australia, but the appointment of a new England captain would need the authorisation of the management board, and with Gatting's term due to expire after the one match for which he was suspended, that authorisation would never be given. 'We just wanted to get back to square one as quickly as possible after it [the suspension]' continues Stewart, 'but they wouldn't have any of that, helped by those who were anti-him when he was given the job in the first place.'

When Peter May said 'he has lost it for the next match. It does not rule Gatting out from being captain again', it was no simple obfuscation for the sake of the press: it was an expression of the belief he shared with Micky Stewart that Gatting might return to lead the side once his one-match suspension was over. Neither man had yet gained a sense of the vehement opposition to this idea held in particular by Ossie Wheatley and Raman Subba Row, or quite how long-standing that opposition was.

One year later, Gatting's nomination for the captaincy by Ted Dexter was vetoed by Ossie Wheatley. In Alan Lee's biography of Dexter, *Lord Ted*, Lee quoted Wheatley some years later giving his reason for exercising the veto:

> I had thought for some time that it would be totally wrong to have as England captain someone who was forever being shown on television wagging his finger at an umpire. What influence was that on the young? One of the absolutely unbreakable rules of cricket is that no-one, but no-one, disputes anything with the umpire, least of all the captain of England. There are no excuses.

It is open to question just how long Wheatley had held this view. He had not seen fit to veto Gatting's reappointment at the start of the summer, but it seems reasonable to assume that once Gatting found himself on the wrong end of yet more embarrassing headlines the view began to take concrete form in Ossie Wheatley's mind.

That evening, Gatting and his wife Elaine appeared at the door of their North London home to deliver two separate statements to the waiting press. In the first, Gatting dismissed the sex allegations and announced that his solicitors had been instructed to prepare writs for libel, while in the second he declared his intention to try and prevent his publishers from including the controversial Shakoor Rana chapter in his book. He probably knew how futile such statements would be.

The book had already been printed, the scandal was already public knowledge and his job already forfeit. Nothing he could say or do now would change that. Perhaps it was in the nature of the man to reject the idea of accepting his fate without a fight, perhaps he felt he owed his family the strongest possible denials, perhaps he thought that indicating a willingness to take the part of the TCCB against his publishers might ward off any further action by the board. Gatting said his piece then turned back into the family home, which would remain under siege for several days. The libel writs never went to court and *Leading from the Front* was published on 30 June with the chapter attributed to Angela Patmore intact. Mike Gatting would never captain England again.

But Mike Gatting's downfall did not bring down the curtain on the scandal that led to it. For *The Sun,* Gatting was now 'the shamed ex-skipper', Ms Shipman the 'shapely Louise.' The paper took Micky Stewart to task for accepting Gatting's account of events without speaking to Louise Shipman. 'We have seen all this before in the past' responded Stewart, 'we do not think it is relevant to speak to that girl.' The paper seemed to be trying to portray Ms Shipman as a wronged innocent, gagged by an all-powerful establishment but given her own voice by *The Sun*, despite not having a single quote from the woman herself to its credit.

Above Stewart's comments, *The Sun* exclusively revealed, in a story illustrated by a photograph in which Ms Shipman displayed what it called 'the charms that bowled over England's skipper', that the Leicestershire barmaid was keeping the score of her lovers and that the Rothley Court affair had left her just two short of an audacious fifty. While the headline seemed to proclaim that the paper remained on the side of Ms Shipman, the story itself indicated a very different attitude. Based on yet another interview with 'friends', it first paid tribute to her 'amazing score of lovers ... 48 NOT OUT', but then went on to describe in detail some of her exploits while asking her friends to pass judgement on her behaviour. 'She thinks it is hilarious,' said one, 'but she does not realise what a terrible reputation she has. She's just man mad.'

'Some of us think she just does it to get attention' said another. 'She's got no shame' they concluded at last. *The Sun* seemed to be asking its readers to admire Ms Shipman's physical attributes, while condemning her behaviour.

Twenty-four hours later, the paper delivered its *coup de grace* –

'GATTING'S GIRL ATE ME ALIVE SAYS CHEF – "But she isn't so hot in bed".' *The Sun's* John Askill and Andrew Parker had tracked down one of Ms Shipman's alleged conquests, twenty-year-old chef Dave Massey, and asked him for a review of her performance. He remarked that 'she goes for volume not quality' and, even more uncharitably, 'I thought, "it's either Louise or a few more pints of beer."' In the space of two editions, *The Sun* had taken Louise Shipman from the good-time girl next door, to shameless man-eater, and not even a very gifted man-eater at that.

For anyone who has found themselves the subject of unwanted headlines, the wounds run deep; the scars continue to nag away long after they appear to have healed. Former England football manager Graham Taylor, subject of the scathing 'turnip-head' abuse in the 1990s, told the *Daily Telegraph* of its lasting effects in an interview in 2013:

> I remember I met Kelvin Mackenzie, who was editor of *The Sun* at the time, and he told me I was being over-sensitive to complain about his paper calling me a turnip. He said it was a bit of fun. Well, I was at a match in Brentford several years later, making my way to my car after the game, when I saw out of the corner of my eye two yobbish looking people coming out of a pub with a pint in each hand. They were shouting 'there's the effin' turnip!' and they chucked the pints over me. If it hadn't been for the action of the Brentford security people, I reckon it would have been worse. Was that just a bit of fun, Kelvin?

Gatting and Taylor both lost their jobs after their journeys through the tabloid headlines, and their travails remain well known, but the forgotten victim in this sorry tale is Louise Shipman. It would be easy to consider Ms Shipman as being part of the hostile party, but the exposure she suffered had a devastating effect on her life too. Two stories that ran on Friday 10 June offered the first indication of this. 'I feel so ashamed,' *Today* quoted her as saying. 'I never intended any of this to come out. It has embarrassed my family and I have been hurt by people exaggerating stories. There have been times when I felt like suicide. My nerves are a mess.' In a two-page spread, the *Daily Mirror* offered more of Ms Shipman's side of the story, but her apparent remorse – 'I'm so sorry, Mike!' – was greeted with contempt by the outside world. 'How nice,' wrote *The Guardian's* Matthew Engel. 'Was she speaking through a grille from a nunnery as she prepared for a lifetime of penitence? Or even from behind dark glasses and high walls at a discreet Leicestershire cottage? Not exactly. She was posing prettily for pictures, apparently in the *Mirror* office.' Just as Micky Stewart had thought from the outset, when he thought it unnecessary to speak to 'that girl', Ms Shipman now stood condemned as the kind of femme fatale who deliberately ensnared a celebrity victim in order to sell her story to the papers. But Louise Shipman's story of how she came to be posing for those pictures in the offices of the *Daily Mirror* is perhaps the darkest part of this whole affair.

For Louise Shipman, the first indication that something was about to go seriously wrong in her life came on Tuesday 7 June when she had a call from an old friend asking if she could meet him for lunch. She had known Nic since childhood and he was now working as a freelance reporter with the Mercury East Midlands news agency. He told her that he had heard some gossip about goings on involving the England team at the Rothley Court Hotel. Ms Shipman adamantly denied that anything had happened, but when she arrived for work at the Red Lion that evening, something was most definitely up. 'There were loads of strange people everywhere' she told me. 'Then the phone calls started. They kept calling the restaurant and asking to speak to me. There were loads of them hanging around outside and eventually the manager asked me to go out and get rid of them.'

Back outside the pub, she quickly found herself accosted by a reporter:

> He asked if he could speak with me in his car, and I agreed, hoping it would get rid of him, but suddenly the doors were locked, there were wires everywhere and he was really pushy and unpleasant. He wouldn't let me out of the car. He kept saying 'we want you to tell us about your affair with Mike Gatting,' but I kept saying back 'I haven't had an affair with Mike Gatting!'

It was only when she claimed she needed some time to think before speaking about it that the car door was unlocked and she managed to escape. The photograph that accompanied *The Sun's* 'GATTING MADE LOVE TO ME' story is of Louise Shipman fleeing from the car for the refuge of the pub, but the pub was still surrounded by reporters and, in desperation, she called the man she thought she could trust most to keep the press at bay – Nic.

Nic told her not to say anything, to stay put and wait until he arrived. When he got there, he must have seemed to Louise Shipman like a knight in shining armour, but this would be no fairy-tale rescue. Her experience over the next few days was to be very different from that which might have been imagined by any reader of the newspapers that would cover her story.

When Louise Shipman got into Nic's car on Tuesday 7 June, the story had yet to break. Forty-eight hours later, almost everyone in the country had read something about her in the press. It is not possible to reconstruct an exact chronology of what happened to her over the next few days. 'It's all very hazy now,' she remembers, 'it was very confusing at the time and I've blocked so much of it out over the years.' However, some incidents, places and emotions remain to provide some insight into her experience.

For more than a week, Louise Shipman was shuttled around by car, cocooned in a series of anonymous hotel rooms, quizzed by a variety of journalists, sometimes moving location suddenly without explanation, and kept in almost complete isolation from the outside world. For the first couple of days she had no change of clothing, having only had time to grab a toothbrush before leaving Leicestershire. At one point, she is no longer sure exactly when or where, a friend was picked up with the idea that she could collect some clothes for her, 'but then Nic's pager went off, the car was stopped and she was told she had to get out.' Only after arriving in London two days later did Nic manage to purchase some 'essentials' for his passenger. The progress of their road trip seems to have been governed by the beeping of Nic's pager. 'We'd be in a hotel somewhere, then the pager would go and he'd say "we've got to move", and we'd be in the car again off to another hotel. Or he'd look at it and say "that's the *Mail*" or tell me that it said "we know you've got her". I felt that I was in so much trouble and he was my only hope. I didn't dare do anything.'

On Tuesday 7 June, they drove to Birmingham and checked in to the Copthorne Hotel. From there she was taken to the Corporation Street offices of solicitor Andrew Mandleberg where, after being offered alcohol to help her calm down, she was questioned by Mr Mandleberg and Wayne Francis of *Today*.

I didn't really know what was happening. I thought I was making a statement to protect myself and my family and that if I told them the truth everything would be OK. They asked me questions and I responded. It wasn't a case of me telling my story or anything like that. After that I was taken away for a while, then brought back to swear on the Bible that what I had said was the truth.

What she was swearing to was the eight-page affidavit whose summarised contents appeared in *Today*. It had, she assumed, been based on the answers she had given Francis and Mandleberg. She signed it without hesitation. 'But I never read it,' she told me. 'I didn't even know what an affidavit was.' It was only later, when she finally read the stories attributed to her, that she realised how significant were the differences between what she had said in that room and what subsequently appeared in print. The whereabouts of the affidavit today are unknown. In 1990, Ms Shipman hired a solicitor to write to Andrew Mandleberg and ask for a copy to be sent to her, but Mr Mandleberg's office replied that the firm had not retained a copy of the document and she would need to apply to *Today* itself. No copy was forthcoming from that source either. The paper ceased production in November 1995.

On Wednesday 8 June, Louise Shipman and Nic headed to Cheltenham, 'but something changed and we didn't stay there.' The next day, Thursday, she was moved again to London and driven to the offices of the *Daily Mirror* for the glamorous photo shoot that helped to paint her in such stark terms as the woman who brought down an England captain. Looking at that photograph years later, Louise Shipman remains bewildered by it all. 'I remember being very upset and protesting a lot, but in the end they wore me down. I don't know how they got me looking like that. I just remember crying all the time, mascara running down my face, then being fed more alcohol.'

Drink seems to have been a constant feature of those few days for Louise Shipman. Frequently, at crucial moments, it was supplied to calm her nerves. She had no contact with her family or friends, no TV or radio, and was kept as far as possible away from the newspapers that were carrying stories about her. She does remember seeing two copies of *The Sun* – those carrying the headlines 'GATTING MADE LOVE TO ME' and 'I'M 48 NOT OUT.' 'I remember challenging Nic about that, about how he'd said he would keep my name out of it all. He made some excuse, saying he didn't know they were going to do that.' These, of course, were the stories based on third-party accounts. She was yet to see any of the stories supposedly based on her own words. She remained in isolation, at the still, silent eye of the media storm that raged all around her. 'That was when things changed,' she recalls. 'I was so upset by that 48 not out story. For several days I was very near to having a complete breakdown. I remember being in such a state at one point that I tried to get out of the car on Putney Bridge. Nic drove me to the house of some friend of his in Fulham and just left me alone in a room to calm down.' Although the media storm was now blowing itself out, her odyssey would continue for some days yet.

Hearing Louise Shipman describe what happened to her today, it is apparent how disorientating the experience was. Isolated from the outside world and dependent upon a single source for information, she found her world shrunk to the confines of Nic's car and the four walls of whichever hotel room she was cooped up in. Within that world she sought protection from a hostile environment beyond, within it too she lost all sense of the passage of time. Even today she is uncertain how long her ordeal endured. 'I still look back and wonder how I could have been so naive, so trusting' she says. She had little awareness at the time of how much exposure she had been subjected to, and it was some time before she understood how comprehensively she had been let down. 'It was only much later, seeing that story in *Today* about me feeling suicidal, that was how the penny dropped. As far as I was concerned, they were not comments made to a journalist. I said those things in a private conversation with Nic. He was the only other person in the room at the time.'

After several days without any contact, Ms Shipman at last spoke to her mother by telephone. Back home in Leicestershire, things had not been much easier for Ms Shipman's mother. Finding the family home under siege, just as the Gattings had, she had quickly learned not to answer the door. Soon, she learned not to answer the telephone either. Some journalists had discovered the names of school friends of her daughter who had gone off to university, and they rang up pretending to be those same friends asking after her.

The following day, perhaps ten days after leaving the Red Lion with Nic, Louise Shipman's nightmare odyssey at last came to an end. A friend had offered her sanctuary and Nic drove her up the A1 to his house in Colsterworth, just south of Grantham. 'Perhaps that was a sign of some compassion from him, driving me there.' Nic then drove off, back to his life and career, leaving Ms Shipman to what was left of hers. Lifelong friends up to that point, they have not seen each other since from that day to this.

Even after she left London, it was clear to Louise Shipman that she could not really go home. 'I spent some time sleeping in a friend's spare room. I had left my job and struggled to find another one because everyone knew who I was. Eventually I got a job in a clothes shop but it didn't last long. I was mostly unemployed for a long time.' Contrary to reports that she had been sacked by the Red Lion, Louise Shipman states that the pub management, old friends of her family, had been extremely supportive and kept her job open for her, but she felt she could not stay on, being sure that some of the staff she would be working with had been the sources of the stories that had painted her so black.

Not only had her own words been spun into a web of exaggeration, so too had the character assassinations based on the testimony of her 'friends.' The idea that she boasted of the number of her 'conquests' is, she insists today, quite outrageous. 'I was young, convent educated, yes, there were a few dalliances, but nothing like that.' Most of the stories, she insists, were untrue or misleading. One example of the many betrayals she endured was the topless photograph which accompanied the '48 NOT-OUT' story. This had been taken on holiday with a female friend. 'I had never done any topless sunbathing,' she recalls. 'That was her thing, but she persuaded me, and when she took some photographs later this was one of them. I went out with her brother a couple of times and when the story blew up, he went into her bedroom and took this photo to give to the press.'

However much such humiliation hurt at the time, Ms Shipman has a forgiving word today for those who let her down so badly: 'I was young and stupid. So were they. They probably didn't realise the consequences of what they were doing. They probably just saw it as a chance to make some quick money.' It was widely assumed that Louise Shipman too had sold her story, and that, just like the 'affluent young ladies' Micky Stewart had encountered in Brisbane, she had been a willing participant in a tabloid 'sting'. In *A Lot of Hard Yakka* Simon Hughes summed up the popular theory of a conspiracy with Mercury East Midlands: 'she had recounted her story as agreed and the agency had auctioned the story on the open market. *The Sun* were the highest bidders. The figure bandied about was £10,000.'

When I showed this quote to Louise Shipman, almost twenty-seven years after the events it describes, she was surprised and upset to discover what sort of person she had been assumed to be for all those years. Some time later, to her surprise since she had never asked for money, she did receive a cheque for £500 from Mercury East Midlands, but far from conniving in a profitable tabloid 'sting', Ms Shipman had been trying to protect herself and her family from the effects of a tabloid scandal whose factual basis she denied. The method she chose was naïve and counter-productive, and the effect on her life ruinous. Louise Shipman had been working at the Red Lion to fund some preliminary study prior to taking up a place at the London College of Fashion. That ambition was destroyed by the scandal, her self-esteem gravely damaged.

It can never be easy to recover from such public humiliation, but it is perhaps easier for those already in the public eye. To the wider public there is more to them than just the embarrassing scandal or the vitriolic criticism. Graham Taylor was a successful football manager; he went on to become a well-regarded pundit and columnist on the game. Mike Gatting was a world-class cricketer who had led his country to Ashes triumph; he had another ten years' cricket in him before retirement brought other honours in the game, including a one-year term as President of MCC. For the ordinary person caught up in a media storm, however, such public redemption is more difficult. Louise Shipman retreated into obscurity. That may have saved her from further exposure, but it also meant that if she were remembered at all beyond her own private circle it would be as the saucy barmaid who brought down an England captain. It is a sad public legacy, and one she did not deserve.

Across the media, reaction to Gatting's downfall ranged from moral puritanism to outrage at the excesses of the press, mingled with a deep sense of sorrow that the game of cricket should have come to this. Friday's *Daily Express* thought Gatting had no one to blame but himself, and advised his successors that the England captaincy was 'an arduous job, demanding great seriousness of purpose. And it is best carried out, during Tests, not with the help of women and hard liquor, but with early nights and a cup of cocoa.' *The Sunday Times* declared with breath-taking pomposity that Gatting had 'betrayed all our young dreams.' *The Observer* considered Gatting's record of only two Test victories and his shameful row with Shakoor Rana and concluded that 'the selectors have at last done the right thing for entirely the wrong reason.' The selectors' claim that they entirely accepted Gatting's version of events but had deposed him anyway was met with widespread scorn. Perhaps Melbourne's *The Age* summed it up best with its famous headline: 'Gatting, caught rumour, bowled hypocrisy, o.'

In *The Sun*, Fiona Macdonald Hull drew an unfavourable comparison between the paragon cricketers of old – Ted Dexter, Richie Benaud, Garry Sobers and Basil D'Oliveira – and the generation of 1988. Her selective memory had clearly erased all recollection of Bill Edrich, Wally Hammond and others who made conquests almost as easily as they made runs. Blessed were they who played the game in an era when only performance on the field was thought to be suitable matter for the breakfast table. 'I'm sick of sporting stars who, because they have a little bit of fame and fortune, start behaving as if they were born in a sewer' she wrote. 'Forget temporary bans and wimpy fines – fire the lot and start again.' As the summer went on, cricket fans might have been forgiven for thinking that Ms Macdonald Hull was also acting as consultant to the England selection committee.

While the news media had their fun, the cricket press were left to reflect on the suddenness of Gatting's demise and to try and work out just who had been most at fault. Was it, as Mike Selvey suggested, the England management team, for not clamping down on team discipline as early as Gatting's Ashes tour when he had received only a reprimand for oversleeping and arriving late to the Melbourne Cricket Ground during England's match with Victoria? Was it Gatting himself for the poor Test record which called his ability to forge a winning team into question and for the row with Shakoor Rana, which did the same for his judgement? Or was it 'the mandarins of Lord's', as Frank Keating named them, for their inability to treat the tabloid press with an appropriate level of contempt? Keating called it 'The Lord's Syndrome': 'It's OK as long as it doesn't get in the papers.'

According to Scyld Berry, the TCCB had brought the scandal upon itself by issuing its instruction that selection would now take into account off-the-field behaviour as well as on-the-field performance. 'In effect, since the relationship between international cricket and chastity is not close, the Board thereby issued a challenge to certain newspapers to rake up all they could.' The Board's misjudged moral stance had meant it was simply a matter of time before a player let his guard down and ended up gracing the wrong pages of the wrong newspaper, and when it happened, the board would not be able to 'snap its fingers at *The Sun* and say "so what?"' without exposing itself to a charge of blatant hypocrisy. Their new firm line on player behaviour probably sounded good in a committee meeting, but when exposed to the brutal reality of modern news gathering it had been no more than a rod for their own backs.

Scyld Berry's view that the TCCB's actions led directly to a deliberate campaign aimed at the England cricket team seems consistent with the reputation of the tabloid press, but there is no real evidence to support it, any more than there is of an attempt to direct a campaign against Mike Gatting in person. The truth is probably more prosaic, that, as Henry Blofeld later wrote 'all the world loves a gossip and a good scandal' and that headlines such as Rothley Court produced were 'impossible to resist'. All the more impossible in the aftermath of all the outrage over England players' behaviour in the months before. As captain of the England cricket team, Gatting was naturally a high-profile target, but the evidence of Louise Shipman suggests that this was more a case of opportunism than deliberate plotting. Had it not been for some unguarded gossip reaching the ears of a local reporter, it is probable that the story would never have seen the light of day, but it cannot be very surprising that to Mike Gatting it felt like a personal vendetta. Gatting's Middlesex teammate Simon Hughes recalled meeting him at Lord's on the day he was relieved of his duties: 'I met him wandering the Lord's corridors the following morning, moments after he'd been sacked as England captain. "I've been stitched up," he muttered, looking thoroughly downcast.'

This stitching up, thought Gatting, had been provoked by his own reluctance to engage with the press on the terms they demanded:

> Even before that Test match began I went to the board and said 'after the treatment we got in New Zealand from the press, why should I do press conferences? They don't want to write what I say, they want to write what's sensational and nowhere near what's happening in the middle. So, why are we bothering with these press conferences? Can you make me do them if I don't want to do them?' There was nothing in the contract really. You just did it. So I said 'give me one good reason why I should talk to these guys.' And that was it. You don't

take on the press. They stuffed me out of sight.

Whether this was, as Gatting thought, retribution for his refusal to play the game by press rules, or simply an opportunistic reaction to the TCCB's new stance on player behaviour, Gatting's most serious misjudgement was that he failed to see it coming.

The manner of Mike Gatting's downfall won the former skipper no small measure of public sympathy. The audience of the BBC's *Question Time* showed themselves to be firmly in Gatting's corner, and when the Middlesex batsman came out to bat for his county at Tunbridge Wells on Saturday 11 June he was greeted by generous applause from the Kentish crowd. The day before, Gatting had been at the Armoury House ground of the Honourable Artillery Company in the City of London for a six-a-side match in aid of his benefit fund. The timing for such an event could hardly have been worse, and the rain which restricted play to a few overs before lunch did not help. Gatting managed to crash one massive six through a nearby third-floor window, before spending most of the rest of the day in the marquee politely avoiding any mention of the one subject uppermost in everybody's minds. Avoiding too the paparazzo lurking outside behind a camouflaged Land Rover. When the Master of Ceremonies announced that Gatting would not be making any speeches at this event, no-one took exception to his reticence. Indeed, the 400 guests gave Gatting a rousing cheer when he was introduced at the start of the lunch.

One man who had an awkward subject to raise that day was Gatting's colleague John Emburey. Emburey was the obvious choice to take over from Gatting at Lord's. He had been vice-captain on the winter tours, and while officially there was no equivalent post for home Tests, Emburey was widely perceived as being next in line to Gatting's throne. Indeed, Emburey might well have got the nod over Gatting in the race to succeed Mike Brearley as Middlesex captain in 1982 had he not been serving a three-year Test ban for touring South Africa the previous winter at the time. The selectors wasted no time in identifying their man. Before lunch in the match at Armoury House, the news came through that John Emburey had long dreamed of, but had never wished to hear in such circumstances.

'I got a call from Micky Stewart, saying "we would like you to be captain. Would you accept?"' Emburey recalls. 'I said "yes, I would."'

There was no hesitation. For Emburey, the England captaincy was an opportunity which 'when it comes along, you don't turn it down.' On hearing that Emburey was in London, Stewart asked him to report to Lord's immediately, where the side was being chosen for the Second Test. Emburey somehow had to break the news to Gatting that he now had to leave Gatting's benefit match to take up the job Gatting had been removed from less than twenty-four hours earlier. 'I went up to Gatt and said, "Look, Gatt, I've been asked to captain England and I've got to disappear". And Gatt said, "all right then, hurry up."'

John Emburey's first duties as England captain did not take very long. After helping to pick the side for the second Test, he had time to dash back from Lord's to Moorgate and rejoin the festivities. 'I don't know whether to congratulate you or commiserate,' Elaine Gatting was heard to say. Rarely in its passing can the England captaincy have seemed more like a poisoned chalice.

8

Cricketers Under Curfew

The England selectors had found little difficulty in choosing an appropriate replacement as captain, but in selecting Emburey they had clearly not made a long-term appointment. Emburey was in his mid-thirties and, by his own admission, not bowling anywhere near his best. The selectors must have considered whether he was likely to remain in the side as a player for the remainder of the series if his form failed to improve. In the end, they hedged their bets and appointed Emburey for just the one Test. Micky Stewart explained that the selectors wanted to stick as closely as possible to the policy outlined at the start of the summer, and reassess the captaincy after the first two Tests. Privately, they retained the hope that Mike Gatting could return to captain the side at Old Trafford. Whoever the selectors had appointed for Lord's, an appointment which lasted beyond that match would have been a direct contradiction of the statement that Gatting's suspension as captain was for one game only. Appointing Emburey for Lord's alone meant they could simply allow Gatting's term to expire and then choose afresh for Old Trafford.

In an unusual step, an official vice-captain was also announced for a Home Test: Graham Gooch, one of Emburey's oldest and closest friends. 'Graham is the ideal man,' suggested Peter May, 'an excellent first lieutenant to have at your elbow and in such good form himself.' A cricketer of Emburey's experience would not normally need a little help from his friends when generations of England captains had gone without such help at home. But here the selectors, to their credit, had acknowledged the unusual pressures now making themselves felt on the England team and its new captain. The wider responsibilities could be shared around the team, the better it might be for everyone.

Perhaps the most crucial decision the selectors had to make with John Emburey in his first selection meeting was how to replace Mike Gatting as a batsman. Gatting's form with the bat had not been particularly impressive in recent Tests, but he remained one of the team's most accomplished senior professionals and, perhaps most vitally, a man who had the skill and technique to prosper in the troublesome number three position. Against the West Indies, England's selectors had found this position, requiring a batsman with the technical soundness to cope with coming to the wicket in the very first over, but also the ability to accelerate the scoring later in the innings, almost impossible to fill.

Given these criteria, it is surprising that the popular choice to step into Gatting's shoes was Glamorgan's Matthew Maynard. Maynard had been invited to spend the first two days of the Trent Bridge Test with the England squad 'to soak up the atmosphere' in advance of a likely debut in the not too distant future. Maynard had attended the pre-match team dinner, and enjoyed net practice with the team. It was a sensible and progressive move, which the Glamorgan youngster had relished. 'It was a real thrill,' he told *The Guardian's* Frank Keating. 'Everyone was really generous and encouraging, Mike Gatting especially.' Keating was a keen supporter of Maynard's credentials, citing his 'stomach for the challenge, the most feline swing off the tee, and a yeoman's vigour with it.' Also in Maynard's favour were his skill as a slip fieldsman, an area in which England had not distinguished themselves of late, and a record of scoring runs against some of the great fast bowlers at county level, Richard Hadlee and Michael Holding among them.

In an era when legions of fast bowlers had pinned a generation of batsmen in their creases and forced them into statuesque, robotic techniques, Matthew Maynard was a refreshing reminder of earlier decades, when batsmen got their feet to the pitch of the ball, and moved forward and back with fluidity and commitment. Where Graeme Hick impressed by sheer weight of runs and by the seemingly unstoppable metronome of drive, pull and cut, Maynard's breezy and unpredictable strokeplay had 'whisked up gales around the cheering shires on the most placid, somnolent afternoons.' The veteran *Times* correspondent, John Woodcock, agreed with Keating. To his eye, Maynard's batting was 'quite exhilarating; crisp, instinctive, and simple; and although he is not as still as he ought to be as the ball is delivered, his footwork after that leaves nothing to be desired. Ah me, how the Australians would love to have Maynard at their disposal.'

Maynard's time was surely approaching fast, but would the selectors have been wise to rush him in to the side when so much attention was still directed at the man he had replaced, in a role which might see him facing Marshall or Ambrose for the second ball of the match? This was surely not what they had had in mind when giving him a taste of the big time atmosphere at Trent Bridge. Another batsman with some support was Derbyshire's Kim Barnett; Micky Stewart had been hoping to see both Maynard and Barnett play when he drove down to Swansea straight after the Nottingham Test. Barnett was more of a top-order player than Maynard, with greater experience, and, having impressed since taking over the Derbyshire captaincy, a possible longer term bet for the England job. But Barnett, too, would be a debutant. If the selectors picked either man and let him settle in further down the order at number five, who would move up the order to fill Gatting's slot? Gower? Lamb? Downton?

The selectors' eventual choice was perhaps unimaginative, but surely correct: Yorkshire's Martyn Moxon. As a specialist opening bat, Moxon fitted the bill as a man used to coping against the new ball. He had been given his first lengthy run in the side over the winter, playing in four consecutive Tests in Australia and New Zealand. His calm temperament and solid-looking technique had won him many admirers, not to mention an average of almost 55, before he made way for the returning Gooch at the start of the summer. 'Moxon impressed us last winter and deserves this chance' commented Peter May. 'If he can get a good start he is just the right person to play the long innings we are looking for.'

Other changes to the squad were minimal. With John Emburey sure to play, there was no place for Nottinghamshire's Eddie Hemmings. England were never going to play two spinners, remembers Emburey: 'In those days Lord's pitches didn't turn a huge amount; certainly the Test pitches didn't, the county pitches did, but the Test pitches were pretty flat.' In 1988 prospects for spinners were even worse than usual. By the time the Lord's Test started not a single first-class wicket had fallen there to a spin bowler that season. Hemmings' place in the squad went to Gladstone Small, who had only missed out at Trent Bridge through injury. He would replace the unfortunate

Phil DeFreitas in the final eleven. Both Moxon and Small had been around the England side for at least two years, so despite the loss of Gatting the squad retained an appearance of stability. But just how much the situation had been destabilised since Trent Bridge was apparent from the merest glance at the headlines in the days leading up to the match, which focused more on the challenges England's players would face off the field than on it.

Micky Stewart's enquiry had come to the conclusion that all the Rothley Court affair had amounted to was one England player sharing a drink with a woman in his room. 'Millions have read the stories but the players and selectors know the truth and four innocent players have been dragged across the pages' despaired Micky Stewart. 'We are convinced their conduct was above reproach' said A. C. Smith of the four. Yet, for all this, the unfortunate press coverage led the TCCB to feel that their spring offensive on player behaviour needed further reinforcement. There would be a clampdown on what the *Daily Express* called 'after-match activity' while the team was in London for the Lord's Test. A curfew would be in place. 'A sensible time will have to be emphasised to them for returning to the team hotel, though I haven't yet decided what that time will be' said Stewart. How much effect such a curfew would have is open to question, since events at Brisbane in 1986 and at Rothley Court had proven that team hotels were not always the safe refuge they ought to be.

There was also concern that securing the players in a sterile environment would be going against the nature of their sport. As John Emburey himself put it, 'having a few beers after the day's play is part of cricket.' Writing in his *Express* column, Clive Lloyd worried that the players' relationships with journalists, indeed with anyone on the periphery of the game, might be permanently damaged: 'they will be frightened to speak to people, to socialise, and their relationship with journalists – built up over so many years – will be altered for ever. We must not reach the stage where a cricketer sees a conversation with someone in terms of enormous and alarming headlines.'

The West Indies had warmed up for Lord's with three-day matches against Lancashire and Northants. Rain had ruined the match at Old Trafford and the Wantage Road game offered little in the way of entertainment as the tourists opted to bat out the final day rather than declaring to offer Northamptonshire a target. Since winning at

Somerset before the Texaco Trophy they had lost three and drawn five of their eight fixtures. But any worries they might have had about their continued inability to find their best form were surely offset by the knowledge that England's preparation for the second Test had been far more catastrophic.

Clive Lloyd told *Daily Express* readers that the pitch at Lord's looked 'a belter', but after Viv Richards won the toss on a sultry morning, his decision to bat was one that took him several minutes of consultation. 'It was a balmy day, that first day against the West Indies at Lord's. Hazy, but warm, and having experienced those conditions before, you always knew the ball was going to swing around' recalls John Emburey. Although cloud was forecast for later in the day, at the time the two captains met up in the middle there was little sign of its approach. 'Viv won the toss,' says Emburey, 'and wasn't sure what to do. He approached his bowlers, and the bowlers suggested they bat. Then he spoke to Gordon Greenidge and Desmond Haynes and they said "we should bowl". In the end Viv decided to bat, and of course the ball swung immensely.'

The start of the match was all that Emburey, and England, could have hoped for. By the sixth over, the bright sunshine that had encouraged Richards to bat had disappeared as clouds rolled in from the west. The conditions were perfect for England's new ball pairing of Graham Dilley and Paul Jarvis. Dilley bowled unchanged through the morning; a total of 13 overs bringing him four wickets for 35 as the tourists were reduced to 66 for 5 by lunch. After all that had happened in the last ten days, to be back on the field of play and actually doing well must have seemed an almost unbelievable relief to the England players, and their new captain in particular: 'I remember thinking in my head "this actually isn't bad!"'

Desmond Haynes was the first to fall, playing and missing at three successive outswingers before clipping an in-swinger to short leg where a diving Martyn Moxon stretched his fingertips under the ball a fraction of a second before it went to ground. Gordon Greenidge had found the boundary five times in just over an hour at the crease when he edged a defensive prod at a Dilley out-swinger to Paul Downton for 22. Richie Richardson found progress rather more difficult, managing just the one four past cover point, but mostly finding the ball darting disconcertingly away from his bat or nipping back off the seam to rap him on the pad.

He managed to add just one more run to that boundary before another away swinger from Dilley flew off the open face of his bat straight to Emburey at third slip.

Carl Hooper lasted just four balls before Gladstone Small found his edge and Downton pouched another safe catch. Two balls later, Gus Logie inside edged a boundary just past his leg stump. A becalmed Viv Richards had observed the last part of the carnage from the non-striker's end, barely able to face a ball. But after Logie had seen out the rest of Small's over, the West Indies captain found himself on strike again, facing the destructive Dilley. He decided it was time to counter-attack, but his cavalier drive at Dilley's first ball produced only a thin edge through to Downton, who claimed his third catch of the session. West Indies were 54 for 5, Dilley had taken four wickets in 28 balls and England were jubilant. The tourists' last pair of recognised batsmen, Logie and Dujon, were together. The next wicket could easily be the breakthrough that would see the West Indies bowled out for less than 150 after winning the toss on the first day. Emburey now set Dilley one of the most attacking fields ever seen in Test cricket. Five slips and a gully, with just one man providing cover on the leg side. But when the chance came, it was spurned. Dilley found the edge of Logie's bat, but the ball flew right between Derek Pringle at first slip and Graham Gooch at second and carried on to the boundary. 'Neither of them really went for it,' remembers Emburey.

It seemed like a minor aberration in a session of great success for England, but it was a lifeline for Richards' men, and one they grasped willingly. Crucially, as the final overs of the session ebbed away, Emburey's attacking field told against England. Dilley, lacking any sort of cover on the leg side, began bowling wider outside the line of off-stump and Dujon and Logie began to find the ball easier to leave. 'He was bowling from the Nursery End,' remembers Emburey,

and the ball was swinging and then just going a little bit more off the pitch. Graham said 'can I have another fielder across?' and I think at the time we had a six-three off-side field with three slips and a gully. Then he asked for another man across so we had four slips and then he asked 'can I have another man?' Well, I thought, that makes eight men on the off-side, we've only got one man on the leg side. He was down at fine leg, so we brought him round a bit further to square leg. But immediately we went to that eight-one field I felt a little bit uncomfortable. I had never played in a side with eight fielders on the off-side before and here I am captaining the side. I think for a short while it did warrant it, but unfortunately Graham, because he didn't have the protection on the leg side, didn't bowl at the stumps to make the batsman play, he bowled a little bit wider and the batsmen were able to leave it. I probably allowed it to drift. I think he bowled it like that for about 3 overs when I should have changed it back after one, given him that little bit of protection on the leg side and said to him 'look, I want you to attack the stumps and make the batsmen play.'

Dujon and Logie were able to see out the last few balls before lunch without any further scares. A score of 66 for 5 was by no means a healthy position, but with Dilley tired after his heavy morning workload, things promised to be easier for the batsmen after lunch. 'The other bowlers in the side didn't swing the ball as much as Graham Dilley did' continues Emburey. 'It was a great spell of fast, swing bowling.'

Dilley carried on through another 4 overs straight after lunch, but the zip had gone. And where Viv Richards had failed in his attempt to launch a counter-attack, Gus Logie was beginning to succeed. Gladstone Small's opening over after the interval had been a nagging maiden, but he soon began to take punishment. Straying too close to Logie's pads he found himself clipped through midwicket for four. In his next over, he over compensated and was struck for two off-side boundaries. Two more followed through the covers from consecutive balls in Small's next over, then three more all around the wicket from his next. Suddenly, Logie and an almost strokeless Dujon had brought up a fifty partnership in seventy-three minutes and all the value of England's fine morning's work seemed to have gone.

The batsmen rode their luck at times; trying to pull a short ball from Jarvis, Logie got a top edge which grazed Downton's glove before flying down to the boundary. One over later, Logie almost edged into his stumps for the second time in the innings. With tea approaching, the partnership reached 130. Things looked to be getting beyond England, but while Jarvis toiled against in-form batsmen and hostile fortune, at the other end John Emburey was bowling an impressively tight spell. As the last over before the interval drew to a close, England's captain found just a fraction of turn and the ball squeezed through Dujon's gate and bowled him.

Logie could only add another fifteen in partnership with Marshall before losing his wicket in unfortunate fashion, a well-timed square cut off Small hung on to at backward point by Emburey. Soon afterwards Marshall pushed out at Dilley and edged to Gooch at second slip. Small then swept up the tail, Ambrose caught by a diving Gower at backward square-leg and Patterson bowled by an in-swinger, to the great relief of Allan Lamb who had shelled a towering skier from Walsh three balls before. The West Indies last five wickets had fallen in the space of 11 overs for just 25 runs. Without the contribution of the Logie-Dujon partnership, the entire West Indies batting line-up would have mustered just 79 runs.

For England's bowlers it had been quite a day. Despite that, and the successful rearguard at Trent Bridge, England knew that their batsmen still had a difficult task ahead of them. John Emburey summed expectations up : 'there was always a feeling that whatever you did to the West Indies, their bowlers would do just as much, or even more, to you.' England found themselves with just over half an hour to bat that evening before bad light brought an eventful day to a close. While Graham Gooch was swiftly off and running with the help of a boundary edged through the slips, Chris Broad lasted just nine balls before Marshall nipped one back down the slope and trapped him lbw for nought.

'That's got to be one of the plumbest things ever' commented Richie Benaud on BBC television. Broad himself may not have agreed, as the cameras caught him muttering his displeasure at the start of his lonely walk back to the dressing room. In his notebook, Christopher Martin-Jenkins recorded a suspicion of an inside edge, almost certainly in reaction to Broad's displeasure; it would have been hard to divine such an edge from his broadcast position in the Pavilion. Colin Bateman thought the ball might have pitched outside leg-stump, but called Broad 'foul-tempered.' 'Broad seemed extremely disappointed,' wrote a tactful Peter Deeley in the *Daily Telegraph*.

At the close of play press conference Micky Stewart was keen to stress that the England opener had simply been expressing disappointment with himself: 'It was a normal reaction and happens in any sport. You may as well not go out there if you're not going to show that kind of commitment.' Stewart said that he too would be 'angry and sad' if the newspapers made anything of the matter, but Broad's previous form in disputing decisions together with the heightened scrutiny the TCCB had imposed upon player behaviour meant that this little bit of lip-service was bound to attract more attention than it really warranted. The unsympathetic press coverage obliged the selectors to issue Broad with a final warning about his conduct.

Disastrous though the first day had been from a West Indian point of view, there were two rather large crumbs of comfort for them to feast upon. The Logie-Dujon partnership had shown once again that while they might have bad days in a series, they would never roll over easily, and going into the second day the improved fitness of Malcolm Marshall gave them hope that they could bowl England out just as cheaply. Marshall had sat out the West Indies' two tour matches since Trent Bridge in an effort to guarantee his fitness for Lord's and the rest of the series, and in the 3.4 overs he delivered from the Nursery End that evening, he had indeed looked back to his skiddy, nippy, unpredictable best. Chris Broad had been beaten for pace as much as overbalanced by sharp movement off the seam. If Marshall could prove himself capable of bowling long spells on day two, then the England batsmen would find it a struggle to survive.

To cap it all, England would have to face this test in conditions that were far from ideal for batting. The cloud that had rolled in twenty-four hours earlier still hung persistently over Lord's. Only now it was cooler and a hint of drizzle moistened the morning air. Add to this a pitch containing far more pace and bounce than the 'doctored' strip at Trent Bridge, and it was clear that for all their tremendous efforts in the field, England would have a hard task in setting any significant first-innings lead.

Yet, through the initial exchanges they survived. Gooch, continuing his secure form from Nottingham and the admirably correct Moxon rode their luck and saw off the early assault from Marshall. There were not many positive strokes to delight the capacity crowd, but with almost an hour gone both batsmen were still there and Marshall and Patterson had withdrawn to be replaced by Walsh and Ambrose. It was Ambrose who made the first breakthrough. Having had an appeal for caught behind against Gooch turned down from his second ball, in his second over he drew Moxon forward to a ball which just left him a fraction down the slope. The edge flew waist-high to Richards at second slip.

This brought together Gooch and Gower, the two experienced batsmen whose partnership at Trent Bridge had saved the Test for England. Gower had had little opportunity since to consolidate his fragile promise of form into something more solid. Hopes of some Championship runs at the Oval had been scuppered by an uncharacteristically seam-friendly pitch and an lbw decision in favour of the eighteen year-old Graham Thorpe, making his first-class debut for Surrey. Gower had made only 3 in the first innings, followed by 19 not out as the match dozed to a drawn conclusion. Back at Test level, he was off the mark first ball and raced to 31 from his first 16. But his strokeplay was by no means clinical, once again mixing grace with skittish eccentricity. One over from Ambrose produced a four pulled through midwicket, another edged along the ground to third man, a bouncer deftly avoided and an airy waft outside off-stump. Gooch, meanwhile, was struggling to get on strike, and struggling to lay bat on ball when he made it. Walsh, in particular, seemed to have mastered the art of making the ball hold its line from the Pavilion End, beating the outside edge as the batsman anticipated the movement down the slope.

England's score passed 100 and the 50 partnership came up in just over an hour. It was the sort of position that encouraged England fans to think that a platform might be set for the building of a big innings, but it was not to be. Having reached 46 from 60 balls, Gower tried to pull a ball from Walsh from outside off-stump. Perhaps this time the ball did dart down the slope just a fraction, perhaps Gower simply couldn't roll his wrists sufficiently to keep the ball down; either way, the result was an ugly lob to midwicket, where substitute Keith Arthurton ran in from the boundary to take the catch.

Not long afterwards, Marshall returned from the Nursery End and, having run his first ball down the slope and away from Gooch's searching bat, nipped his second ball back off the seam to bowl him through the gate. Gooch had made just 11 runs in the 15 overs since lunch, tied up by a very deliberate West Indian plan to avoid giving him any width or anything to clip away off his legs. At 129 for 4, England were not so very far behind the West Indies, but the two new batsmen at the crease were Allan Lamb, without a hundred in his last twenty-six Tests, and Derek Pringle. Suddenly, the tail seemed horribly exposed. Pringle managed a single off his first ball, but then struggled to lay his bat on anything before gloving a catch down the leg side trying to pull a short ball from Walsh. Lamb, footwork never his strongest point, was trapped lbw by a fast breakback from Marshall for 10. Emburey, greeted at the crease by a vicious bouncer from Marshall that struck him over the ear, tried to pull a ball from Patterson that was far too full and lost his off-stump. Downton battled gamely for 32 balls before he unluckily played back to a ball from Marshall that kept low and was lbw.

Marshall then claimed the last two wickets with successive balls. Having packed his off-side field, he bowled a straight, slower ball to Jarvis, drawing the Yorkshireman into a mistimed on-drive that lobbed gently to Haynes at mid-on. The next ball to Dilley was fast, straight and ripped the left-hander's off-stump from the ground before his defensive prod was complete. Marshall's wonderful bowling had induced a disastrous England collapse, the last eight wickets going down for 53 runs. His figures of 6 for 32 were amply deserved; they took him into the top ten of all time Test match wicket-takers and helped West Indies to an unlikely first-innings lead of 44.

Perhaps most frustrating for England, on a day that was never bright, once the West Indies began their second innings at 4.50 p.m. the cloud quickly loomed lower and the light became gloomy. Just twenty minutes into the innings, the umpires offered the batsmen the light, an offer England's batsmen would have grasped with delight at any time in the previous three hours or so. When they resumed half an hour later, only nine balls were bowled before they all trooped off again. After another twenty minutes they came back out, only to turn back to the Pavilion after two balls from Dilley. This time, there was no coming back, leaving a packed Lord's crowd fuming at the loss of more than an hour's play with the match so delicately poised. The umpires, Ken Palmer and David Shepherd, had not helped the mood of the crowd by appearing on the field during each break to check the light dressed only in their blazers. Even if the light were good enough to resume immediately, there would be a further delay while they returned to the Pavilion to collect their white coats. The crowd made their frustrations felt by pelting the outfield with seat cushions. 'We'd had cushions on the field before,' recalled PA announcer Alan Curtis recently, 'but never in such numbers.'

Any hopes England had of ending the day on a positive note had been frustrated by the weather. After all the strides forward at Trent Bridge and the positivity and elation of Thursday, Friday had taken England back to their familiar nightmares of facing the West Indies. Now their curfew cricketers had a long and lonely night ahead in which to relive them all again.

Having been bowled out cheaply under chilling, grey skies, the last thing England's players would have wanted to see when they pulled back the curtains in their hotel rooms the next morning – bright and early no doubt – was glorious June sunshine. That they did perhaps foretold to them that a long day of chasing leather in the outfield lay ahead. They had an early breakthrough when Dilley found the edge of Haynes' bat and Downton took a good low catch, but by then Gordon Greenidge was already into his stride and showing signs of the form that had destroyed England's glimmering hopes on the same ground four years earlier. His was a beautifully judged innings, filled with punchy drives through extra cover, riding the bounce 'on the up', but just as impressive was his skill in knowing which balls to let go just outside his off-stump. Richie Richardson stayed with him in a partnership of 83 in just 102 minutes. Richardson contributed just 26 of those runs and was dropped twice before Pringle trapped him lbw playing across the line. He still seemed to be struggling with English conditions, but that only placed Greenidge's supremacy in even sharper relief.

Viv Richards was soon playing in similar vein. Having prodded a couple of balls from Emburey gently back to the bowler, he gave the next a playful tap towards midwicket and stood and watched it sail into the Tavern Stand. Pringle almost had him bowled off the inside edge soon afterwards – and rapped him painfully in the box soon after that – but the old master still managed to find the gaps on the leg side with ease. Rarely can any batsman have looked in more control than when he lofted the persevering Dilley over extra cover for another boundary. Gladstone Small had bowled tidily enough that morning, but now he was taken apart, first Greenidge driving him past mid-off, where Pringle failed to field the ball with his boot, to bring up his hundred off 177 balls, then Richards easing another boundary through mid-off before reeling off four boundaries in succession through cover and straight midwicket.

England had a breath of relief when Dilley had Greenidge caught at slip for 103, but already the West Indies were 242 ahead, with seven wickets in hand and Richards still at the crease. Perhaps England knew already that the match had gone. Two quick wickets after tea, Richards bottom-edging a cut at Pringle into his stumps and Hooper caught behind off Jarvis, might have given England renewed hope, but it was soon snuffed out by a renewed partnership between Logie and Dujon. If there was one difference between their partnership in the first innings and this one it was that Dujon played with greater fluency than before. After a couple of early wafts at Jarvis that nearly caught the edge, he caressed boundaries all around the wicket with sublime timing. Logie, meanwhile, was his usual impish self, impossible to predict, and, it seemed, to get out. Emburey rotated his bowlers and kept his fielders on their toes, but to no avail. A sharp throw from Moxon almost accounted for Dujon on 19 but flashed narrowly past the stumps. The luck now seemed to be running against England, and they took another blow when Gladstone Small, having returned to the attack to take the second new ball, retreated to the Pavilion clutching his thigh after just 2 overs. It was a recurrence of the injury that had kept him out of the Trent Bridge Test and would keep him off the field for the rest of the innings.

As a glorious Lord's Saturday eased gracefully, and perhaps for the revellers in the Coronation Garden a little drunkenly, towards its close, Logie and Dujon batted on blithely in the soft light of evening. Their second century partnership of the match came up in 111 minutes shortly before the close, and by the time stumps were drawn, West Indies had reached 354 for 5, the lead a distant 398.

England suffered little more damage on the fourth morning. Jarvis and Dilley cleaned up the last five wickets for only 43 more runs in less than an hour. Logie was stranded desperately close to a place on the Honours Boards with 95 not out from just 124 balls. It is doubtful whether any bar the wildest optimists expected England to mount a serious challenge at their unlikely target of 442 runs for victory. Most would have doubted their chances of batting through five and a half sessions, a probable 172 overs, to save the match. True, they had achieved a similar rescue mission at Trent Bridge, but on a far less docile surface, and with the West Indies fast bowling attack now operating at something like full power, the odds were greatly stacked against them.

If anything the pitch looked to have quickened up a touch when England began their long trek towards safety. Or perhaps it was just that Marshall and Patterson steamed in with even greater pace and intent than in the first innings. The clouds were low, the light poor and the humidity high. Short of the pitch being uneven, conditions were as bad as they could reasonably be for batting in a Test match. Marshall's first two balls to Gooch were both bouncers and when Gooch got off the mark with a single through point, Broad received the same greeting. It was not much easier facing Patterson – in his first over Gooch played and missed once and was dropped at short leg by Logie.

England's openers had no hesitation when, after 4 overs, the umpires offered the light, but conditions were little easier when they resumed after lunch. The first ball of the afternoon session was edged by Gooch between Dujon and Richards at first slip. Gooch's luck would not hold for long. Three overs later Marshall found some late in-swing and trapped the Essex opener plumb in front of his wicket. Broad followed soon afterwards, edging low to Dujon's left to end an innings which had never looked likely to be a long one. Gower too was soon gone, slicing a cut at Patterson low to third slip where, after a short conference between the umpires, Richardson's catch was confirmed. England had lost three wickets for 4 runs in the space of twenty balls and all their most reliable batsmen were out. That there would be no repeat of the defiance of Trent Bridge already looked certain.

The pressure on Martyn Moxon and Allan Lamb must have been immense. For Moxon, stepping into Gatting's shoes and knowing that he might return to occupy them once again at Old Trafford could well have been his only chance to play that long, mature innings that Peter May had suggested he was capable of. For Lamb, many such chances had already passed. If he could not now add to his tally of seven Test centuries then he might have to resign himself to playing county cricket in future. Moxon got off to anything but a racing start, remaining scoreless for his first thirty-five minutes at the crease while first Broad and then Gower departed in quick succession. Lamb was beaten outside his off-stump by his fourth ball, but then struck his fifth crisply to the extra cover boundary to get off the mark.

Lamb took ten off Walsh's first over. Neither of his two boundaries was a stroke of real certainty, and at the end of his next over Walsh almost had his man, Greenidge at first slip not quite able to get his hand on a low chance. The ball sped to the boundary once more. It was nervy stuff, but Lamb had reached 33 from 36 balls. He was off and running.

Perhaps these two batsmen in combination offered England's best hope of salvation. Not simply because they were the last two specialists at the wicket, but the fact that their contrasting styles of play seemed to offer the right sort of blend. The brisk, counter-attacking style of Lamb meant that Moxon could trundle along in his accustomed manner without worrying about forcing the pace, and Moxon's orthodoxy and calm temperament allowed Lamb to offer an offensive thrust without worrying about uncertainties at the other end. Lamb was beginning to play exactly the sort of innings that had brought him three hundreds against the West Indies four years earlier. It was not easy to forget, however, that all his heroics in 1984 had been in vain.

By tea the pair had moved the score on to 89 for 3. Rain during the interval caused the loss of another 13 overs. Perhaps if England could get through to stumps without losing another wicket, and go into the final day with seven wickets still in hand, there might still be hope. Perhaps the rain might even come to their rescue. It was not to be. Twenty-five minutes after tea, Moxon called Lamb through for a single to Patterson at midwicket. There was probably a run to be taken, but Lamb sent him back. As Moxon span round and tried to regain his ground, he saw Patterson's throw shatter his wicket. Moxon had spent 133 minutes compiling just 14 runs, but his vigil had ended in the most unfortunate fashion.

Pringle fell quickly, lbw to Walsh when he failed to get forward to a straight ball, but solid resistance from Downton and Emburey helped Lamb take the match into the final day. Downton hung around for an hour and a quarter, despite offering two sharp chances to Logie at short-leg and nearly becoming Patterson's second run-out victim of the innings. Twice during their 56-run partnership Lamb and Downton watched in hope as the umpires discussed the light, but the longed-for offer never came. Downton fell at 6.40 p.m., still an hour before the close, when a full ball from Marshall nipped back and trapped him in front of his stumps. Emburey nearly followed him the very next ball, an inside edge slipping narrowly past the wicket, but England's captain survived both that and a barrage of short stuff from Patterson, taking his revenge on the big Jamaican by striking him for three successive fours.

As ever, when Allan Lamb was at the crease, the crowd were guaranteed good entertainment. Almost every over saw the ball flash past the edge of the bat, but boundaries came almost as frequently. The 50 partnership came up in just forty-five minutes when Emburey pulled Ambrose past square leg for four, but three balls later Emburey was surprised by a high full-toss; as he tried to duck away, the ball struck his glove and cannoned down into his wicket. It was 7.30 p.m. As if in mockery, the sun came out and Lord's was flooded in bright evening light.

There was time for just one more scare before the umpires called an end to the day's play, Marshall finding Lamb's outside edge only for the ball to drop short of first slip. Lamb faced a nervous night, stranded on 99 not out, but at least he was still there. Had the West Indies bowled their overs at a faster rate than around 11.2 per hour, the chances of England having survived into the final day must have been much slimmer. Now, with only Small, Jarvis and Dilley for company, a century the following morning would be about the limit of Lamb's hopes.

As NW8 bathed in balmy evening sunlight, there was at least one bit of good news for John Emburey. What the selectors had seen so far during this match had convinced them that he was the right man for the England captaincy. This, surely, cannot have been a move aimed at inspiring a miraculous fifth day rearguard from the team. With the weather forecast suggesting a full day's play in store, it was too much to hope that England's final three wickets might occupy the crease for that length of time. Nor was it exactly a vote of confidence in Emburey for the longer term. The reappointment was for just one match. Clearly the selectors did not want to upset team spirit still further with another change of captain after just two matches, but with the fourth Test scheduled to be played at Headingley, and worrying reports already emerging about the state of the pitch there, they were evidently anxious to retain the option of going in to the fourth Test without a spinner in the side. And no spinner meant no Emburey.

It took Allan Lamb twenty-five minutes the following morning to punch a ball from Patterson wide of mid-off for the single that brought up his hundred. Small did not stay with him much longer, Marshall switching his angle of attack from over the wicket to round with annoying versatility and inducing an edge to Richards at slip. Paul Jarvis survived the traditional three-bouncer greeting and stayed with Lamb as early morning cloud gave way to sunshine. The game now entered a cat and mouse stage as Lamb attempted to retain the strike wherever possible and the West Indies sought to offer him singles to bring Jarvis on strike. For several overs it worked for England, until Lamb confused himself over the choice of whether to come back on strike for the last two balls from Walsh or stay at the non-striker's end ready to face Ambrose. He was still some yards short of his ground when Courtney Walsh took Hooper's throw and swept the bails off with a flourish of forearms. Jarvis and Dilley took the match into the afternoon, Dilley swiping six boundaries with some of the spirit of Headingley `81 before he sliced a drive at Patterson to Richardson at third slip. The West Indies had won by 134 runs.

Perhaps Viv Richards' tongue was worrying at the inside of his cheek when he claimed after the match that the two teams seemed 'evenly balanced.' Perhaps he had seen his young team squander too many advantages in recent series and wanted to keep their feet on the ground. But Micky Stewart too felt that the match had been decided on a handful of narrow margins, Logie's chance through slip in the first innings being a major case in point. But the truth was surely closer to the view of Peter Deeley, writing in the *Telegraph* that morning. Far from this year being a rare chance for England to hold their own against the West Indies, 'little in these encounters seems to have changed: gallant, backs-to-the-wall English resistance gradually worn down on the relentless high tide of speed.'

It was not just speed that the West Indies had in their favour. Malcolm Marshall's ten wickets in the match had been a masterclass of skilful, intelligent fast bowling, with accuracy, swing, unpredictable changes from over to around the wicket and back, sometimes just for a couple of balls and sometimes for an over or more, and bouncers, seam movement, late swing into or away from the bat and subtle changes of pace. Everything adjusted to fit the conditions, or the opponent. Far from a combination of the technical solidity of Moxon and the brave, cavalier strokeplay of Lamb, it seemed that England needed a blend of all those ingredients in every batsman in order to survive. A Ted Dexter perhaps. Or, perhaps, a Mike Gatting.

9

Three Options for Defeat

Since standing down for the Lord's Test, Mike Gatting had prospered once more for Middlesex. An attractive 104 at Basingstoke was followed by 76 at Tunbridge Wells, 54 at Northampton and 67 at Chelmsford. There had also been another hundred and an unbeaten 80 in one-day cricket, and although none of those matches had offered a challenge anywhere near the level of facing the West Indies in a Test match, an in-form and newly motivated Gatting would be a proposition the selectors would be foolish to ignore. It was debatable, however, just how motivated Gatting could be until the events of recent weeks had been put well and truly behind him, and despite the evidence of some handy scores for his county, at least one of his recent controversies remained stubbornly in the news.

In what was now an unfortunate piece of scheduling, Gatting's much disputed autobiography was scheduled for publication on the very same day that the Third Test was due to start at Old Trafford. The TCCB had formed a three-man board of inquiry to establish what, if any, disciplinary proceedings should be started against Gatting. Their deliberations promised to drag the affair out for some time yet. 'Gatting will be able to play [at Old Trafford] without either side losing face. The reckoning is for another day,' wrote Peter Deeley in the *Telegraph*.

If that was one consideration for the selectors to concentrate their minds on, another more structural issue was whether to strengthen the batting line-up, probably by adding a sixth specialist batsman at the expense of Derek Pringle and accept the consequent risk of weakening the bowling attack. Although Pringle had offered little penetration in the first two Tests – taking just three wickets for 162 runs – his control had been greater than any other seam bowler and, in the role of fourth seamer, he had certainly done his job. On the quicker pitch, however, at Lord's he had looked horribly exposed against the high pace of the West Indies bowlers and his solid 39 at Trent Bridge seemed a distant memory, as did all his heroics in the Texaco Trophy games. Scyld Berry clearly supported the inclusion of a sixth batsman; that five specialists 'followed by assorted cannon fodder' would not be enough against the West Indies was, he wrote during the Lord's Test, the most obvious lesson of the last dozen Tests between the two teams.

There was, of course, a halfway option: find another all-rounder to bat at six who was capable of wielding the willow for longer than Pringle. This might strengthen the batting, if only a little, and if it also weakened the bowling, well perhaps that would only be a little bit too. The obvious candidate for this role was David Capel, who had recovered from his early season fitness problems and was at least batting well for Northamptonshire; wickets were, admittedly, a little hard to come by. Some other candidates were mentioned too. In *The Mail on Sunday* Bill Frindall championed the cause of Chris Cowdrey, who had just captained Kent to their sixth successive Championship win, but Frindall's case was based more on promoting Cowdrey, who had not played a Test since 1984/85, as a possible candidate for the captaincy in the near future than on any claim that he was a superior player to Pringle with either bat or ball. With England just 1-0 down with three matches to play, it sounded as though Frindall was writing off this series already. In the *Telegraph*, Peter Deeley suggested a more short-term option in the person of Leicestershire veteran Peter Willey. Willey, renowned as a stubborn and brave cricketer, probably spent more of his career than he wished being slipped into the England side whenever the West Indies were in town, rather as if he were a pair of steel stays reinforcing a shirt collar. The tactic had often produced stiff resistance in the manner of Brian Close or, more recently, Paul Downton. But it had never offered a sniff of victory against the Caribbean foe.

Willey's off-spin would at least offer England the chance to add variety to their attack on an Old Trafford pitch with a reputation of being more amenable to spin than Lord's. Both Richard Illingworth and Vic Marks had claimed five wicket hauls there already this summer, but the general view seemed to be that the pitch was more conducive to seam bowling than in recent years. But there was, according to Peter Deeley, another reason for hoping England might supplement Emburey with a partner in spin – it would allow England to 'set an example to the West Indies over the visitors' abysmal over rate'. England's ambitions were clearly more limited than they had been a few weeks earlier.

The case for Willey was also discussed, if not recommended, by Mike Selvey in *The Guardian*. Selvey also considered Glamorgan's Rodney Ontong as an alternative who could bat at no.6 and bowl respectable off-breaks, but the general view in the press was that England's batting needed to be reinforced. After Lamb at number five, no-one in the England team at Lord's boasted a Test century to his name, and the efforts of Logie and Dujon in both West Indies innings had shown the value of having players at six and seven who could recover the innings from a shaky start. The likely return of Mike Gatting, a move supported in the press by John Emburey, made this the easiest and likeliest choice.

The balance of the bowling attack offered further problems for England, and it was here that England began to suffer more severely from the bad luck that would add to the inconsistency in selection throughout the series. Gladstone Small might well have been dropped after an erratic performance at Lord's and his recurring thigh injury was a major cause for concern. The selectors offered him the benefit of the doubt and gave him until Tuesday, two days before the next Test, to prove his fitness. This was a hard task for Small, since his county did not have another game until the Wednesday. In the end, Small withdrew. Perhaps the selectors might have left it at that; Small out, Gatting in. One extra batsman and Pringle batting a place lower at seven. But there were further complications. Paul Jarvis, selected in the original squad of thirteen, strained his back playing in Yorkshire's Championship match at Hove and was forced to withdraw. On the same day, Nick Cook, called up as second spinner, turned his ankle on a boundary rope while performing twelfth man duties for Northamptonshire and was also forced to withdraw from the squad.

The loss of both bowlers was a heavy blow for England. Jarvis had bowled with spirit at Lord's and had deserved better luck. Cook had plenty of Test experience behind him and his record of twenty-seven wickets at 25.96 so far that season suggested reasonable form. But the selection of Cook also raised questions about the thought processes of the selectors. As a slow left-arm bowler, Cook was an obvious candidate to complement Emburey's off-spin. But where did that leave Eddie Hemmings, Emburey's fellow off-spinner who had been part of the squad at Trent Bridge? If, in playing two spinners, the selectors now wanted to ensure that they didn't both turn the ball in the same direction, why had the same consideration not applied earlier in the summer or when Hemmings was retained for the second part of the winter tour while Cook went home?

Perhaps it came down to form, something Peter May had said at the start of the summer would be the major consideration in selection meetings. But in his last two Championship matches, Hemmings had recorded figures of 47-16-104-5. There was little reason on that basis for not recalling him to the squad. Similarly, in choosing replacements for their injured bowlers, the selectors seemed to have mislaid their own yardsticks. The obvious choice to replace Jarvis would have been Jonathan Agnew, with fifty-three first-class wickets so far that summer, who had taken 6 for 39 at Gloucester on the same day that Jarvis strained his back, his fifth five-wicket haul of the summer. Instead they close Greg Thomas again who, despite claiming career-best figures of 6 for 68 two weeks' previously, had claimed just five more in his last two matches. And, in looking for a replacement for Cook, the selectors continued to ignore Hemmings and focus on finding a left-arm spinner. According to Bill Frindall they first enquired about Gloucestershire's David Graveney, who felt that his long-standing back problem might not stand up to a Test match, then about Lancashire's promising twenty-five-year-old Ian Folley. 'Lancashire had advised that Folley was in no sort of form,' wrote Frindall in *10 Tests for England*. The selectors might well have countered by pointing to Folley's performance in the latest Championship match. He had claimed 6 for 20 as Lancashire bowled Glamorgan out for just 47.

The selectors seemed trapped between choosing on the basis of current form and seeking consistency in their selections. If they went on form, surely Agnew would have replaced Jarvis; if they sought consistency, surely Hemmings would have returned to the squad. The replacement spinner eventually announced was a surprise to everyone: the bowler included Essex's thirty-six-year-old veteran John Childs. He would be England's oldest debutant since Dick Howarth in 1947. Childs recalled how he learned of his selection in Essex's 1989 yearbook:

The first I knew of my England call-up was when we came off the field for bad light against Middlesex on the last day of our Championship match at Chelmsford and Peter Edwards caught me at the top of the Pavilion steps and said 'congratulations'. I told him my birthday was not until August but his reply was that I had been called up into the England squad as Nick Cook had twisted his ankle ... my mind was in a spin and I felt about 10 feet tall.

In selecting a squad containing Dilley, Emburey, DeFreitas, Thomas, Childs and Capel England had, as Peter May put it, given themselves every option. 'We are concerned about our batting at six' he said, 'and with this squad we have given ourselves three options. We can play all six batsmen, with Lamb at six, or we could have Capel or even Downton at six.' Perhaps England wanted to have a final look at the pitch before deciding whether to go in with two spinners, a choice which would surely rule out the option of picking all six batsmen. But giving yourself three selection options going into the match could also be regarded as indecision. Spinners aside, it was clear that the tactical choice between five or six batsmen had yet to be completely resolved within the England hierarchy, and yet, the day before the match, Peter May and John Emburey offered near unified views on the issue.

'I know we need to get twenty wickets to win' said May, 'but we have to get the runs first, which we have so far struggled to do. I don't consider six batsmen to be a negative approach and we see this as a vital game.' Emburey too, sounded keen on playing all six batsmen: 'conventional teams with five bowlers have not done well in recent years and, if we can get the runs, two spinners might come into their own on a turning wicket.' Still, it was no surprise when England took the field with just five specialist batsmen and David Capel in at six. Emburey's suggestion the previous day, that England might play six batsmen and still go in with two spinners, had clearly been a step too far. That, of course, meant that one of the six batsmen in the squad would have to miss out. The man to go was Chris Broad. Despite Micky Stewart's defence of Broad's 'disappointment' at Lord's, the England opener's verbal misdemeanour had not gone down well with either the press or Peter May. There were continued murmurs too about his failure to record a single century in home Tests. Those two factors, combined with Martyn Moxon's solidity in partnership with Allan Lamb at Lord's, meant Broad had to go.

Broad's omission confirmed that John Childs would make his Test debut. Just twenty-four hours earlier he had sped up the motorway to meet his new teammates for the first time, spend the afternoon in net practice, then join the rest of the team in the pre-match dinner.

It is apparently the custom for any 'new boy' to sit next to the Chairman of Selectors so that is how I found myself alongside Peter May at the dinner table, while the old boys, i.e. Gower, Lamb, Gooch, were selecting the wines at the other end of the table! As it turned out, that was the only time I sat next to the Chairman as the following two Tests Mr. May had new men sitting on both sides of him!

It was only one hour before play began that Childs learned for certain that he would play. 'After they had looked at the wicket – it was about 10 o'clock – John Emburey, our captain for that Test, came across to me and said "good luck, you're in." Then Micky Stewart called me into the captain's room and I received my sweaters, cap and "Peckham Rye" [tie].'

It was a questionable decision for several reasons, most notably the fact that when the covers were removed on the first morning, the pitch revealed beneath them had a distinctly greenish tinge. A raging turner it was never going to be, and nor did it look like the kind of pitch where you might be forgiven for thinking that two spinners were worth a punt. England had given themselves as many options as possible, but the one major factor which should have informed their choice between those options had been most curiously ignored.

'It can only have been panic,' wrote Mike Selvey. 'Broad... would not have been brought into the squad had it not been intended for him to open.' Panic does not always involve making a sudden, irrational choice when confronted by an unexpected situation, sometimes it can show itself in a determination to stick to a pre-arranged plan despite the evidence suggesting it would be wiser to change course. England had selected their squad for Old Trafford in the light of the ground's reputation as a friendly surface for spin bowling, and in the five first-class matches held there so far that season fifty-four of the 124 wickets to fall had indeed fallen to spin, the highest proportion on any of the main county grounds. Perhaps too they felt that catching the West Indies on a turning wicket offered the best hope of snatching a win at some point in the series. They certainly couldn't hope to out-bat or out-pace them.

Playing two spinners had been the bedrock of England's strategy for the match. Now, confronted by a greenish pitch clearly more suitable to seam and swing, they found themselves unable to abandon their plan. And yet they appreciated the absurdity of going in to a Test match on a pitch like this with only two seamers, so the extra batsman made way for the third seamer. The extra batsman was Chris Broad, a man with six Test hundreds to his name, all of them admittedly overseas. The third seamer, expected to bat at six, was David Capel, who had none. Tellingly, it was not a decision that either England's captain or manager were happy with. 'I would have played him,' remembers Micky Stewart. John Emburey too recalls arguing for the retention of Broad at the top of the order: 'perhaps I didn't fight hard enough for that. Perhaps that says something about me as a character, that I'm not confrontational enough.' For all the talk about Broad's poor record in home Tests, something that was raised against him with regularity throughout the summer, is seems clear that his omission had more than a little to do with his visible displeasure at the lbw decision against him at Lord's.

Further evidence of England sticking rigidly to a plan came at the toss, when Emburey won it and decided to bat first. Batting first meant England would, in theory, have the opportunity to bowl last when the pitch should be at its most helpful to spin. But with England's batsmen now going in to face Marshall, Walsh and Ambrose with the pitch at its greenest, the skies overcast and the air thick with humidity, would the match even get that far? As David Capel made his way out to the wicket ten minutes before lunch, it certainly didn't look as if it would.

The West Indies had also made changes to their team. Missing Desmond Haynes with a hamstring injury, they moved Richie Richardson up to partner Gordon Greenidge at the top of the innings and brought in Roger Harper, whose off-breaks had just claimed seven wickets at Canterbury in a two-day victory over a Kent side weakened by injury and squad rotation. In a move that suggested an appreciation of the type of wicket the match would be played on, they replaced the outright pace of Patrick Patterson with the greater control and movement of Winston Benjamin.

The tourists took an immediate grip on the match. Martyn Moxon, moved up to his more natural position of opener, never looked like scoring a run and was bowled, stiff-legged, through the gate by a straight ball from Marshall. Gatting almost played on to his second delivery; his fourth nipped back as he shouldered arms and struck him on the pad. Marshall's strident appeal was upheld, and Gatting trooped back to the Pavilion having revived vivid memories of a previous recall against the West Indies, when he was twice out in identical fashion at Lord's in 1984. The former skipper cut a disconsolate figure. 'Gatt was fine' recalls John Emburey of his teammate's mood during the Test, but Gatting himself would subsequently concede that the last few weeks had been the very worst kind of preparation for batting against the West Indies in a Test match.

It would soon get worse for England. David Gower glided a four through gully, and then slashed another wildly over the slips. A third attempt to attack outside off-stump brought a thick edge to the giant hands of Roger Harper at fourth slip. Just over half an hour later, Gooch edged a firm-footed drive at Benjamin to Dujon and England were in dire straits at 55 for 4.

As so often in these contests, without the reassuring presence of Ian Botham in the middle of the batting order, the loss of four England wickets meant one front-line batsman was left trying to eke out a few precious runs with the tail. After Capel fell soon after the interval to a breakback from the nagging Benjamin, his feet cemented to the crease, Lamb and the stubborn Downton offered hope of some resistance. Downton played straighter than most and cut ruthlessly when offered the opportunity of anything wide of off-stump. He was, however, only given the opportunity twice. Lamb proved his return to form at Lord's had been no illusion, straight driving Benjamin for four twice in three balls before lunch. There were some hairier moments after lunch when he persisted in trying to cut as the ball nipped back at him off the seam, but as long as he and Downton stayed together, there remained some hope of a competitive total.

The pair put on 33 in three quarters of an hour before Lamb cut once too often at Ambrose and, failing to get over the tall Leeward Islander's extra bounce, sent a chest-high catch to gully. After a three-hour rain break, 94 for 6 became 98 for 7 when Emburey nibbled at a lifter from Walsh and was caught behind. DeFreitas and Dilley offered brief aggression before, left with only the debutant Childs for support, Downton also succumbed to the temptation to cut and sent Greenidge his third catch of the innings. England had been bowled out for 135 in just over 60 overs. Their seam attack of Dilley, DeFreitas and Capel were going to have to bowl out of their skins if they were to keep England in the match long enough for the spin of Emburey and Childs to have any effect.

The loss of almost half the day's play meant that Greenidge and Richardson had only 3 overs to face before the close. Enterprisingly, Emburey bowled the second of them himself. His first ball gripped, took Richardson on the glove and offered Downton a sharp leg side chance that the England wicketkeeper could not accept. Four times in the next five balls Richardson prodded forward uncertainly and saw the ball turn past his bat and thud into his pad. After anther twenty minute weather delay, Emburey continued to bowl on the second morning. But after Richardson unluckily bottom-edged a bouncer from Dilley into his stumps and was replaced by the more fleet-footed Carl Hooper, Emburey took himself off in favour of DeFreitas.

That first session of the day probably gave the West Indies their most comfortable period of batting in the match as they made easy gains on England's meagre total and went in to the interval on 73 for 1. 'Greenidge grafting patiently, Hooper coolly impressive' recorded Christopher Martin-Jenkins in his notebook. John Childs had been given his first bowl in Test cricket in the traditional spinner's slot, five minutes before lunch. Continuing after the break, he bowled without nerves and with superb flight and control and soon claimed his first wicket, Hooper padding up to a ball that pitched on middle and off and straightened. Two balls later, Childs found the edge of Viv Richards bat with a ball that turned and lifted. Rather than going to hand, the ball ran through a gap in the slips and got the West Indies captain off the mark with two runs.

Richards was visibly discomfited. It later emerged that he was running a fever and struggling with a damaged right wrist, but at the time there was encouragement for England in the sight of a veteran county spinner tying the world's greatest batsman up in knots. There was a fraction of turn, and a hint of uneven bounce offered the batsmen further challenges and many observers wondered why Emburey did not take the step of bowling in tandem with Childs. That, after all, would have been the greatest tactical justification for picking a left-arm spinner to complement the captain's off breaks. Instead, Childs wheeled away at the Warwick Road End while first DeFreitas then Capel bustled in opposite.

Both seamers used the conditions well and both had their reward. DeFreitas nipped one back into Greenidge's pads, which kept it low, and beat the batsman's urgent defence for a clear lbw. Capel too took advantage of the uneven bounce, with Richards forgetting the perennial instruction to avoid cross-bat shots on an uneven wicket and cutting a wide ball into his stumps. He was three short of a hard-earned fifty, but had passed Wally Hammond's aggregate of Test runs on the way. Batting was far from easy for the West Indians, and the anticipated Logie-Dujon partnership this time failed to materialise, Logie too falling lbw to a ball that kept low. Logie had already battled eighty-two minutes for his 39 runs. All of the West Indies' first five wickets had fallen bowled or lbw, four of them to movement off the pitch or uneven bounce. By comparison, six of England's ten wickets had fallen to catches from attacking strokes. The tourists were clearly determined to sell their wickets dearly. At the fall of Gus Logie's wicket they had reached 187 for 5 – 52 ahead of England. Worse for the home team was still to come.

All through the evening session a stiff breeze blew brooding clouds, sharp showers and sudden bursts of brilliant sunlight across Old Trafford. Three times the players trooped off the field as rain or bad light made play impossible, and three times they returned – twice within a quarter of an hour of going off. In between the interruptions, Dujon and Roger Harper took the score on to 242 at the close. It was not thrilling stuff. The batsmen struck only three boundaries in 23.4 overs of play, and the only other excitement came when DeFreitas surprised Harper with a short ball and the tall all-rounder, fencing at it in panic, almost got a glove on it before it sailed through to Downton.

Harper had not bowled a ball in England's first innings, but his solid batting and loose-limbed presence in the field made him much less of a passenger in the side than any non-bowling English spinner would have been. Even after the departure of all their front-line batsmen, the West Indies continued calm progress towards a significant first-innings lead, showing once more a degree of professionalism and discipline that they were too rarely given credit for. When Dujon and Harper were eventually parted soon after lunch on day three, they were just six runs short of posting their team's third consecutive sixth wicket partnership of 100 runs or more.

The third morning saw, at last, England's two spinners bowling in tandem. Unchanged for the entire session, only a rain break of almost an hour truncated their spell. Despite the stoppage, Emburey's short run-up and Childs' busy, enthusiastic approach saw England get through 22 overs in the session, conceding just 35 runs in the process, but England's captain took the new ball immediately after lunch and in the third over of the session Dujon's patient 67 came to an end, looping a leading edge up to Capel running in from mid-on, a wicket for Graham Dilley making up for a wasteful spell at the start of the innings. Although Childs returned after just 4 ineffective overs from DeFreitas, Emburey did not bowl again in the innings.

'I probably underbowled myself' Emburey now concedes. 'When you've got two spinners in the side you want to give the other guy an opportunity to bowl and therefore you don't bowl yourself enough as a senior spinner, which wouldn't have done me any favours.' As at Lord's, Emburey had seen the role of spin as being to contain and help the seamers remain fresh. England needed wickets, and impressive as Childs' and Emburey's containment had been, they had not claimed any. Emburey could not afford to disdain the new ball as soon as it became available, but allowing himself to play second fiddle to the debutant Childs would have immediate consequences for his own Test career.

Rain wiped out almost two hours of play either side of the tea interval and allowed just one more hour's play before stumps. Emburey kept Childs wheeling away at the Warwick Road End, rotating Dilley and DeFreitas in snappy, three-over spells at the Stretford End. Capel appeared to have been forgotten entirely. He had not bowled since tea the previous day. Childs found just enough grip to make the batsmen play for a fraction of turn, hitting the pad time and time again when the ball went straight on, but although he struck the pad three, sometimes four times per over, it was never close enough to justify an appeal for lbw. The cricket remained attritional, with Malcolm Marshall hitting only two fours and Harper one as they took the score to 357 for six at stumps, but it was yet another frustrating partnership for England. Twice at Lord's they had worked a crack in the West Indies façade only to be unable to widen it further. Here at Old Trafford it looked as if they were trying to cut a diamond with a stick of celery.

The morning of the fourth day was lost to yet more rain, but the tourists batted on to a formidable lead of 249 before more rain forty-five minutes into the afternoon session finally brought a declaration from Richards. They lost just one more wicket on the way, Harper yorked by Dilley for 74 – his highest Test score. As rain continued to sweep across Manchester, only at 4.15 p.m. did England take the field again to begin their innings. They had 41 overs to survive before the close of play. Facing such a deficit and with just four sessions remaining in the match, any thought of victory would have been delusional even against lesser opposition. Against the West Indies, surviving even one of those sessions was by no means an easy task.

In the end, more bad light meant that England faced just twenty-nine of those overs before the close, Roger Harper and Carl Hooper bowling the last three of them as the light closed in before 7.00 p.m., but it was enough for England to lose three crucial wickets. Gooch, his feet slow to get going, lasted just nine balls before shuffling across the crease and stopping a straight ball from Marshall with his pads. Gatting, beaten twice in successive balls by Ambrose, then struck a painful blow on the shoulder, pushed forward at Marshall and edged to Richardson at third slip. Moxon, who hung on gamely for eighty-three minutes, was also struck a blow by Ambrose, in his case on the arm, and dropped at slip by Richardson off the same bowler before he got a thin edge to Winston Benjamin's first ball of the innings and was caught at first slip. Ambrose suffered a second missed slip catch off his bowling when Gower slashed him to Marshall. His nine-over spell ended wicketless, but there were worrying signs for England of the young paceman beginning to find his feet at Test level.

After Benjamin's first ball success, he saw his next ball tickled down to the fine leg boundary by Allan Lamb. His third lifted and struck Lamb painfully on the glove. For the rest of the evening the Northamptonshire batsman seemed unable to find his timing or placement, hitting the ball straight at fielders and able to add just two more runs. Gower did manage to strike a couple of boundaries, one thanks to an unfortunate bounce, which made the ball shoot past the surprised Walsh on the deep cover boundary, but none of England's batsmen had occupied the crease with the same level of security as had their West Indian opponents, and despite having the vast experience of Gower and Lamb to begin the final day at the crease it was hard to believe England's batting might hold out for the draw. Only two niggling concerns might have disturbed Vivian Richards' sleep that night – the Manchester weather and the fact that his key strike bowler had already received two warnings from umpire Nigel Plews for running down the pitch in his follow through. If the umpire spotted a repeat of the offence, Marshall would be removed from the attack for the rest of the innings.

Few may have expected England to repeat their Trent Bridge resistance, but even fewer would have expected them to collapse quite so miserably on the final day, losing their last seven wickets in just 14.4 overs. Gower, having got off to a positive start and taken his score on to 34, threw his bat wildly at a widish ball from Marshall and was taken by Richardson at second slip. Capel lasted, scoreless, for just seven balls before pushing forward at Marshall and squeezing a bat-pad catch to silly mid-off. Lamb, having added just a single to his overnight score – and having made just 9 from 53 balls – fended a lifter from Ambrose off his ribs to short leg. Downton fell next, then DeFreitas and then Emburey, and at last, with forty minutes still to go before lunch, Dilley was late on a defensive stroke and turned to see his off-stump flying towards the Warwick Road End.

The West Indies had sealed an embarrassingly easy victory in less than seventeen hours' actual playing time. Malcolm Marshall, yet again, had been the destroyer, using the conditions perfectly to claim 7 for 22 in the innings and 9 for 41 in the match. Anyone other than this most gifted and intelligent of bowlers might have struggled to amend his follow through successfully without compromising his effectiveness with the ball. But Marshall somehow managed to make minute adjustments to his approach, to curtail his follow through down the pitch and veer towards the off-side of the wicket without these moves removing his concentration from the important business of how to attack each batsman, and how best to manipulate the ball towards that end. The result had been one of the great fast bowling spells.

Marshall's approach to the crease was a long, graceful parabola that began somewhere near long-off. Where Michael Holding glided soundlessly across the turf, Marshall's feet skipped off it in a series of light, rapid quicksteps, like a flat stone skimming over calm water. The rate of acceleration was so dizzying that it seemed the final leap into the delivery stride – a triple jumper's leap, surely – must take him well beyond the crease, but it rarely did. The curving run-up brought him to the crease at a slight angle, but there was no other effort to avoid being chest-on. The leap into the delivery stride seemed to leave him hanging for a split second in mid-air, his body arched backwards, left arm raised high. Front foot followed back foot so quickly in landing that they almost came down as one, then the sudden whiplash rotation of the shoulder, and the low trajectory that meant you would pick up the length that vital fraction later than with most bowlers, and most deadly of all, the fatal impossibility of predicting whether the ball would slide away from the bat or dart back in at the stumps until it was nearly upon you. All through the process the bowler's head remained perfectly, supernaturally still. It must have been like watching a bullet coming towards you in slow motion. Never mind what the ball itself looked like.

Could any batting line-up have resisted him that day? England's humiliation was that their lack of capability had been so apparent that it had begun to look like a lack of will. If their morale hit rock bottom the moment Graham Dilley's off-stump was removed from the turf, within five minutes it was lower still. Almost before the players had made it back to the pavilion the heavens opened. Soon, a torrent of rain was falling. It did not cease for the rest of the day.

10

A Present from Uncle Peter

The appalling ease of England's defeat at Old Trafford gave new strength to the voices calling for change. Almost without exception, the cricket press demanded new blood for the team in wholesale quantities. Emburey, Gower, Gatting, Lamb (just one Test after his Lord's hundred), Moxon and Downton found their heads on Colin Bateman's block, with Kim Barnett, Tim Curtis, Matthew Maynard, James Whitaker, Jack Richards and Neil Foster to line up like a fresh regiment of 'Pals' and head up to the front in their stead. This time it was not just the players who found themselves facing calls for their heads. Peter May's selection panel now found that the period of goodwill that had followed their surprise success in the Texaco Trophy had come to a sudden end. And with the team having gone fifteen Test matches without a victory, their future had gone beyond the sports pages and become a question of national interest.

In its leader column, the *Daily Express* supported its correspondent, Colin Bateman's, proposals for significant changes to the team, but questioned whether the evidence from county cricket suggested that anyone stepping up to Test level now would really do better. The paper blamed the selectors for having failed to develop new talent and accused them of 'out-dated, gentlemanly amateurism', a natural line of attack for a popular paper facing a target like the Charterhouse-educated P. B. H. May. But the subject of the selectors also found air-time on the BBC's *Newsnight* programme, which invited former England skippers Bob Willis and Ted Dexter to offer their views on Peter May and his panel.

Dexter suggested that part of the problem was May's well-known difficulties as a communicator, something he may well have experienced first-hand when making his first tour of Australia under May's captaincy in 1958/59. Dexter called for the sacking of the entire committee: 'I think the whole selection committee should stand down. It should be disbanded forever.' Bob Willis, while not avoiding criticism of May's failings, thought that the sheer weight of that criticism throughout the media was as significant as the failings themselves: 'The press are making his position untenable and it would make things easier if he were to hand over the reins' he said. For Peter May, who had begun the summer with the firm intention of keeping negative coverage of English cricket out of the news media, seeing this sort of material aired on BBC Television's premier current affairs platform must have been a bitter blow. He was not the sort of man to surrender mid-campaign, but the pressure for wholesale change had beyond all doubt become irresistible.

The first signs of upheaval came in the absence of any news at all from the England camp. If John Emburey's tenure as captain was to be extended, an announcement ought to have followed soon after the conclusion of the Old Trafford Test. No such announcement came. Days passed. By Thursday 7 July, it was known that the selectors would meet over the two following days, the Saturday being the date of the Benson & Hedges Cup Final at Lord's. This raised the possibility that the selectors were deferring the decision until they had observed two potential captaincy candidates in action against each other: the final that year would be between Kim Barnett's Derbyshire and Mark Nicholas's Hampshire.

The possibility of a new captain being chosen from outside the current team was now widely accepted. Options within the team itself were looking increasingly poor. Few of the senior players were now certain of their places, and indeed Mike Gatting had once again declared himself unavailable for selection. Graham Gooch, whose captaincy credentials remained in doubt after his resignation from the Essex job the previous year, was known to be contracted to play in South Africa during the coming winter and would therefore not be available to captain the tour of India. Perhaps he might be a stopgap for the rest of the summer prior to Emburey taking over for the India tour, but neither could be seen as a long-term choice.

There were three outside candidates: Barnett, Nicholas and Kent's Chris Cowdrey, Colin Bateman's early support for Peter Roebuck having waned. As a player, Barnett had the strongest credentials and the greatest support, but as a captain there was a suspicion that, as with Gatting, his face would not entirely fit the pro-forma desired by the TCCB hierarchy. 'Barnett,' wrote Colin Bateman, 'a down-to-earth Northern lad, is not favoured by some at Lord's who want a return to a "gentleman captain."' Although neither Nicholas nor Cowdrey were generally considered to be Test-class players, either would be, in Bateman's words, 'the right sort of chap.' Of the two, Cowdrey's brief experience of Test cricket on David Gower's tour of India in 1984/85 perhaps gave him the edge.

Strictly speaking a 55-overs a-side knockabout would have told the selectors little about either captain's ability to command a side at the highest level, except for offering a hint as to how they might conduct themselves in a big game atmosphere. The Final itself proved a disappointing match, with Derbyshire being hustled out for just 117 thanks to a spell of four wickets for 1 run in just 8 balls by South African left-arm seamer, Steve Jeffries. It was a total that even Derbyshire's formidable new-ball pairing of Michael Holding and Devon Malcolm could do little to defend. Mark Nicholas, playing despite a broken nose, saw his team home with a patient 35 not out, but it was twenty-four-year-old Robin Smith who really caught the eye, thumping seven boundaries in making 38 from 27 balls. That showing, at least, seemed to make an impression on the watching selectors.

The captaincy question remained unresolved, however. Sunday passed with no announcement other than the announcement that no announcement would be made before Tuesday. Speculation was rife that the delay was due to the selectors attempting to persuade Graham Gooch to pull out of his contract with Western Province and take the job on a long-term basis. However, on Tuesday Gooch himself, reaffirming his commitment to his South African winter, denied having had any contact with the selectors about the captaincy. This was true, if a little disingenuous. The selectors had not contacted Gooch directly, but an intermediary had been asked to sound him out on their behalf. In his autobiography Gooch revealed that after the Old Trafford Test former Essex and England player Doug Insole had made an informal approach. 'I wasn't actually asked if I would be prepared to captain the side,' wrote Gooch, who immediately foresaw a potential conflict with his arrangements for the winter. 'I had to tell Doug that it might prove awkward. Giving me the captaincy now would mean that they also had me in mind to lead the side on the tour of India that winter, when I had already contracted to play for Western Province.'

The withdrawal of Gooch from contention left the selectors with little option but to look outside the current team if Emburey were to be replaced as captain. And with the selection meeting for Headingley scheduled for Friday; on Thursday at last their decision was revealed. For John Emburey it was the news he had dreaded but expected: 'I got a call from Peter May. He said that they were going to make some changes for the next match, that they felt I wasn't bowling particularly well at the time and that it would do me good to go back to county cricket for a while, take some wickets and come back into the side later in the summer.' Emburey had been unfortunate that the timing of his appointment had coincided with a dip in his form as a bowler. Although still bowling with control and guile, technical problems had crept into his action, which were affecting his ability to take wickets. 'I was getting too far around, my front foot was getting too far across and I was bowling around my body instead of over it, and although I felt okay in terms of control I wasn't getting the bounce and I wasn't getting the spin.' With the Headingley Test match approaching, few observers expected England to carry in to the match an out-of-form spinner when even an in-form one would be unlikely to have much impact on the game. But if the timing was poor in Emburey's case, it was little better for the man chosen to replace him.

Chris Cowdrey's Kent side had been unfancied at the start of the 1988 Championship season. 'We were about fifteenth favourites out of seventeen counties' he recalls – a status backed up by their first three matches, which produced heavy defeats to Essex, Hampshire and Leicestershire. A radical change in the team's fortunes was about to take place, as Cowdrey remembers:

> We had a new Chairman of Cricket, the late Jim Woodhouse, who became a really close friend. We sat down at the beginning of the season and examined why we were not doing better on the field. We'd lost something like eight or nine international players over a three year period, but Jim was bemused why people weren't doing better. We didn't have any world class fast bowlers, we were a bit of a makeshift side but with some really nice players.

With Kent in Leicester, and about to lose their third game in a row, Woodhouse called a meeting where the players could air their views. The results were not what either Woodhouse or Cowdrey had expected.

'We had an amazing meeting listening to the team tell us why they were unhappy, everything, as a team.' There were three complaints: the meal money they were being paid on away trips was insufficient; they had complained about it before but nothing had been done; they felt that practice facilities were inadequate; and they didn't have a top coach who could get the best out of players in different areas. Woodhouse said to the players 'if I sort those things out, can you get on with it? Can you win the Championship?' The players' response was a guarded one – they wanted to know who Woodhouse would bring in as coach. 'You tell me. Who do you want?' he replied. Cowdrey and Chris Tavaré then jumped in and said 'the best is the Australian John Inverarity.'

Kent had a two-week gap between the defeat at Leicester and their next Championship match, at home to Yorkshire, interrupted only by a practice match against Oxford University. About halfway through that fortnight, Cowdrey remembers, Woodhouse called another meeting:

> He said, 'OK, the meal money's gone up. We've got the right figure. We've sorted out the practice facilities for you, and John Inverarity is arriving on Monday. Is there anything else?' We then said, look, the excuses have gone out of the window, the club are looking after us now, we should start playing a bit better. But that was Jim's style. He was a table thumper. He'd say, 'look, I've done this for you, what are you going to do for me?' He was really amazing, and he got me going more than anyone else had ever done before.

The results were immediate and a new vigour was quickly apparent in Kent's cricket. Inverarity, realising that it would be impossible to inject new quality into the side's batting and bowling in the short term, worked hard on improving the team's fielding. In this he was backed up by Cowdrey's lively on-field captaincy style, which kept players on their toes and relied upon rapid reaction to changing situations in the game. 'As a leader, I never liked to plan too much,' says Cowdrey, 'I preferred to play it as I read it.' Cowdrey's tactical flexibility and the team's new alertness in the field helped to give them the edge in several close games.

They beat Yorkshire in a tight match at Canterbury, just squeezing over the line to reach their target of 104 with three wickets to spare. A week later another last-gasp victory was sealed over Nottinghamshire at Dartford, Cowdrey himself hitting the winning run from the last ball as his team reached the target of 111, the winning margin this time just two wickets. More comfortable wins over Glamorgan, Middlesex and Lancashire followed before Kent travelled to Warwickshire and thumped the hosts by an innings and 46 runs in just two days. Kent had gone from losing their first three games of the season to winning the next six. They were now thirty points clear at the top of the Championship table.

With such *esprit de corps* and such a sense of momentum having developed in his side in little more than a month, by early July Chris Cowdrey would have been forgiven for considering an England call-up for any of his team an unwelcome distraction. He certainly had little real indication of his own imminent elevation to the most prominent, and precarious job in English cricket.

It was my ambition as a cricketer to win the County Championship with Kent. After those six consecutive wins, we went top of the table and I actually thought at that point that we would win it. The players were playing right at their capacity, playing how they should have been playing [earlier in the season] when they were going through the motions. Now people were playing for each other 100% and it was exactly what I had always wanted from a team. I have to be honest, when the England job came up it was the last thing I wanted. It's a funny thing to say, but it was the last thing I wanted because of this run that we'd had.

With the newspapers, filled in those days with cricket reports and comment, an ever present feature of county dressing rooms, Cowdrey had been aware of the growing sense that John Emburey's time as captain was coming to an end, but the idea that he himself might take over had not developed beyond a passing thought in the back of his mind. 'I suppose I saw that as a sort of possibility, but I was so focused on the Kent job, and also having gone through a good spell I was now going through a bad spell. I wasn't making any runs at all. I had one or two press boys coming up to me and saying "you know, you could get that job," but still it didn't really dawn on me that I was a leading candidate. Even when I saw some of the names being bandied around I thought, I don't think any of us are leading candidates!'

Cowdrey heard of his appointment through an unexpected source. 'It was Brian Luckhurst, who was with the Second XI somewhere [Sittingbourne, where a match against Essex Seconds was in progress] who rang me up and asked "how far away are you? I've got something to tell you, can you come into the game?"' Arriving at the Sittingbourne ground, Cowdrey was told by Luckhurst 'you need to phone Peter May. Well done, you've got the job.' Just as John Emburey had found, initial misgivings were soon overcome. He had no hesitation in accepting. 'I have to admit, I got in the car and thought, oh no, this is just the worst timing. We were on fire at the time.' But as for turning the job down, 'you just can't do it'.

Cowdrey had to drive to the Oval for a meeting with the Chairman of Selectors in order to be formally offered the job. Much was made in the press of the fact that Peter May was Chris Cowdrey's godfather, but the relationship was not such a close one as that implies. Although Cowdrey still sometimes refers to May as 'Uncle Peter', the pair had not met frequently in recent years and at the time Cowdrey felt he 'didn't really know him that well.' The manner of Cowdrey's appointment was typical of Peter May's style. 'He wanted, in a rather old-school way, to break the news to me in person, to tell me why I had been appointed and wish me good luck.' May went on to outline to Cowdrey his expectations for his new captain and to offer a tantalising glimpse of a long-term future in the role. Cowdrey recalls the meeting as one which held the key to everything that later happened during his short tenure as England captain. 'He said to me "I didn't really want to pick you for this game. We were forced into a corner. We wanted you to lead the side in India. We feel, unanimously, that you're the man to lead the side this winter, but if we're changing the captaincy again, we're going to find it difficult to put someone else in for two games and then send you to India."'

What May said next left Cowdrey stunned:

'I don't mind' he said, 'what happens at Headingley or The Oval. You're going to lose these games anyway.' Well, I had never, ever played a game of sport where I had gone into the game thinking I was going to lose. I had always been one of those people who always thinks he's going to win. I had great confidence in my ability as a captain and as a fielder where I always wanted to be remembered as the best.

May explained that the remainder of the West Indies series was merely an opportunity to break himself into the role, and that his reign would begin in earnest on the tour of India. Honoured as he had felt to be offered the job of captaining his country, this was not what Chris Cowdrey had wanted to hear.

> I left that meeting feeling pretty deflated. I was playing in a team that was well clear at the top of the Championship, a team that thought it was going to win every game, even against sides much better on paper. I'm not really criticising him, because I know exactly what he was saying. He was trying to say 'don't panic' he was trying to take the pressure off and in a funny sort of way it probably did. But it didn't help me when I got into the England dressing room thinking it doesn't matter.

It was another example of Peter May's misfiring communication skills. Cowdrey's meeting with his godfather certainly did not have the same invigorating effect as his meetings with the determined Jim Woodhouse earlier in the season.

Cowdrey's next meeting was perhaps even more important. It was the meeting, at Guildford, where Kent were playing Surrey, which would select the team to play at Headingley. Just as the pundits were hoping, it would result in wholesale changes of personnel. The mild indecision of the first half of the season was about to turn into a large-scale cull of the old guard. Over the next few weeks, a series of young hopefuls would find themselves loaded into the breach as the selectors aimed a series of long shots towards the seemingly bulletproof West Indians.

'We sat round the table' recalls Cowdrey, 'and the first thing Peter May said was that Paul Downton and David Gower aren't playing. So they wouldn't be entering the discussion. I imagine they had had a pre-meeting meeting.' This is certainly borne out by May's comment about making some changes when he relieved John Emburey of his burden.

> That was a pretty shocking thing for me, because my two best friends in the game were Paul Downton and David Gower – I was best man at both their weddings and David was mine. They were my best mates in the game and I was being told to leave them out. You know, when you're sort of going in to World War Three, you need your allies with you. When I was heading there in the car I was trying to think of

everyone I could get together to rally round and try to get a bit of the spirit going which we had at Kent. But it didn't feel right, me saying to experienced England players 'well this is what we do at Kent so this is what we're going to do here'.

For a captain stepping uncertainly into a new dressing room, the presence of his two closest friends would have helped give him precious leverage with other senior professionals in the side. Their absence, he worried, might leave him seriously short of authority.

Bravely, Cowdrey did his best to argue the case. It was an argument that dominated the meeting, lasting well over an hour. Eventually, Peter May relented just a fraction and offered Cowdrey a compromise: 'you can have one of them.' Cowdrey now had to choose between his two great friends. For him, it was purely a cricketing decision. 'I kept thinking, it will be David Gower's hundredth Test match. People raise their game for occasions like that.' So Gower stayed, and Downton went. To this day it hurts Cowdrey that Downton would not play for England again.

The rest of the meeting was a comparative formality. Emburey and Gatting were both out of contention. Martyn Moxon, technically solid though he had been in the last two Tests, had shown little sign of producing a big innings, so he also made way. So too did Chris Broad, left out of the final XI on the first morning at Old Trafford, and now left out of the squad entirely. Not only was Broad demoted from Test duty, but he now found himself banished to the Nottinghamshire Second XI at the behest of county captain, and Broad's erstwhile England colleague, Tim Robinson, for having acted as a subversive influence in the dressing room. 'Broad has shown a total misunderstanding of what is required in a cricket club' commented team manager Ken Taylor in a judgement Peter May would no doubt have had sympathy with. It was a remarkable comedown for a cricketer who, just six months earlier, had become only the second English batsman to have notched Test hundreds on four separate Australian grounds.

That left three batting vacancies if England were to give themselves the option once again of choosing six specialist batsmen and just four bowlers. Replacing Gatting in the No.3 slot was Bill Athey, who had earned a recall with some fine recent form for Gloucestershire. Athey was a talented batsman who had never quite shown his best form at Test level, and he was currently enjoying a purple patch. A score of 91 not out in a rain affected draw at Worcester had been followed by a wonderful 168 not out in a desperately close one-run defeat at home to Northants, with West Indian paceman Winston Davis rampant with 6 for 92 for the visitors. The man to become Graham Gooch's third opening partner of the series was Worcestershire's Tim Curtis, who had impressed with his steadfast support work for Graeme Hick that season. 'Technically he is sound and he has learned his craft well,' commented Clive Lloyd. Cowdrey concurs about Curtis's solidity, but concedes that on reflection the Worcestershire opener was 'not quite good enough at Test level.'

The final batting place went to the man who had impressed everybody with his decisive, powerful strokeplay in the Benson & Hedges Final at Lord's – Robin Smith. The decision was 'a no-brainer' as Cowdrey recalls, but Smith himself was less sure of his credentials for Test cricket at the time: 'Don't mention me in the same breath as other young players because they have scored runs consistently and I haven't. I know I have the ability but I don't deserve my chance yet' was his modest response to suggestions of a Test call-up after his innings at Lord's. Since breaking into the Hampshire side as a nineteen-year-old, Smith had managed to compile thirteen first-class centuries, and overall his record bore comparison with any of the other young talents in England. At the time of his selection, however, his first-class average for the season stood at a meagre 29. The selection of Smith for this game proved yet again the value of scoring runs in high-profile matches.

There was one great boost for England in the bowling department. Neil Foster was at last considered fit enough to bowl through a five-day Test match, meaning that for the first time that summer England would have their first choice new-ball pairing of Foster and Dilley available. Sadly, Paul Jarvis' back strain now looked serious enough to keep him out of action for the rest of the summer. Phil DeFreitas lost his place again and, in a curious parallel with Chris Broad, also found himself playing second XI cricket before the month was out, Leicestershire captain Nigel Briers having dropped him for failing to give 100 per cent in a Championship match against Derbyshire. David Capel made way for Cowdrey's inclusion in the XI, while the dropping of DeFreitas offered a chance of a recall for Derek Pringle, who was unlucky to have missed out at Old Trafford and was regarded as something of a specialist on the Headingley wicket.

Paul Downton's exclusion from the side also meant a recall for Surrey's Jack Richards – well known to Micky Stewart both through their county association and the wicketkeeper's part in Mike Gatting's successful Ashes tour. Richards had been in fine form with the bat and would go on to top Surrey's first-class averages at the end of the season. John Childs retained his place in the squad, but was left out of the XI predictably on the morning of the match. 'We didn't want to go overboard with the changes, but some had to be made' said Peter May. The number of players who had represented England in the summer's four Test matches had now reached twenty-one.

Kent's match at Guildford ended in a draw on Tuesday 19 July. The following day, twenty-four hours before the match, Cowdrey arrived at Headingley to take charge of the England team. From that point until the game began, everything passed in a blur for the new England captain. There were press interviews, lasting an hour and a half or so, net practice, the team dinner – everything it seemed that could be done to prevent the new captain from sitting down calmly to focus on the game ahead. 'I have to be honest' recalls Cowdrey.

> By the time that match started my mind was completely fuzzy. You don't really get any warning of the media attention, for one; the shortage of time to prepare for the game; the opportunity to think of how you're going to put over your own style of captaincy when you're playing against a side so good that everyone thinks you're going to lose in three days. As a result, I didn't do anything. As a result I thought I'll just go in and enjoy the game.

For Chris Cowdrey, the only way to prepare himself for the challenge of captaining his country was to go into this Test match 'as just another player'.

Fortunately for Cowdrey, he was not the sort of captain who would go into any match with a well-researched dossier on how to combat the opposition. 'I always preferred to try and get the best out of my team rather than worry about how the opposition would play.' Nor was he unaware of the inherent absurdity of coming in to the England dressing room and issuing instructions on how to play the West Indies to players who had far more experience of facing them than he had. Not only had he taken no part in the series before now, he had not even seen that much of it on TV. 'What's the point of me telling Gooch, Gower, Lamb, how we're going to play differently, how we're going to spank the West Indies when I've never played against them? What's the point of me, OK I was fine with the bowlers on the field, but trying to put together a plan of bowling at Viv? Well, everyone always had the same plan for him: don't bowl straight!'

The fuzziness in Cowdrey's head can't have been helped when he lost the toss and asked Viv Richards what he was going to do. 'I don't know man,' came the reply. 'I'll go and speak to my team and let you know.' It was the same tactic John Emburey had encountered at Lord's, presumably designed to keep the mind of an uncertain new captain in ferment for as long as possible, to stop him focusing on the job ahead because he did not yet know what the job would be. Perhaps it would have been easier for Cowdrey to take charge of his team for the first time in the field, with everyone together. But this was Headingley; they had lost the toss, they would be batting.

Overnight rain had left the outfield wet and delayed the start of play for almost an hour. The pitch too was an unknown quantity. After England's home defeat against Pakistan the year before the main Test strip had been subject to a TCCB inspection. It had not played much better during the Texaco Trophy match in May and, amid worries that the future of Test cricket at the ground could be in jeopardy, a reserve strip was called into service. Runs had been scored on it during county matches earlier in the season, but no one knew how it might behave in a Test match. England would find out quickly enough.

At first, everything seemed normal. Marshall bowled a maiden at Gooch, and Ambrose bowled one at the debutant Curtis, but at the end of his over Ambrose trooped sullenly up to umpire Dickie Bird and complained that the ground under his run up was sodden. Bird duly examined the turf a short distance behind the stumps at the Football Stand End. To his surprise, he saw water bubbling up to the surface as if from an underground spring. He glanced up at the heavens, in his usual manner of trying to divine the nature of approaching clouds, and was met by the kind of dazzling sunlight that a Yorkshire cricketer expects to see only three or four times in a lifetime, unless called upon to tour overseas. By now the water was bubbling over Ambrose's boots. A swift conference with fellow umpire David Shepherd brought the unavoidable conclusion that the players would have to leave the field while the ground staff mopped up the water. Bird could not believe his bad luck. Spectators at Headingley were better used than most to Bird's fretful moods and his unwanted reputation for dragging a personal weather system around the country with him for the express purpose of ordering the players back to the Pavilion at the first hint of rain or poor light. Now, in a Test match on his home ground, Bird was in the position of having to lead them off in bright sunshine with barely a cloud in the sky.

Unbeknownst to either the umpires, players or the spectators who jeered them all from the field, the reason for the unexpected quagmire was a decision made by Yorkshire County Cricket Club. Acutely aware of the poor reputation of Headingley's pitch, especially the way it had developed serious cracks during recent Test matches, the club had decided to prevent the cracks from forming by finding some way of helping the playing surface to retain moisture. The method they came up with involved blocking the drains beneath the ground so that water could not escape. It might have been fine if there had been a light shower, but the heavy overnight rain had overloaded the drainage system, and all the work done by the ground staff to clear water from the outfield and prepare the ground for the start of play had simply put more water into a system from which it had only one escape – upwards, and directly at Dickie Bird's feet.

It was not until 2.30 p.m. that play could resume. For the next hour and forty minutes until the tea interval, it looked as though the change of captain had not altered the momentum of the series one jot. Gooch didn't quite get far enough forward to a good length ball from Marshall and edged it to Dujon for just 9. Athey and Curtis then, together for almost an hour, seemed to prove the prophecy of the *Express* leader writer entirely. Each did almost exactly what Martyn Moxon might have been expected to do – hold out solidly for a decent length of time without ever really getting 'in'. The tall, white helmeted Curtis showed an admirably straight bat and good judgement of where his off-stump was, but there was something rather robotic about his batting. He had one of those stances fashionable at the time: straight legs, bat held high, almost at the top of the back-lift, left elbow pointing down the wicket at the bowler, ready to lead the stroke, with the bat coming through with the rigidity of a pendulum rather than the fluidity of a golf swing.

Curtis struck one impressive four, pulling a barely short ball from Walsh off the front foot, but soon afterwards was trapped lbw by

Benjamin playing across his front pad. Gower now came to the crease amid generous applause for his hundredth Test. There were less than twenty minutes to go before the tea interval, but it was a frenetic innings from England's most experienced batsman. Off the mark first ball, he was caught at short leg off a no-ball from his third. He then proceeded to take nine off Benjamin in one over – one glorious off-drive chased to the boundary by ten thousand memories of years gone by – before, with just four balls to go before tea, he nibbled at a ball angled across him and was caught behind. England were 58 for 3.

Allan Lamb struck the second ball after the interval through cover for four, and although he soon lost the company of Bill Athey, trapped lbw on the back foot by Ambrose for 16, there was now a visible shift in the tempo of the innings. Together, Lamb and Robin Smith put together a partnership that became one of the great 'if onlys' of English cricket. They ran singles with an urgency not seen from England batsmen all season. Lamb stood up straight and drove straight, sometimes leaning back and hooking when all a spectator's instincts said that he should duck. Smith showed no sign of first Test nerves. As his career progressed he became well known as one of the best England batsmen when it came to standing up to a barrage of pace and bounce, and although he never claimed actually to enjoy short-pitched bowling it was clear from this first innings that he relished the physical challenge.

Smith, too, was a batsman who favoured the pre-raised backlift, but in his case it was married to a low, crouching stance that kept him on the balls of his feet rather than his heels and helped him to launch into a generous forward stride against good length bowling. That big forward stride sometimes brought him so close to the ground that he could cut the ball on width as well as length, his forearms thick as serrano hams coming down on the ball and crunching it to the boundary with a crack like a rifle shot. No one since Norman O'Neill had cut the ball with such power and ferocity. Sometimes it seemed likely to bounce off the advertising hoardings and return itself to the wicket without the need for a fielder to intervene. It was that cut shot, played once that evening to a wide ball from Marshall that announced Smith's arrival as a Test player. After that stroke, nobody could doubt that the selectors had, in his case, made an inspired choice.

Lamb and Smith took England to 137 for 4 at the close, and continued in the same vein the following morning. Lamb brought up his 50 from 70 balls and looked well set for his second hundred of the series. They had added 45 to the score at a run a minute – an unheard of rate for England against this attack – when disaster struck. A leg bye off Ambrose took the partnership to 102 and brought Lamb on to strike. The next ball was just short of a length and just outside off-stump. 'I played the ball into the covers, but my feet were in a funny position,' said Lamb that evening. 'I set off for the run and felt something in my leg. I thought it was cramp, but when I got to the other end I knew it was something more serious. I couldn't stand up.' Lamb had completed the run almost hopping. Supporting himself on his bat he tried to massage his calf muscle back into life, but to no avail. Team physiotherapist Laurie Brown raced out to the middle and was soon escorting Lamb back to the pavilion; the batsman had torn his calf muscle. It was a bad tear, thought Brown. 'The normal recovery period is two to three weeks but it could be even longer.'

Chris Cowdrey came to the wicket for his first innings as England captain with his team well placed on 183 for 4. He had never faced Curtly Ambrose before. 'And I didn't face him then,' he remembers. 'Marshall and Walsh were enough for me.' Cowdrey watched from the non-striker's end as Smith played out the rest of Ambrose's over. Cowdrey then took guard and waited for Malcolm Marshall to run in.

'If we were going to talk about my strengths as a batsman,' he told me, 'they would not include playing fast bowling.' He was able to let his first ball go through to Dujon without playing it, but the second nipped back into his pads and produced a loud appeal for lbw. Umpire Shepherd shook his head. Cowdrey managed to keep out the third and fourth balls of the over. The fifth seamed and lifted and struck him on the thigh pad, the last he played safely out to square leg. Marshall took his sweater from David Shepherd and walked back to his fielding position. If Cowdrey then breathed a sigh of relief, his relief did not last long.

The next ball from Curtly Ambrose was similar in line and length to the ball Lamb had played out to cover the over before, but the seam bit into the turf and the ball lifted and darted away from the middle of Smith's bat, caught the edge and flew safely to Dujon. It was typical of the West Indies that, offered a fraction of good fortune, they would shift into a higher gear and turn it swiftly into a windfall. Suddenly, it was a very different game. It was something John Emburey had witnessed in many earlier Tests:

> If somebody got in, and they were playing strongly square off the back foot they'd put a man back to cover it so you were only picking up one, you weren't getting four. They were slowing down the game in terms of you you getting on top of them. But as soon as they took a wicket, by golly everyone came in and all of a sudden that new batsman was under immediate pressure.

Cowdrey survived five more balls before Marshall beat him for pace and trapped him lbw. Derek Pringle lasted just three before he gloved a lifter to Dujon. Jack Richards, his stance open towards mid-on, seemed to be facing in completely the wrong direction as Ambrose nipped one back off the seam and bowled him through the gate. Dilley and Foster then managed to scrape the innings past 200 before Dilley edged a drive to second slip to give Ambrose his fourth wicket. Since Lamb's injury, England had lost five wickets for just 18 runs in 51 minutes. It looked like the old, old story once again – give England fans a glimmer of hope, then collapse in disarray before they can get used to the idea. However, despite being bowled out for just 201, England were not out of this game yet, as Cowdrey and his team were about to prove.

The West Indies' batting was again weakened by injury, with both Greenidge and Richardson absent from the roster. Carl Hooper was pushed up the order to fill Richardson's No.3 berth while the honour of replacing Greenidge and partnering Desmond Haynes against the new ball went to the man who had just unbuckled his other set of pads after taking four catches as wicketkeeper – Jeffrey Dujon. It was the first opportunity for England to see how much more effective their bowling might have been if both Dilley and Foster had been fit for the whole series. The initial signs were promising with Dujon falling in the third over of the innings, and the first after lunch. Batting as if against a tired attack on a flat pitch using a ball 60-overs old, Dujon had roared out of the starting gate, striking two boundaries from his first eleven deliveries. But he mistimed a drive at Dilley and was caught at cover by Robin Smith for 13. Dilley, feeling a twinge in his hamstring, was not quite at his sharpest, but Foster bowled with great control and intelligence off a short run. By the time he stepped down from the attack he had bowled 19 of the first 42 overs and claimed the wickets of Hooper and Richards, with the West Indies captain falling to a superbly athletic catch at short leg by Tim Curtis. With Pringle having also trapped Haynes lbw for 54 soon after tea, England were right back in the match.

Only 2 more overs were possible before bad light brought an early end to the day's play. In that time Gus Logie, after a lively 44 from 51 balls, failed to spot Pringle's slower ball, got a thick inside edge and fell to a head-high catch by Neil Foster at mid-on. None of the West Indian batsmen had been able to dominate in the way that Lamb and Smith had done. England's bowlers had used the conditions well and been supported by sharp fielding and sound catching. Nobody watching the game could have failed to notice the definite buzz of fresh energy that had suddenly instilled itself into the England team, and yet Chris Cowdrey 'didn't do anything' to effect this change.

Perhaps it was not so much anything that the new captain had deliberately said or done. Perhaps, in combination with the unprecedented sight of two England batsmen biffing the West Indies fast bowlers around and standing firm against their short-pitched bowling, the fact that Cowdrey went about his business with the unaffected joy of playing cricket for a living had reminded his team that this was supposed to be fun. 'Chris brought real energy to the job and was a natural leader,' remembers Graham Gooch. It was just what a world-weary team needed. England's new found vigour in the field and success in claiming the first five West Indies wickets cheaply had blurred the memory of their batting collapse earlier in the day and helped Cowdrey avoid the sort of unpleasant headlines that might have got the knife sharpeners whirring in the TCCB offices before the ink was even dry on his contract.

More heavy overnight rain kept the 15,000-strong crowd waiting until 2.45 p.m. for play to begin on the third day. In a tense first hour, Foster and Dilley beat the bat repeatedly as Roger Harper and the left-handed Keith Arthurton, playing his first Test of the series, nudged the score forward by 35 runs. In the end it was Pringle who got the breakthrough, with Arthurton edging a prod at a wideish ball through to Richards behind the stumps. Harper nearly went soon afterwards, with Foster finding his edge at last, only for Bill Athey at second slip to pull out of the catch as if leaving it to a colleague. It was England's first serious fielding lapse of the innings and it would prove to be a crucial one.

Harper lost Marshall and Ambrose before rain brought an early end to the day, then Benjamin departed early on the fourth day having been run out by substitute fielder Neil Fairbrother. Harper, left with only Courtney Walsh for company, hung on. Two tactical choices made by Chris Cowdrey at this point brought him some criticism. After Neil Foster completed his interrupted over from the previous day, Cowdrey replaced him with Graham Dilley who bowled in partnership with Derek Pringle. Foster, though, had bowled 31 overs so far in the innings and Dilley, just 15. England's captain also used the tactic of spreading the field when bowling at Roger Harper, inviting him to take the single. Eight times during his partnership with Courtney Walsh Harper refused easy runs in the early part of an over, only to take one later in the over. He was happier to see his partner face Pringle than Dilley. In Pringle's final over Harper took a single from the third ball. Walsh played and missed at the next, but then clubbed the fifth ball straight back past the bowler for four. It was the final hurrah. Foster returned to the attack and had Harper caught by Gower at backward point off a skied drive, but Harper had done his job well, adding 53 runs with the final two wickets to raise his team's score to 275 and his own to 56. He had been just eighteen when missed by Athey.

It could have been worse. England's first innings deficit was not the mountain it might have been after their first innings collapse, but against the West Indies even a molehill could be difficult to climb. Nevertheless, when England wiped out their first innings deficit for the loss of only one wicket in less than two hours' batting, there were plenty of reasons for their supporters to be hopeful. Curtis, despite taking twenty-four minutes to get off the mark, reinforced the solid impression he had made in the first innings. He again made only 12 runs before playing across the line at a full length ball from Ambrose and losing both middle and leg stumps, but by that time he and Gooch had brought up only England's second first-wicket partnership of more than 50 in the series. Gooch and Athey then added 24 more in just under half an hour, with Gooch bringing up his 50 in the process, before the experienced opener tried to drive a ball that was a little too wide and edged low to second slip.

From that moment, the vision of a rejuvenated England team vanished as if in a desert haze. Gower had just enough time to clip his seven-thousandth Test match run off his pads before overbalancing in trying to repeat the shot and getting a thin edge through to Dujon. Walsh then bowled a brute of a ball that reared up off a length and Athey could only edge for another catch to the wicketkeeper. Smith and Cowdrey hung on pluckily, adding 20 together before both came up against fast seaming balls that were simply too good for them. Due in next would be Pringle, but astonishingly, in hobbled Lamb, his right leg painfully immobile, and Robin Smith trotting out to act as his runner.

It was probably to Allan Lamb's advantage that day that he had never been known as a batsman who used his feet very much – an advantage, too, that his entrance had come as such a surprise. He had said that he would bat if needed, and Laurie Brown had conceded that he might be patched up to bat on one leg at the risk, he warned, of making the injury even worse. But few had taken the suggestion seriously, and the way the West Indies bowled to him indicated they had done little in the way of planning. His right leg being immobilised, Lamb could not play back; he remained propped in the crease, with all his weight on his left leg. There was nothing wrong with his hand-eye co-ordination however, and after he slapped Marshall through the off-side to the boundary twice in one over, the West Indians decided to bounce him.

Curtly Ambrose's first ball struck Lamb on the wrist – a blow that required treatment before play could resume. More short balls followed. Lamb could not play back, so he could neither hook nor block such bowling. He was too immobile to get properly out of the way, so just had to hold his head up as long as possible, keep his eye on the ball and rely upon his reactions to sway head and upper body out of the way at the last moment. It was a display of extraordinary pluck. From a tactical point of view, persistent short-pitched bowling generally has two purposes: either the bowler wants to entrap the batsman into an uncontrolled stroke, or he wants him to anticipate more of the same, and keep his weight on the back foot, unprepared for the full-length ball to follow. But Lamb was not capable of placing any weight on the back foot, let alone playing shots off it, so the tactic seemed ill-thought-out. Pretty soon it became apparent that its prime cause was frustration. Whatever was happening at the other end, Lamb would not budge.

By the end, Lamb was receiving at least two bouncers every over. After sending down two in succession, Ambrose found himself officially warned by umpire Shepherd for intimidatory bowling. His next over began with another bouncer and finished with two more. Shepherd stepped in again with a second and final warning. Still Lamb was there, but for all his resistance matters at the other end were making clear that it was all in vain. Richards had been skittled by another Ambrose breakback that kept a little low. Pringle had gone the same way to Benjamin and Foster had edged the same bowler to slip. Lamb was now left with only Dilley for support. After almost an hour and a half of stubborn resistance, with England's lead just 64, Lamb's arms reached for a square cut, but his legs couldn't take him across to it and the ball just kissed the top edge of his bat on the way through to Dujon. Lamb's wonderful effort had achieved little more than allowing England to take the match into a fifth day. The West Indies knocked off their meagre target without losing a wicket.

Despite Peter May's claim that he didn't care about the result of this match, another heavy defeat produced a glut of public reaction. In the post-match press conference, Micky Stewart conceded that England had been 'stuffed out of sight' in the last three games. Reluctant to criticise the players, Stewart instead blamed the county system at the heart of their development: three-day cricket on bowler-friendly pitches and an over-abundance of overseas players, echoing comments made by Peter May before the match. It was not a view that went down well with Vivian Richards. 'Your players can only benefit from having big stars around them,' he said. 'When I first came here I learned from people like Brian Close and it must be great practice for your batsmen to have faced Malcolm Marshall. The system works vice versa and helps the world.' He might have added that if three-day cricket were such poor preparation for Test matches, why did most of the great West Indian stars of the past twenty years set such great store by the development they enjoyed through playing county cricket? Peter May pointed to the fact that the one specialism in which English cricket remained self-sufficient, wicketkeeping, was the one area where it could claim superiority over the rest of the world. In *The Observer*, Vic Marks reflected on his own cricketing education: 'back in 1968 observing Gary Sobers at Trent Bridge was I guess marginally more instructive and inspirational for a young player than studying Brian Bolus.'

For Chris Cowdrey there were mixed feelings about the match. He had had little time to think of what success might look like on his debut as Test captain, but this surely was not it:

You can't call it success when you lose a game as badly as that. I didn't get any runs. I only made 0 and 5 in the Test. If you play against that attack and make 20, 20 is not a great score but you still feel that you've achieved something, that you've played a part in the game. But all I did was make 5 and have a little knock with Robin Smith. I was the fourth seamer, but only bowled when they were chasing 45 or so just at the end. To go in as the fourth seamer and not bowl, and not make any runs, lose the toss; you can't call that success.

Cowdrey remains reluctant to take any credit for the good positions England got themselves into earlier in the match, preferring to give credit to individual performances. He had not come into the dressing room with any kind of game plan, nor told his bowlers how to bowl at particular players. But what he had brought in was a kind of spark, and in the positive batting of Lamb and Smith resulting in England's newfound vitality in the field, the Headingley crowd had seen a glimpse of what might have been. Graham Gooch called it energy. It was also fun. 'Trying to enjoy it, I think, that was the only thing, if anything, that I achieved on the field.' It was an attitude that certainly found favour with Cowdrey's old friend David Gower, who remarked to *Test Match Special* commentator Henry Blofeld during the rest day that it had been many years since he had enjoyed playing for England as much as this.

More than the result, Cowdrey's biggest regret of his one match as captain was that he did not manage to concentrate on the job. 'My mind was in turmoil,' he remembers.

We had that issue at the start with Dickie Bird, the water coming up, it's bright sunshine and he takes them all off. In that interval I was on the phone to Kent to find out how we were getting on down at Folkestone. Calls were coming in all the time saying 'we've got a wicket'. Can you imagine Wayne Rooney at half-time playing for England phoning up to find out how Man United are getting on? It's not going to happen. Your mind has got to be focused. When you're playing against the West Indies, unless you're really, really fired up and sharp you've got no price. I'm really blaming myself for buying in to this fact that if I got the tour job that winter, that would definitely be the place I'd be at my strongest. I was a better player against spin than pace, I was comfortable on tours, I would have enjoyed building a team, which you can't do when you're a makeshift captain in an England home series.

On a more positive note, Cowdrey remembers the magnanimity of Viv Richards at the end of the game: 'my hero of all time as a player, a sportsman and a person. He was very generous and wished me good luck. I don't think he wanted me to be pulverised into the ground, never to reappear.' Of course, for all anyone knew at the time, Cowdrey was due to reappear with his England team at the Oval in just nine days' time.

11

Taking the Team Out

Three days after the defeat at Headingley, England's selectors met once more at the Oval to pick the team for the final Test of the series. This time, Chris Cowdrey could not defend the position of David Gower. A season of erratic innings, glorious boundaries sprinkled randomly amid less well-executed strokes, had at last resulted in the exhaustion of the selectors' patience. The phrase 'laid-back' had stalked him like a spectre for several years, linking, rather unfairly, his relaxed demeanour with the idea that he did not guard his wicket jealously enough. On the third day at Headingley, *Test Match Special* broadcaster Brian Johnston clearly had the phrase in mind when he asked Gower, on air, whether he would like 'any two words' to be expunged from his career record. Gower, having in the first innings fallen as so often against the West Indies to a catch at the wicket, responded with lightning wit: 'yes, caught Dujon.' It raised a laugh, which perhaps only added to the devil-may-care image. But taken literally the words suggest deep wounds at professional failure, and an awareness that such failure would not much longer be tolerated. Those two words claimed him again, in that most desperate of ways, a leg side 'strangle', in his very next innings. Now, Cowdrey would have to do without his other great ally as well. Mike Gatting had finally decided to declare himself unavailable for England for the rest of the summer, ending hopes that a ready-made replacement for the injured Lamb might be found in his form. In the circumstances it was hardly surprising that Lamb's appeal to be included in the squad and given time to prove his fitness found a receptive audience in that Oval meeting room.

Without Lamb, Gatting and Gower, England's batting order at the Oval would have a decidedly inexperienced look. Following two sadly

passive innings and a crucial missed catch, there was agreement that Bill
Athey's final chance had come and gone. He had, according to Scyld
Berry 'again fallen at the final hurdle, which only the self-confident will
cross.' Most writers seemed to accept that change was inevitable, even
desirable, while at the same time approving Viv Richards' suggestion
that the real flaw in English cricket lay in the very idea of a selection
committee. In *The Guardian*, Mike Selvey noted that Peter May had
now handed out Test caps to fifty-seven players during his tenure as
Chairman, about 10 per cent of all those issued since 1877, but he
refused to blame May personally, arguing instead that it was in the
nature of a committee process to produce such inconsistent thinking.
Given the sole responsibility for selection, he argued, Micky Stewart
would surely not have selected twenty-one different players in just four
matches. The same paper's leader writer, however, took a more personal
view of selectorial culpability:

> If cricketers who consistently fail to deliver the goods at the highest
> level are customarily dropped, in the hope that others might do rather
> better, so selectors who fail to deliver should surely expect to make
> way as well. A system in which those down the line are fired when
> they fail, but those at the top survive unscathed, is unhealthy in any
> context.

Perhaps the only obvious flaw in this view was the idea that it required
consistent failure before a Test player would be dropped. The evidence
of 1988 was that once or twice was quite enough.

Three names had dominated press discussions about the batting
vacancies for the Oval: Matthew Maynard, Kim Barnett and
Northamptonshire's Robert Bailey. Despite failing in a tour match
against the West Indies, Maynard had largely maintained his strong
early season form, hitting four sparkling half-centuries in his last five
innings. Bailey had just recovered from a poor trot with 63 against
Kent and 127 not out against Sussex, while Barnett had just made what
Wisden called a 'peerless' career-best 239 not out against Leicestershire.
Both of the latter two, however, were known as front-foot players, and
not particularly as specialists against fast-bowling. Were they really
the type of player who should be offered a debut against Marshall,
Ambrose, Walsh and Benjamin on a fast, bouncy wicket at the Oval?

Thoughts of the bowling attack were dominated by one major consideration – the question of the captain himself. Cowdrey had been a barely used fourth seamer at Headingley. On a fast and true pitch at the Oval, could he really play the role of third seamer if England chose to play a spinner – as they surely would – or would he remain fourth seamer in a five-man attack and find himself batting one place higher in the order at six?

By allowing Allan Lamb until the morning of the match to prove his fitness, and including Matthew Maynard as cover in the event that he failed, the selectors retained the option of playing six batsmen on a technicality – the hope that Lamb might recover in time was perhaps their longest shot of all that summer. Kim Barnett got the nod over Rob Bailey at no.3 and to the Headingley attack of Foster, Dilley, Pringle and Cowdrey – with John Childs in reserve – Gladstone Small was added to provide an extra seam option. Jack Richards retained the wicketkeeper's position despite the growing clamour for a chance to be offered to Gloucestershire's 'Jack' Russell. 'If there are any cricket followers outside the selection panel who do not believe that Russell should be keeping wicket for England, I have yet to meet them,' wrote Alan Lee in *The Times*. Lee was even more scathing about the recall of Small, pointing out that while prior to his selection for Lord's he had claimed thirty first-class wickets at less than ten apiece, he had since taken just 10 at 380. 'If the selectors were not aware of this it was an extraordinary oversight. If they were, it was a remarkable selection.'

It is just about possible to follow the selectors' logic in choosing this team. Athey failed at Headingley, Gower had failed since Lord's, Gatting was not available, so what better time to give a chance to young hopefuls like Maynard and Barnett, than here on a fast, true, batting wicket in a dead rubber with all the pressure off and tour places there for the taking? England went in with three-and-a-bit bowlers at Headingley, but at the Oval an extra bowler would certainly be required – a spinner, presumably – and Chris Cowdrey would need to bat at No.6.

In the process England's selectors had chosen a batting order which looked like the epitome of fragility. After Gooch would come Curtis, Barnett, Smith and Maynard – two Test caps between the four of them – followed at Nos 6 and 7 by Cowdrey and Richards, neither of whom had lasted more than a few balls in either innings at Headingley. At no.8 would come Pringle, who had made 43 runs in three Tests so far, followed by Dilley, Foster and Childs. It was not so much the triumph of hope over experience as that of despair over realism.

Obvious though the flaws in the team's original selection were, there was little the selectors could do about the rash of bad luck that followed. The team was announced on the Saturday before the Test. That very day, Graham Dilley withdrew due to a 'stressed condition in his right knee.' Dilley, who had struggled with hamstring problems at Headingley, had been unable to recapture his best form since his wonderful spell at Lord's, but having only just seen Neil Foster return to fitness, to lose the other half of their first choice spearhead was a dreadful blow for England to bear.

Five bowlers were discussed as possible replacements. Four were thought to be Jonathan Agnew, Norman Cowans, Greg Thomas and David Lawrence. Lawrence, Gloucestershire's bustling, muscular, twenty-four-year-old fast bowler, had benefited hugely from having bowled alongside Courtney Walsh over the last couple of years and had added accuracy to undoubted hostility. He was also known to be a 'trier'– someone who would willingly charge in all day no matter how flat the pitch, no matter how hopeless the situation. This, however, was clearly not a quality that the selectors considered significant enough to swing their final decision.

To widespread surprise, the nod went to Phillip DeFreitas, who was recently dropped by Leicestershire for not trying and the possessor of twenty-three Test wickets at an average of 42. He had recently been restored to his county's first XI following a brief penance in the seconds. Leicestershire assured the selectors that the issue had been resolved, but it was nevertheless curious that such a misdemeanour could so swiftly be forgiven by those who picked the England team. On his recall to the side at Worksop against Nottinghamshire he had shared the new ball with Agnew and taken 2 for 62 while Agnew, in 9 more overs, bagged 6 for 117. It was hard to justify his recall on the grounds of bowling or temperament, but when Leicestershire batted, DeFreitas smashed a hundred from 82 balls – the fastest first-class century of the season. If it was that performance that earned him another Test cap, then the selectors were only too well aware of the weakness of the batting line-up they were ushering out to face the West Indies.

That batting selection was about to get even weaker. Kim Barnett sustained a bruise to the base of his thumb while fielding in a Refuge

Assurance League game against Warwickshire at Derby on the Sunday. Although he then came out to open the innings for Derbyshire and made a rapid 74 before being caught behind off Gladstone Small 'with the hand so stiff and painful I could hardly hold the bat.' He, like Lamb, was officially given until Wednesday to recover. If the selectors had a momentary thought of recalling Bill Athey to take Barnett's place, the choice was quickly taken out of their hands. On the same day, at Cheltenham, Athey was struck on the hand by a short ball from Surrey's Sylvester Clarke. Like Barnett, he batted on to a fifty, but an x-ray later revealed that the blow had fractured his knuckles. He would not play again that season.

The worst blow of all came on Monday. Down at Canterbury, Chris Cowdrey was in the process of discovering just how much momentum his Kent side had lost while he was absent leading his country. Having lost the toss to Peter Roebuck, Cowdrey watched as Somerset ran up a total of 452 for 4 declared, thanks largely to an innings of 161 from their young Australian batsman Stephen Waugh. Kent's reply got off to a disastrous start against the nagging seam of Neil Mallender and the hustling pace of Adrian Jones, and Cowdrey found himself walking to the crease with the total 32 for 4. He had made just 8 when he received an in-swinging yorker from Jones full on the instep. 'I carried on batting, although I didn't get any more runs,' Cowdrey remembers. 'But at the end of my innings I couldn't get my shoe off. So we put some ice on it and the physiotherapist said "I don't like the look of that, I think you'd better zip off quickly and have an x-ray." It wasn't until I got there that I began to think it was broken. The way I was walking, it felt like a break.' However, the x-ray revealed nothing more than bruising. Cowdrey returned to the ground, and found that the Kent medical staff were waiting for him with the news that Peter May had telephoned. 'He's ringing back in another five minutes, what are you going to tell him?' they said.

The Chairman of Selectors came straight to the point. 'He told me he wanted to hear the truth, he didn't want any flannel.' May told Cowdrey that he wanted to know exactly how he was feeling. Cowdrey replied that his foot was only bruised, but a bit sore. May then asked another question: if the Test match was starting in two hours' time, would he play? 'Two hours' time, I thought? This was when I was still hobbling. Bruises can get better quite quickly but two hours' time – of course I said I definitely wouldn't play in two hours' time, but I thought I would be probably be OK given a day's rest. They had told me [at the hospital] rest it for a day and it might be all right.'

May's response to that was immediate: 'Might be all right', he said. 'You're not playing.' Cowdrey's first thought was not to protest that he was being given no time to recover when Allan Lamb was being given all possible time to get fit after a more serious injury; it was a legitimate concern for his future in the job and the prospect of leading the team in India. 'It was a nightmare really, because I thought, if I don't play, am I going to come back and captain the side? I thought that if they went for a new captain again they would probably stick with him, but if they went back to one of the old ones and said "do this Test", I thought I might still have got the tour. That was my thinking.' Only one thing gave Cowdrey some comfort: in the poor form he was in, it was no bad time to be missing an appointment with the West Indies. 'The one good thing was that I wasn't getting a run. Although I always made runs at the Oval, to be honest I wasn't going to back myself to make runs against that attack.'

Officially at least Chris Cowdrey remained the England captain and Peter May's decision to rule him out of contention for the Oval was not made public. As it turned out, giving Cowdrey a couple of days to recover would not have made any difference. Although he hobbled to the crease at number eleven with Kent on the brink of an innings defeat against Somerset, Cowdrey could place no weight on his front foot and was quickly out. He was not considered fit enough to play in Kent's next Championship game, which began the day before the Oval Test.

On Tuesday afternoon, Graham Gooch, playing in a six-a-side benefit match at Hampstead, was called to the telephone. Micky Stewart had been trying to get hold of him all day. 'I was called to the public pay-phone on the wall under the stairs at the Hampstead clubhouse' Gooch recalled in his autobiography:

The phone is next to the bar, but over the din of noisy drinkers I could hear Micky Stewart say: 'Hang on Graham, the Chairman of Selectors wants a word with you.' Obviously they were at Lord's and Micky had Peter May with him. A few moments later Peter May came on the phone and said, 'Christopher is injured. We'd like you to take the team out at The Oval. Would you accept?' 'Yes, with pleasure.' I obviously presumed it was a one-match appointment, since Chris was injured. So it didn't look as if it would affect my contract with Western Province.

The choice of words is interesting: 'take the team out' sounds more like an instruction to a substitute than an offer of a long-term position, and Graham Gooch was not alone in thinking that his appointment as England's fourth captain of the series was a purely temporary affair. Both Cowdrey and the cricket world at large could have been forgiven for thinking that this would still leave open the possibility of his leading the team on tour in India. Gooch himself declared publicly that his appointment for the Oval would not affect his plans for the winter, but the fact that Cowdrey had so quickly been ruled out of the match by Peter May, while Lamb and Barnett were given extra time to recover, adds further weight to a suspicion that was even then gaining ground. Although Cowdrey's captaincy had reinvigorated England in the field, as a batsman and bowler he had been painfully exposed by the best team in the world. Considering the initial selection of Kim Barnett as a certainty for the final XI ahead of Matthew Maynard, Mike Selvey spoke for many when he deduced a bit of forward planning by the selectors. 'Underlying it all,' he wrote, 'is a suspicion that the selectors realise that picking Cowdrey was a mistake, and that the seeds are already being sown for a successor.'

Despite being the incumbent captain, Chris Cowdrey remained absent from the Oval as the team he helped select went into its final battle against the West Indies. 'It sounds crazy,' he remembers, 'but nobody suggested I should be there, so I didn't go.' Instead, Cowdrey remained at Canterbury, where he watched the discarded David Gower make a sudden return to his brilliant best, playing two sparkling innings of 90 and 43 as Leicestershire and Kent fought out an exciting drawn game. But Graham Gooch did not find himself entirely free from the presence of former captains in the home dressing room at the Oval. Before heading north to Manchester where Middlesex were to face Lancashire in a match beginning on the Saturday, Mike Gatting spent a few hours in the company of one or two old colleagues and a host of young hopefuls. TV cameras spotted the two chatting on the players' balcony on the first day.

In the week leading up to the Test, Gatting had first declared himself unavailable for international selection until the following summer and then been fined £5,000 by the TCCB in a disciplinary hearing at Lord's for the breach of contract relating to his book. His subsequent visit to the England dressing room raised the hackles of former Sussex off-spinner Robin Marlar, writing in *The Sunday Times*:

> That Gatting should want to enter the inner sanctum was in questionable taste. But that he should be allowed to do so by the same management whose entreaties to play he had flatly rejected, was bizarre. His presence could hardly assist the motivation of a struggling batting order. Doubtless he was not ejected because no one in cricket wants to be beastly.

If anything can be deduced from Gatting's visit to the Oval it is that the manner of his dismissal from the captaincy had left him with bitter feelings towards those in cricket's corridors of power, but not those in the England dressing room.

Play began at the Oval under heavy cloud and humidity, on a pitch typically hard, fast and true. It was the kind of pitch that against another attack might have been described as a belter, or packed with runs. But it was also the kind of pitch that would bring a malicious grin to the face of a bowler like Curtly Ambrose as he prepared to engage an extra yard of pace. Graham Gooch had far too much time for chatting on the balcony after he won the toss and elected to bat first. Marshall's first ball to him was a bouncer. His second was edged to the third man boundary. His third struck Gooch on the arm. In between the bouncers, Gooch managed to squeeze one more boundary behind square before a snorter from Ambrose left him with no option but to fend it to short leg. Having chosen such an inexperienced batting line-up, England's selectors had been relying on Gooch to lead from the front and shepherd his young charges through the innings. Just half an hour in to the match, he had gone.

Now the senior batsman remaining, Tim Curtis had again taken his time in getting off the mark, twenty-nine minutes had passed before he tickled Marshall down to fine leg for his first single. After Gooch's dismissal there was a brief hint of aggression when the Worcestershire opener hooked Marshall for successive boundaries, but Curtis and the debutant Bailey soon settled for stubborn resistance as the only practicable policy. Known to prefer playing off the front foot, the tall Bailey was kept rooted back on his stumps, but rarely bounced in his first overs at the crease. Only after several minutes, in which he proved his willingness to get in a good forward stride whenever the length justified it, did the West Indies, and Walsh in particular, let fly with the short stuff. Bailey, for the most part, dropped his hands and let it go. Against Curtis, who had shown his mettle at Headingley, they hardly bothered.

After 29 overs, England reached lunch in the relatively secure position of 56 for 1. Positive batting it had not been, but there had been few signs of obvious discomfort. Although Curtis fell half an hour after lunch for 30, Robin Smith came to the crease and hooked his first ball from Benjamin for four. Such a powerful hit was it, that umpire Bird at first signalled six in error. It was a partnership that confounded expectations: two young batsmen left unshepherded by their captain's early departure refusing to be cowed by the fearsomeness of their adversaries; Bailey, the supposed front-foot specialist, showing coolness and good judgement against the fast, rising ball; Smith, reputedly a nervous starter, smiting his first ball to the boundary as if he were bringing up his hundred. Marshall tried going around the wicket to Bailey, and a successful bid to change the ball was made. Ambrose bounced Smith just as Walsh had bounced Bailey – hitting him once on the shoulder blade – but still England's innings progressed. Past the three-hour mark it went, past 50 overs, past the point where Richards decided to give pace a break from one end and bring Roger Harper on for a spell, until the kettle was on the hob and the crumpets under the grill for the tea interval.

Perhaps it was the sight of Dickie Bird, agitated as ever, shooing a stray pigeon from the pitch that broke the mood and the concentration. Or it may be that the approach of an interval tempted Bailey to think about how he should play. One run, eight balls later, two balls before tea, Ambrose found some extra lift with a good length ball on off-stump and Bailey edged a drive to Dujon. A score of 116 for 3 still represented respectable territory in the context of England batting performances against this opposition, but it was a very different England that emerged from the dressing room for the evening session.

Matthew Maynard had earned a reputation not just as a promising and prolific young batsman, but as a cricketer worth watching. His first Test innings, just six balls long, offered as much drama as many a fine century has done. Ambrose's first ball, a no-ball, was a searing bouncer that the young Glamorgan man could only just whip his face out of the line of in the last fraction of a second. The next was struck forcefully to extra cover, where Carl Hooper, spotting Maynard setting off for a risky first run, provided a rocket-like return that had him scurrying back into his ground like a startled squirrel. A single from Smith then saw Maynard down at the Vauxhall End facing Roger Harper. He prodded nervously at his first ball and inside edged it to short leg, where Gus Logie put down a regulation catch. The next ball, uncharacteristically, was blocked. The next gave him a slightly fuller length and a little extra width to swing his arms through, and a glorious, full-striding cover-drive almost made it to the boundary. Perhaps that might have settled him, but the three runs he took saw him back at the Pavilion End with Ambrose beginning another over. The first ball was a bouncer, wide of off-stump. He might have let it go, but perhaps feeling that he ought to play his natural game, he tried to uppercut into the vacant third man position and succeeded only in giving Jeff Dujon yet another catch. It had been a frenetic innings, and one obviously driven by nerves, but the light had flickered brightly enough to suggest a rare talent that would surely come again.

It was not quite the end. David Capel stayed with Smith for forty-nine minutes, adding 39 runs, but after he edged Harper's arm ball to Marshall at slip England's innings quickly fell away. Richards went to a bat-pad catch off Harper for a duck. Pringle was caught behind off a firm-footed drive for one, and DeFreitas carved his way to 18 from 26 balls before gloving a catch to silly mid-off. Foster launched a drive halfway to orbit that substitute fielder Keith Arthurton managed to station himself underneath at cover point. It gave Malcolm Marshall his thirty-fourth wicket of the series – a record for a West Indies bowler in Tests. Robin Smith had battled his way to a maiden Test fifty before being ninth out, one of those terrifying short balls from Marshall that seemed to home in on a batsman's throat flicking off a defensive glove and looping to second slip. Having fielded such an inexperienced batting line-up against a rapidly improving West Indies attack, perhaps it was only to be expected, but it was still a demoralising collapse. After approaching tea at 116 for 2, England had lost their last eight wickets for 89 runs in little more than a session. Worse still, they had collapsed while the devastating off-spin of Roger Harper was enjoying an unbroken spell of 19 overs from the Pavilion End. This was, at least, some sort of variation on the old, old story.

What happened next, however, surprised everyone. In a spell of intelligent, controlled fast-medium bowling that rivalled Dilley's spell at Lord's, Neil Foster reduced West Indies to 57 for 4 in less than eighty minutes. Desmond Haynes was the first to go, Foster finding bounce and movement to find the edge of the opener's pushed drive. Greenidge then was early on a pull and found DeFreitas waiting under the resulting lob to mid-on. Richards was defeated by one that nipped back at him, lifted a little and went from inside edge to thigh pad to Tim Curtis at short leg. Then, after a brief flurry from the ever annoying Logie, Hooper edged a drive at the last ball of an over from which Logie had taken 15 runs and Gooch pouched the catch at first slip.

It must have been a shock to the crowd, basking as they were on perhaps the first really hot day of a sodden, sorry excuse for a summer, expecting no doubt to witness the early end of England's innings followed by a festival of Caribbean strokeplay on one of Harry Brind's fast, true surfaces. There were flashes of it, sure enough; the six that Hooper cannoned over extra-cover for his last scoring stroke was played off the back-foot in a way that could not have been risked on most pitches, or by any English batsman, and the two upright straight drives that Jeffrey Dujon later played in his elegant, high-elbowed way were an equal testimony both to the groundsman's and the batsman's art. With England in charge, and the West Indian fans unusually quiet and becalmed, the Oval had an unexpected air of a bank holiday heatwave at a seaside resort, all melting ice cream and floppy sun hats.

England and West Indian fans alike would have admired the quality of the West Indies fightback after lunch as Logie and Dujon yet again set about reasserting the upper hand. Gus Logie had raced to 32 from 24 balls while Hooper was with him, but now he was content to sit back and let Dujon make the running. Happily for the West Indies, and the watching crowd, Dujon was in the kind of form where every stroke of his bat seemed to have been choreographed by Petipa, the very balance of his form coached by Nureyev. It was not just pretty, it was also effective. Of their partnership of 69, Dujon made 50 before a lapse in concentration persuaded Logie to follow a lifting ball that left him. As Gooch held the catch at slip, Logie threw his head back in despair, knowing what a promising position had just been squandered.

It was Foster again. All five wickets had now fallen to the Essex paceman. His new ball partner, Phil DeFreitas, had been economical enough, but as so often either the length had been a fraction too short to really trouble the batsman, or the line a fraction too wide. Even with their opponents tottering at 126 for 5, it was all too easy for England to wonder what might have been achieved with both Foster and Dilley fit, and in form, in the same match.

Dujon batted on until tea in company with Roger Harper, but when he fell soon after the interval, lbw to a Pringle delivery that came back off the seam, the tourists' innings collapsed in alarming fashion. Malcolm Marshall began by using his pads against John Childs, but when he tried to get off the mark with a single into the leg side he was through the shot too early and the leading edge went straight back to the bowler. Harper had nearly run himself out just before Marshall went, but he was now the victim of a miscommunication with Curtly Ambrose. Harper thick-edged Pringle to third man. He ran the first one hard, then turned and started off for the expected second. By the time he realised Ambrose was going to stick for one and not twist for two, Neil Foster's throw was already skimming back to the bowler's end. The throw went wide of the stumps but was gathered by the alert Capel at mid-on and quickly returned to Pringle, who had time to remove a bail then, worried that he had not put the wicket down correctly, pull out a stump for good measure with Harper still short of his ground.

Winston Benjamin lost his off-stump first ball to a Pringle yorker, and Courtney Walsh lasted just six balls before skying a drive to mid-off where DeFreitas took a good catch on the run. The West Indies were all out for 183 and England had claimed their first first-innings lead against them since Lord's in 1984. Not that this was an especially encouraging precedent. In a remarkable statistical anomaly, all of the West Indies' wickets had fallen to the Essex trio of Foster, Pringle and Childs except, that is, for the run-out, which would have been an entirely Essex affair had it not been for the backing up of Northamptonshire's David Capel. Joined by their skipper, Graham Gooch, it was the first time a quartet of Essex players had played in a single Test for England. Gooch, of course, had played no part in selecting the side.

The crowd's sense of disbelief can only have been enhanced when Gooch and Curtis added 34 to England's lead in the first 6 overs of their second innings. Marshall could do nothing to stop the England captain taking 8 off his first over and even Curtis, who hitherto had begun every innings like an overburdened locomotive on a steep incline, was off the mark quickly, spoiling a hostile first over from Ambrose by hooking him to the fine-leg boundary. Ambrose was removed from the attack after leaking 19 runs from 3 overs, and with Marshall lacking his usual rhythm, and Walsh leaving the field for treatment before having bowled a ball, everything seemed to be going England's way.

It might have been the perfect summer's day for an England fan, but clouds – metaphorically – returned before the close of play. After playing out a maiden from Marshall, Gooch found himself stranded at the non-striker's end while first Curtis, then Bailey, and finally Smith, departed in quick succession. Curtis, having again laid a solid platform in a fifty partnership with Gooch, was trapped on the back foot by a ball from Marshall that came back a vast distance off the seam. Bailey was bowled through the gate by a Benjamin in-swinger and then Smith, inexplicably, shouldered arms to his fourth ball and was lbw. England had lost three wickets for 5 runs in just 5.1 overs. Gooch had faced just nine balls as his partners fell one by one.

Gooch and nightwatchman Neil Foster saw out the last 6 overs before stumps with understandable caution. The next day promised what most people, even England's selectors, had expected from the start: an inexperienced England batting line-up led by a determined Graham Gooch, trying to eke out every last run they could. But England were 86 runs ahead with seven wickets still in hand; it was a position of unexpected strength after two days in which their untested team had more than held their own. If there was one nagging concern that prevented any real confidence in an English victory it was that however much of a lead England could work towards, would their bowling be strong enough to force the win on such a good pitch? Up to now, England had put Richards' men under pressure when inspired by a devastating spell by Foster or Dilley. Without the lead shown by those two, the bowling had never been as penetrative. If Neil Foster could not recapture his inspired form of the first innings, could DeFreitas, Pringle or Childs do the job instead? The whole weight of England's hopes seemed to be borne on the shoulders of the two Essex men who would be walking to the crease together on Saturday morning.

If Friday had been almost the perfect English summer's day, Saturday felt more like a steamy day in Bridgetown with not a hint of a breeze to take the edge off the heat. Little puffs of dust rose from the bowler's footmarks as the crowd sweltered under their sun hats and tried to gobble their ice creams before they melted. It must have been a good day for a bet on how many wickets might fall before your 99 flake melted all over your hands. For the first hour or so there was nothing but joy for England as Gooch and Foster added another 42 to the lead, but this was not the expected case of dogged resistance from Foster while his captain took the lead. In fact it was quite the reverse. Foster dominated the strike from the first 7 overs, with Gooch tapping a couple of singles and retreating to the non-striker's end. For sixty-nine minutes, Gooch then remained on 40, not stranded exactly, but perhaps, on such a day, just happily beached. It was Foster who seized the initiative, crashing five boundaries in an innings of 34 that lifted the spirits of the England camp and made everyone think that, just maybe, a win was possible. When, in a single over from Marshall, he first hooked the great fast bowler to long leg then creamed him through extra cover, it said a lot about the confidence flowing through the whole team.

When Foster fell just after a drinks break, gloving an attempted hook to backward short-leg off Benjamin, England's total had risen to 108 and their lead to 130. With Matthew Maynard striding to the crease to join his captain – in just the sort of situation he might be expected to capitalise upon – England were well placed to force home their advantage. But however great the domination before it, the fall of a wicket was never really the time when opposing batsmen could increase the pressure on the West Indies fast bowlers. Instead, they scented blood in the water and began to dart in like a shoal of barracuda, their jaws gaping at 90 degrees to reveal uncounted rows of razor-sharp teeth.

Maynard's innings was certainly less frenetic than his first, but it was no more fluent. First Ambrose, then Benjamin bounced him and both bowlers kept him pinned on the back foot, with little width through which to swing his arms. His one moment of glory came when he struck Benjamin square through the off-side to bring up his thousandth first-class run of the season, but his celebrations did not last long as the bowler got his next ball to dart back in off the seam and lift awkwardly to strike Maynard a painful blow in the box. His tortured stay at the crease lasted almost half an hour before he played forward and the ball squeezed back off pad and bat to Benjamin, who held the return catch at the second attempt.

Now it really was all down to Gooch. First Capel, then Richards, then Pringle stayed with him as he edged the score forward, but when the England captain at last brought up his fifty with successive fours off Walsh, it had taken him all of 285 minutes. With Jack Richards at the crease, there was a sudden burst of three chances going down in 3 overs. First Harper put down Gooch at slip off Courtney Walsh, then Richards, having played and missed at Ambrose four times in a row, finally got an edge to the next ball only for Harper to spill the catch again. In Walsh's next over, Gooch edged him even finer, but the usually secure Dujon could not hold the catch in his right glove.

The next time Richards edged it, trying to drive Walsh through cover, Dujon made no mistake. Harper then atoned for his errors at slip by claiming the next two wickets; Pringle bowled through the gate and DeFreitas edging a sweep via pad to silly point. That just left another Essex pairing – John Childs and the unmoveable Gooch. In fact Childs proved equally unmoveable, lingering for forty-seven strokeless minutes as his captain added a further 25 with the help of nine more extras. When, at last, Gooch cut Ambrose to Greenidge at deep backward point, his innings of 84 had lasted a total of 422 minutes. He had come to the crease twenty-three hours and fifty-nine minutes earlier. It was a remarkable innings, even prompting Micky Stewart to declare it the best of its kind he had seen – quite a tribute from a man who spent much of his career batting with Ken Barrington. 'It was the hardest I've had to fight for runs for a very long time,' said Gooch. There would be plenty more hard-fought 'captain's innings' from him in the years to come.

The West Indies were left to chase a target of 225. It was by no means a formidable task on such a good pitch, but England could still be quite satisfied with themselves. For the best part of three days they had competed as equals, and at times had even had the better of things, but in the two hours of play remaining before the close the balance of power shifted decisively in the West Indies' favour. Phil DeFreitas began the second over of the innings with a ball that swung away from Desmond Haynes' bat and found the edge. Jack Richards seemed to move towards it, but then pulled away, leaving Gooch at first slip to shoot his left hand out. He just got his fingers to the ball, but could not hold on. As Haynes and Greenidge ran through for a single, Gooch examined his hand and knew that his game was over. 'My finger had split open like a sausage when you put it in the frying pan' he recalled in his autobiography. It was also bent at an angle that suggested dislocation, and he immediately left the field to have it reset in hospital. It would be in a splint for the next three days. As Kent's Neil Taylor entered the field as his substitute, the England team found itself under the direction of its fifth captain of the summer, Derek Pringle.

There was little that any of his four predecessors could have done to arrest the downward momentum of England's summer, but Pringle had no chance at all. Neil Foster could not recapture his first innings rhythm, bowled too short a length and found himself carted for five fours by Gordon Greenidge in his opening five-over spell. Colin Bateman observed that he frequently ended his follow through with both hands on his knees. Perhaps it was fatigue, or perhaps the recurrence of a too-familiar pain. DeFreitas too was ineffectual, and only the introduction of Childs in the eighth over managed to put a brake on the scoring. Childs wheeled away from the Pavilion End until stumps, beating the outside edge of Haynes' bat several times and only conceding 11 runs from his 9 overs. It was easier going at the other end, and by the close West Indies had laid a solid foundation of 71 for no wickets.

It was much the same story the next morning. Childs bowled another 13 overs, from which the world's most well-established opening partnership could only acquire 21 runs. They went into lunch with their stand still unbroken and only one false stroke between them, Childs having found Haynes' edge at last, only for Richards to spill the chance. Greenidge, however, did get out immediately after lunch, Childs bowling over the wicket into the rough, finding some extra lift and turn and the ball looping up off the opener's glove to silly point, where Jack Richards dashed round to take the catch. It was challenging but negative stuff from Childs, and he kept up the tactic against Haynes and Carl Hooper. Haynes simply left his bat out of the equation and padded everything away. Bill Frindall's scoresheets record that in one over from Childs, Haynes was struck on the pad by every single delivery. It was not the sort of response that Carl Hooper would employ; he danced out to his fourth ball from Childs and struck it back over his head for four. He stretched forward to the next ball and lanced it through extra cover, only a diving stop by substitute Neil Kendrick preventing another boundary. There would be one more flash of brilliance from Hooper, another lofted hit off Childs that carried for six this time, before he tried to late-cut Foster and chopped the ball on to his stumps.

The fall of Hooper would be England's final success of the series. They remained sharp in the field, Smith preventing a boundary with a fine stop at mid-off with less than a dozen runs still needed, but Haynes and the inevitable Logie carried on with no further alarms until, at 4.20 p.m., with almost four sessions' playing time remaining, Logie on-drove DeFreitas for a match-winning boundary, pulled a stump out of the ground and raced towards the pavilion, pursued by half the Caribbean population of south London.

The precedent of England's previous first-innings lead against the West Indies had proven to be a clear guide to how the match would turn out. Once again England had worked themselves into a strong position that against most opponents would have made them slight favourites to win, only for the West Indies to race away to a comfortable victory, leaving them gasping in a cloud of dust. As the tourists took the plaudits on the Oval balcony, only the absence of their captain cast any shadow over their jubilation. Viv Richards had missed the last two days with a severe recurrence of his haemorrhoid problem and could only watch the celebrations on television from his hospital bed.

Gordon Greenidge accepted the Wisden Trophy on his captain's behalf. Fred Trueman gave the man of the match award to Jeff Dujon, while the West Indies' man of the series award went to Malcolm Marshall. If that was a straightforward decision, the choice of England's man of the series must have involved less anguish still. Amid the carnage of injuries and axings, only one England player had survived all five Tests – their captain Graham Gooch. Gooch might also have been in line for one further award after his performance at the Oval, but, as Mike Selvey wrote, 'no decision has been reached on the England captain of the series.' In a moment of supreme humiliation, such gallows humour was all English cricket had left.

12

Victory Without Witnesses

Just as Mike Gatting's tenure as England captain had expired with him conveniently out of the side, so had Chris Cowdrey's. However, while Gatting had been banished by allegations of misconduct, Cowdrey's absence had been a matter of pure misfortune. As far as he was concerned, Peter May's assurances about his future as captain for the India tour still held true. Few observers saw the captaincy question through Cowdrey's eyes; those assurances given to Cowdrey were not public knowledge, and the progress of the Oval Test had seen the initial enthusiasm for Cowdrey's leadership at Headingley ebb away as Graham Gooch displayed an unexpected aptitude and enthusiasm for the job. Cowdrey, it was true, had invigorated England in the field at Headingley, but Gooch had done much the same at the Oval with a far less experienced team and Micky Stewart had seen in him a cricketer with a similar attitude to preparation and fitness, and, crucially, he had made runs. 'For so long as his finger heals,' wrote Scyld Berry, 'Gooch can be appointed [as captain] for the next Test against Sri Lanka and the Cowdrey experiment forgotten as a ghastly aberration.'

But Graham Gooch was refusing to add to speculation about the England captaincy. Asked after the end of the series whether he would consider leading the side against Sri Lanka, he said only 'I haven't been asked yet so I can't say anything.' It was still widely thought that Gooch would be reluctant to tour, and unwilling to take on the burden of captaining his country on a long-term basis. If he did take the job, it would need all the selectors' powers of persuasion. Just two weeks would separate the end of the West Indies series from the one-off Test against the much weaker Sri Lankans at Lord's. To pick one captain for the Sri Lanka Test and then a different one again for the India tour would only have added to the sense of shambolic incompetence that now surrounded the selectors, calls for whose heads now jeered from the top of every sports page across the land. If one thing of value could be salvaged from this disastrous summer, it surely had to be the secure, long-term appointment of a new England captain. That new captain would now need to be chosen without delay.

The very fact that Graham Gooch had been named as his replacement for the Oval had left Chris Cowdrey more confident of being reappointed in the job: 'once they picked Gooch, everyone said to me, "well you'll definitely go to India now, because they won't take him – the tour might not happen!"' Following his badly timed foot injury, he was now back to full fitness and in form with the bat. The weekend after the Oval Test ended, Cowdrey travelled to Chesterfield with his Kent team, having still heard nothing from Peter May or Micky Stewart. His foot remained painful, but he managed 5 overs on Saturday as Kent bowled Derbyshire out for 262. Two days later, Cowdrey came to the wicket with Kent well set on 216 for 4 to face Michael Holding and Devon Malcolm on a typically fast Queen's Park pitch. He made 108.

'I played really well,' he recalls, 'I just freed up from being back with Kent I think.' But as he left the field after edging Bruce Roberts to slip, he had a shock in store. 'A Derbyshire member came up to me, I'll never forget it, and said "bad luck mate, you've lost your job." That's when I knew it was all over.' News that Graham Gooch would captain England for the Sri Lanka Test had been released to the media that afternoon. No attempt had been made to contact Chris Cowdrey and let him know the news directly. 'That was poor,' he told me. 'That was as if you were never going to get the job, did you really think you were going to get it?'

Gooch's appointment was, for now, for one Test only, but it was a clear indication that May & Co. saw Gooch, not Cowdrey, as the man to captain the side in India and were confident of securing his agreement. Gooch's initial pronouncements seemed to back this view up. In fact, he appeared to suggest that it was the prospect of captaincy itself that would persuade him to tour again. 'I could be persuaded to tour India this winter' he told the press, 'it's a possibility I have not ruled out. Much depends on talks which are due to take place at Lord's. Being asked to lead your country is a great honour and when that happens you think again, don't you?'

Something of Gooch's state of mind at the time was revealed in an interview with Frank Keating, published in *The Guardian* during the Sri Lanka Test. To Keating, a journalist he had known since his first England tour almost a decade earlier, Gooch spoke candidly about the difficulties of departing on long overseas tours leaving three young daughters, then aged between two and five, at home. He had opted out of the last tour of Australia due to the recent birth of twins Megan and Sally, and was still trying to balance the competing demands of a cricket career at its peak with a young family. He found accusations from some quarters that his recent reluctance to tour revealed a lack of commitment to English cricket deeply offensive: 'at my age, thirty-five, I must be allowed, surely, to make a judgement between developing my career and developing my involvement with the family.' With family naturally being his first priority, any decision to tour again would remain a tricky one, but captaincy itself was less of an issue than it had been, and his experience at the Oval had clearly been a revelatory one.

Gooch had resigned the captaincy of Essex due to its effect on his form with the bat. 'All the little bits and pieces a county captain has to organise and bother about wasn't giving me time to concentrate on what I wanted to do best for the team – like at twenty to eleven I like to be changed, everything ready, padded up, gear on, and just sit there calm and placid and silent.' But captaining England, with Micky Stewart there to do much of the administrative work, was 'much easier.' Gooch had felt a definite pride in leading his country for the first time, but whether that pride would be sufficient for him to sacrifice another winter watching his children growing up still remained to be seen. For now, he had one little bit of administrative work that he could not leave to Micky Stewart – his first selection meeting.

The sense of a new beginning engendered by England's first performance under Gooch's leadership meant that fewer changes were expected for the Sri Lanka Test than for any Test since Old Trafford. Four of the team from the Oval were probably less than satisfied with their performances – David Capel had been restricted to only 12 overs with the ball and although he had got something of a start in each innings with the bat, he had failed to reach 20 on either occasion. Phil DeFreitas had gone wicket-less as Neil Foster's new-ball partner and his flashy first-innings 18 had hardly justified the hope that he would strengthen the batting. Jack Richards had endured an untidy game behind the stumps and again made few runs. Matthew Maynard had seemed overwhelmed by the occasion, but there had been glimpses of great talent, and he surely deserved another crack against the less formidable Sri Lankans.

When the squad was announced, both Peter May and Micky Stewart stressed that it had been picked purely as the best side available to beat Sri Lanka in this one-off Test, but even this drew enfilade fire from the critics. Bill Frindall, taking the view that this should be the basis for all selections, thought 'this suggested that actually picking a side to win a Test represented new, enlightened thinking', while Mike Selvey derided the selectors for yet again embarking on a new direction and noted that a total of thirty-three players had been named in both Test and one-day squads over the course of the summer. This was more than in the equally shambolic summer of 1921 when, in the first Test series since the First World War, England's selectors threw in a total of thirty-one players against Warwick Armstrong's Australians. The summer of 1988 must have been a desperate one for those on the county scene who were ambitious for an England place, but for whom the call did not come. Selvey imagined a forlorn Jonathan Agnew waiting alone on a platform for the Peter May Special to arrive, and offered him a shred of hope: 'Don't worry Aggers, there'll be another train of thought along in a moment.'

Not only did Capel, DeFreitas, Richards and Maynard feel the ever-sharpened blade of Peter May's axe, so did Rob Bailey, John Childs and twelfth man, Gladstone Small. It was hard enough on Small – it always seems a little unfair when a player selected for one match but left out of the XI finds his place taken away without having had the chance to defend it – but Childs had been England's most consistent bowler in the two Tests he played against the West Indies, and Bailey had shown guts and technique in his first Test innings. Bailey made way for Kim Barnett, whom he had originally been called up to replace, and Childs for the return of John Emburey, who had recaptured his wicket-taking form with two six-wicket hauls in recent weeks.

It was understandable that Gooch should want his most experienced spin bowler and closest friend in cricket alongside him at the start of his proper tenure as captain. Just as Emburey had found Gooch an invaluable right hand during his two Tests in charge, so Gooch would surely find the astute, level-headed Emburey a vital source of ideas and support. But it was desperately hard on John Childs, who had come into the team out of the blue and performed very well indeed. Now he would have a nervous wait for the announcement of the squad to tour India before knowing whether his Test career would continue, or whether the experience of Emburey would be balanced by a younger spinner such as Ian Folley or Surrey's Keith Medlycott.

The return of John Emburey to the side was less surprising than that of another experienced campaigner. Tim Robinson had not had a happy summer as captain of Nottinghamshire, but his form with the bat had been good. He had just made an extremely well-timed, match-winning innings of 134 not out against Gooch's Essex, and therefore, in effect, against the better part of England's bowling attack. The inclusion of Robinson meant that England would again have the option of going in with six specialist batsmen, but was this option unnecessarily cautious against the Sri Lankans, when for most of the summer it had been disdained against the West Indies?

Robinson, of course, had made a spectacular beginning to his Test career on David Gower's tour of India four years earlier, and had formed a successful opening partnership with Gooch against the Australians the following summer. But on the West Indies tour in early 1986 he had been all at sea against hostile fast bowling and his Test career had stalled since then. He had not been risked against the West Indies earlier in the season. Although the replacement of Childs by Emburey could be justified not least on the grounds of strengthening the lower order batting, the choice of Robinson suggested that the selectors had at least one eye on the development of a team that could win a series in India and not just a Test match at Lord's. As it turned out, Robinson would become Graham Gooch's fourth opening partner of the summer, Tim Curtis having aggravated a knee injury two days before the match. Robert Bailey was called up as cover again, but despatched back to Northamptonshire when England decided after play the extra bowler after all.

There were three more newcomers to the squad – David Lawrence, Jack Russell and Phil Newport. Lawrence had been heralded as a potential Test fast bowler since he burst onto the scene in 1985, winning the Cricket Writers' Club's Young Cricketer of the Year award. He finally emerged as a front-line fast bowler in 1988, ending the summer with eighty-four first-class wickets at 27.33. This had also been a breakthrough year for Worcestershire's Newport; he ended the season with ninety-three first-class wickets at 19.82, swinging the ball either way from a fuller length than Phil DeFreitas usually bowled. While perhaps not as naturally gifted with the bat as the Leicestershire man, Newport's record suggested greater consistency.

The selection of Jack Russell as wicketkeeper brought with it a collective sigh of relief from cricket lovers across the nation. The selectors' policy of picking wicketkeepers whom they thought had sufficient guts to face Marshall & Co. in front of the wicket had unquestionably backfired. Paul Downton's series batting average of 21 was respectable enough, but Jack Richards' average of 3.25 was not. Neither had convinced behind the stumps. Moreover, their selections had encouraged the selectors to stack the bowling attack with sub-Botham all-rounders whose batting pretentions had been exposed as just that: the batting averages of Pringle, Capel and DeFreitas in the series had ranged from 7.2 to 7.42, and while Pringle had performed well with the ball, Capel and DeFreitas together had claimed four wickets at 83 apiece. At the Oval, Phil DeFreitas, who now boasted a Test bowling average of 46.95 from twelve Tests, had been preferred to Gladstone Small, who had an average of 22.7 from five. Curiously, Small's Test batting average was also superior – 15.25 to DeFreitas' 11.37.

DeFreitas, like Pringle before him, had first emerged as a player with all-round potential, but in neither case had their batting developed sufficiently to make them all-rounders of genuine international class. The selectors, unfortunately, seemed to have the original billing stuck in their heads, a result of the continuing obsession with replacing Ian Botham. Had Botham been available, and at his best, the selectors would not have felt obliged to consider such far-fetched alternatives, but without him they had failed to appreciate an obvious lesson. In the absence of a true all-rounder, as Matthew Engel wrote just before the Sri Lanka Test, 'the selectors should choose the best six batsmen, the best wicketkeeper and the best four bowlers. The inclusion of inferior players on the off-chance that they might do something or other is an absurdity in Test cricket.' It was a view that Scyld Berry had shared even before the first Test of the summer.

At Lord's on 30 August, England finally ended their sequence of eighteen Test matches without a victory – the longest barren run in their Test history. Sri Lanka did not offer much in the way of opposition. The batting remained theoretically strong: Arjuna Ranatunga was growing in maturity, and Amal Silva, the stylish left-hander who had made such a composed century in the equivalent match in 1984, was still there too, but the experienced Ranjan Madugalle and skipper Duleep Mendis, whose spectacular batting four years earlier had provided probably the only genuine excitement of the match, were now past their best, while young Aravinda De Silva was still finding his feet at Test level. Asanka Gurusinha was struggling with a knee injury and two other heroes of 1984, Sidath Wettimuny and Roy Dias, were no longer on the scene.

But it was in the bowling where the real decline since 1984 could be observed. Between wiry, studious leg-spinner D. S. De Silva, whose best years came before his country achieved Test status, and the legendary Muttiah Muralitharan, Sri Lanka struggled to produce any spinner of real Test class. Their spin department in 1988 was led by debutant off-spinner Ranjith Madurasinghe, who would play only two further Tests and claim just three wickets in total at that level. Of the three-man seam attack that had tied England down for long periods in 1984, only the tall Ravi Ratnayeke remained. Despite four first-innings wickets and an overall Test bowling average in the low twenties, Vinothen John was to find that Lord's in 1984 would be his last ever Test – he was discarded at the early age of twenty-four. The senior member of the trio, Ashantha de Mel, had lost his place after an unsuccessful tour of India in 1986/87. It all added up to what Matthew Engel called 'bowling of quite abject mediocrity: four medium-paced trundlers and an off-spinner who turned not a thing.'

The game was effectively over as a contest by lunch on the first day. The Sri Lankan batting was unable to cope with the swing of Newport, the pace of Lawrence or the sheer class of Foster, and had subsided to 69 for 6 in the first session. It might have been worse still had not a nervous Russell put down two chances – one in Lawrence's third over and another off Newport just after lunch. The tourists were bowled out for just 194 with more than an hour's play left on the first day, only a last-wicket partnership of 64 between Ratnayeke and Graeme Labrooy, giving the score a semblance of respectability.

Released from the shackles of facing Marshall and Ambrose, the England batsmen might have been expected to race away against bowling of sub-county standard, but just as in 1984 they seemed to have difficulty in breaking out of the 'survival first' mentality that they had lived with all summer. The momentum was not helped by the arrival of Jack Russell as nightwatchman when Robinson gloved a half-hearted hook at a Ratnayeke bouncer after spending an hour and a quarter in making 19. Reaching stumps at 47 for 1, Russell and Gooch crawled on through the next morning, adding just 72 runs in the session. Gooch took eighty minutes fewer in reaching his half century than he had at the Oval, but at 205 minutes it was sedate progress indeed. After Gooch fell for 75 midway through the afternoon session, first Barnett then Lamb did their best to increase the tempo, but overall it was dull fare for a meagre Lord's crowd huddled together against an early autumn chill.

Although Lamb's 63 was the more positive innings, Barnett's attractive 66 from 127 balls made for an encouraging debut. He was quick to pull or cut anything short and drove superbly off the front foot, ending each stroke looking like Wally Hammond despite having begun it looking like his boots were on fire. At the other end Russell battled his way determinedly through two sessions, confounding the selectors who had, presumably, not chosen him earlier in the summer on account of his suspect batting. He fell to the new ball shortly after tea, just six short of a century on Test debut. Battling your way to a 202-ball 94 against Ratnayeke, Labrooy and Madurasinghe does not, of course, guarantee similar performances against the likes of Malcolm Marshall, but it indicated at least a potential with the bat that had not, prior to this, been acknowledged. 'It was an innings of great concentration and intent, with some well-struck shots,' wrote Matthew Engel. 'He may not come so close to a Test hundred for many years' thought Christopher Martin-Jenkins. In fact, Russell's maiden Test hundred would come less than a year later, his unbeaten 128 at Old Trafford being one of the few moments of defiance in a summer of sorry surrender to Allan Border's Australians.

England were eventually bowled out for 429 just after three o'clock on day three, having toiled for more than five sessions against the weakest attack in Test cricket. Taking encouragement from this, Sri Lanka put up more resistance in their second innings, setting off at a great pace with Kuruppu and Silva thumping five boundaries from Newport's first 2 overs. Debutant Athula Samarasekera continued the assault, twice hooking Foster to the boundary and once over it in the space of four balls. It was much more stirring fare for the spectators, and brought back happy memories of 1984 for a few sessions before the tourists were finally bowled out for 331 just before the close of day four.

A target of 97 with a day and a bit to spare was never going to challenge England, but they at least showed more urgency about chasing the runs down. Gooch and Robinson knocked off the first 73 in ninety-six minutes and had it not been for the quick loss of Barnett and Lamb – Barnett showing that fallibility outside off-stump that the Australians would exploit the following summer – the match might have been won before lunch. As it was, lunch was taken at one o'clock on the dot, with England still one run short of victory. Few would witness the end of England's long, barren sequence of winless Tests. The crowd, sparse throughout the match, barely numbered four figures and the TV audience was denied a sight of the winning hit when it came at 1.41 p.m. because BBC One was still enjoying its daily dose of *Neighbours*. The Australian producers of that programme would no doubt have been delighted to add in some small way to England's year of humiliation. It was a fitting end to a shambolic summer of Test cricket.

13

Misjudgement and Insensitivity

There was one more ritual to go through before the curtain came down on the English season – England winning a one-day international at the Oval by the comfortable margin of five wickets. The match saw more fine runs from Barnett and Lamb, while the clean, straight hitting of Rob Bailey that saw England to victory 'could not', thought Christopher Martin-Jenkins, 'have been bettered by anyone from Jessop to Botham.' But perhaps this one-off match was most notable for one last statistic – the inclusion of Somerset off-spinner Vic Marks bringing to thirty-four the number of players chosen in various England squads that summer. Thirty-one of them made it onto the field, the exceptions being Eddie Hemmings, Nick Cook and Greg Thomas. It was a good week for Vic Marks. The day after he heard of his selection for England he learned of a reward that would bring a less transient pleasure than his final international appearance. He had been appointed Somerset captain in place of Peter Roebuck. This was, perhaps, the only time that season that a professional cricketer felt only unalloyed joy at being appointed captain of his team.

As soon as he was appointed to captain England against Sri Lanka there could be no doubt that Graham Gooch would be invited to lead the England team to India. 'Sure enough,' recalled Gooch in his autobiography, 'before the end of the Test at Lord's against Sri Lanka, May asked me if I was prepared to go to India as captain. Naturally I said "Yes."' Gooch was still, at this point, under contract to Western Province, and he contacted them and asked to be released from it. 'I owed them that much out of a sense of decency. They were good about it and agreed to allow the contract to lapse.'

They say a week is a long time in politics; the same could often be said of English cricket too. The dizzying speed at which Chris Cowdrey had found himself turned from sprightly new incumbent to dejected discard must have left him feeling as though he had somehow blinked and missed his own captaincy. 'I felt sorry for him,' wrote Gooch later. 'He was pretty upset about it and said so. I don't blame him.' Within hours of learning that his dream of leading England on tour had turned to dust, Chris Cowdrey found himself confronted by *The Sun's* Ian Todd.

'I got collared,' remembers Cowdrey, 'and really because I hadn't heard much from Micky Stewart.' Much of what Cowdrey told Todd of his disappointment would probably hold true today. At the heart of it was the fact that neither Stewart nor May had taken the trouble to tell him either that he was no longer under consideration for the captaincy or why they had changed their minds about his suitability for the job. 'I am deeply hurt because no one has had the courtesy to tell me where I went wrong,' he told Todd. He recalled an encounter with Stewart at Bristol where the England manager was watching Kent play Gloucestershire a few days before the selection of the team to play Sri Lanka: 'we even had a chat, but we talked about everyone and everything except my own position.' It must have been one of those peculiarly English conversations in which both parties talk about anything except the one thing uppermost in their minds.

There was little in the article that an impartial judge would take exception to. Had a little more time elapsed since his rejection, Cowdrey might not have felt the impulse to say 'if that's the way they treat players like Phil DeFreitas, David Capel, Chris Broad and the others who come and go in the England team, no wonder we're doing badly and team spirit is so low', but it was an understandable sentiment at the time. That was about as outspoken as Cowdrey got in speaking to Todd. This being *The Sun*, of course, the headline 'ENGLAND KICKED ME IN THE TEETH' was not a quote from Cowdrey at all. The banner above it – 'EX-TEST SKIPPER'S AMAZING BLAST AT THE MEN WHO SNUBBED HIM' was not exactly designed to promote a healing process either.

Like so many others who have been 'collared' at vulnerable moments by unanticipated journalists, Cowdrey had to take the consequences on the chin. He received a caution from the Kent Committee and found himself the subject of a TCCB inquiry, rather than the recipient of its most prestigious job. The most bitter disappointment of all would come on the field itself. At the end of the summer, Kent missed out on the Championship title, pipped to it by Worcestershire by the margin of a single point.

> Two things happened to prevent us winning the Championship. Firstly Alan Igglesden, who was a great bowler for us, got injured and missed a key part of the season, and the other was me being appointed England captain. It wasn't because we didn't have a good replacement, because we had the best in Chris Tavaré, and it wasn't because I was making huge runs, but it was the whole momentum that we'd built up.

He remains remarkably sanguine about the experience, and although he did once tell Micky Stewart of his disappointment at the lack of communication he never sought any further explanation from the men responsible for his brief tenure at the pinnacle of English cricket: 'I shook hands with Micky. Micky is a friend of mine, he was a friend in the game. We'd been through all that really and nothing needed to be said.' The same was true of Peter May: 'I went to a lunch with him some years later. Lovely, lovely bloke. I don't think anything needed to be said with us two, funnily enough. It was all there, didn't get any runs, lost the game, got injured and I wasn't reselected!'

For Chris Cowdrey's successor as captain – Graham Gooch – the immediate future looked rosy, but he had failed to spot the clouds on the horizon. 'There was no indication at that time that the Indian authorities would raise any objection to the selection of any players in the party who had links with South Africa.' So wrote Gooch in his autobiography, but for those with an eye for the politics of cricket, the signs of trouble had been apparent for more than twelve months already.

In the summer of 1987, the West Indies Cricket Board had put forward a proposal to ICC that any professional cricketer who played or coached in apartheid-ruled South Africa should be banned for life from international cricket. The West Indies had introduced such a policy for their own cricketers on a unilateral basis and so those who, like Collis King, Colin Croft and Franklyn Stephenson, had toured South Africa with a 'rebel' team were now banned, not just from playing for the West Indies but from all domestic competition in the Caribbean too. Fearful of the effect such a move might have on the World Cup later that year, ICC had deferred any action until its annual meeting in July 1988, once a report on the issue had been compiled by a select committee.

By October 1987, a compromise brokered by Australia seemed to be gaining ground. The idea was that, rather than an outright ban, any host nation would have the right to refuse entry to any player on a touring side whom they considered unsuitable. In effect, the proposal gave each country carte blanche to act in exactly the same way that Vorster's South African government had done when confronted with the prospect of an MCC team including Basil D'Oliveira in 1968. The TCCB's attitude remained exactly what MCC's had been then – that it would not tolerate interference in team selection. It was also thought that neither the West Indies nor India would favour this solution.

When the ICC select committee met in Calcutta in November 1987, its members did agree a resolution. They then refused to tell the outside world what it was. ICC secretary Lt-Col. John Stephenson told a disbelieving press, 'The committee have come up with a recommendation which will be put to the full ICC annual meeting at Lord's in the first week of July 1988. I have been told not to say what the recommendation is and the committee have agreed not to discuss it. There will be no further meeting of the select committee.'

Whatever the resolution was, it was likely to affect the TCCB more than any other national board. During the winter of 1987/88, an estimated eighty English cricket professionals were engaged in either playing or coaching in South Africa. With the largest professional base in the cricketing world, and a tradition of contracts running from pre-season training in March through to the end of the season in September, England had for around a century produced professional cricketers who needed either an alternative trade or an alternative location for around six months of the year. South Africa had always been amongst the most popular destinations for those choosing to winter overseas. If the West Indian option of an outright ban had found favour, any of them with international ambitions would be looking for different employment next winter. But with those few people who knew what the ICC resolution was not prepared to say, it might be July before they would know whether their usual form of income post-September would still be open to them.

If the sporting world was seeking a united front in its boycott of sporting links with South Africa, all it got was further confusion when, in March 1988, the International Rugby Board lifted its ban on individuals playing in South Africa. The IRB had rejected a proposal that the British Lions should tour the country in 1989, but in allowing individuals to tour it had left open the option of them clubbing together to make up private touring teams. Almost immediately, plans were generated for a two-Test series between the Springboks and a World XV sometime in the middle of 1988. Just a few days before the IRB's move, the anti-apartheid Supreme Council of Sport in South Africa threatened a major boycott of the Seoul Olympics if Great Britain selected the South African-born runner Zola Budd in its team. Budd was also compelled to withdraw from the World Cross-Country Championships in New Zealand at the end of March. Confronted with such mixed messages from sport's administrators, it was hardly surprising when in April the Cricketers' Association objected to what they felt to be a restraint of trade and reaffirmed their members' rights to play or coach wherever they wanted by a margin of eighty-five to nought.

By the day of the ICC annual meeting on 7 July it became apparent that as well as the West Indian and Australian proposals – the latter of which included the clause that unacceptable players shall be replaced if requested – the delegates would be debating a third option, which replaced in the Australian proposal the word 'shall' with the rather more British 'may.' It was apparent that the highly confidential resolution made in Calcutta had been a resolution against having any resolution. At the end of the meeting it then appeared that ICC had made the decision not to make any decisions. 'It all went very well,' said Lt-Col. Stephenson. 'There was a good debate, views were clearly expressed and we even made some decisions.' But on the question of South Africa, the decision had been that no decision could be made on any of the proposals in their current form. Amended proposals would be put to a special meeting at Lord's on 23 January 1989.

Following the ICC's failure to take immediate action it seemed that, for the time being at least, everything was set fair for individual cricketers to retain their links with South Africa. Although no binding international agreement had been made, there remained the possibility of unilateral action by the more hard-line states, such as India. When, in August, rumours arose of a possible single-wicket competition in South Africa that autumn, featuring several prominent English players, David Gower ruled himself out of any involvement. 'I know of this tournament,' he said, 'but there is no danger of my taking part in it. I want to go to India this winter and there is no way I'd want to make waves by going to South Africa beforehand.'

The South African connections of some of England's top cricketers had found them a place on a blacklist produced by the United Nations Centre Against Apartheid. Although several players on that list, including Gooch and Emburey, had visited India and Pakistan for the World Cup just a few months earlier, 'an ordinary player in a huge competition is not the same as a visiting captain whose South African connections are almost morning fresh,' Matthew Engel wrote in *The Guardian*. When the Indian Minister for Sport, Margaret Alza, was asked whether her country intended to exclude any blacklisted cricketers on the England tour her answer was equivocal: 'until we see the list of England's players we cannot comment.' There was a strong possibility that when they did see the list, they would have several problems with it.

While the TCCB maintained its policy of not taking political issues into consideration when selecting players – it had, after all, taken over responsibility for England tours from MCC in the immediate aftermath of the D'Oliveira affair – it was powerless to prevent other boards taking an entirely different attitude. England's chaotic selection policy had caused sufficient problems on the field already this year, but now it was to have repercussions far beyond the boundary rope. Since ICC's failure to agree a resolution in July, England had appointed the blacklisted Gooch as captain, and while the similarly blacklisted Graham Dilley and Allan Lamb had been regulars when fit throughout the summer, the final two Tests had seen call ups for five more players on the UN blacklist – John Emburey, Tim Robinson, Kim Barnett, Robert Bailey and Phil Newport. To an Indian board said to be co-sponsoring one of the ICC proposals, a squad including all of those players might have looked like a deliberate act of provocation.

At the end of August, the President of the Board of Control for Cricket in India, Sunil Sririman, gave another hint that the tour was in jeopardy. 'Graham Gooch being appointed as the captain will pose some problems to the Indian board,' he told the UK media. 'The policy of the Indian board cannot be different from that of the Indian government. I shall be approaching the government when I receive the relevant communication from England.' In response, A. C. Smith said that India should wait until the ICC meeting in January before taking any action of its own. He would be 'surprised and disappointed' if the Indian government objected to Gooch.

While some Indian officials, such as NKP Salve, coordinator for the previous year's World Cup, suggested that Gooch having been permitted to play in India just a few months before might mean that he would be acceptable this time as well, the atmosphere at higher political levels soon began to make this seem unlikely. Prime Minister Rajiv Gandhi was known for his strong stance on apartheid and his Congress Party colleague Anand Sharma, chairman of World Youth Action Against Apartheid, was threatening to organise a public boycott of the tour if it went ahead under Gooch's captaincy. The situation was further complicated by the meeting of the Commonwealth Games Federation on 15 September, which was due to decide which city would host the 1994 games. With New Delhi having submitted one of the more likely bids, it was thought that if India were to accept an England team led by Gooch it might lead to several African states withdrawing their support for the New Delhi bid.

When the England touring squad was finally announced on 7 September it contained not only Gooch, but also Emburey, Dilley, Lamb, Bailey, Barnett, Newport and Robinson. No fewer than eight of the sixteen-man party were on the UN blacklist for playing or coaching in South Africa. Rajiv Ghandi called the selection an affront to the Indian people, and Margaret Alva said that it indicated that England did not want to play in India at all. Former Indian captains Bishan Bedi and Mansur Ali Khan Pataudi joined in the condemnation. For *The Guardian* leader writer it was 'the crowning crassness in a record packed with misjudgement and insensitivity.'

For some years now many people in cricket had been pointing to the efforts made to create a degree of integrated, multiracial cricket in South Africa, hoping that efforts made on the cricket field itself might lead to a normalisation of sporting relations with the outcast republic. Dr Ali Bacher, executive director of the South African Cricket Union, claimed in July 1988 that the input of English cricketers was vital in promoting this 'cricket revolution' that had brought cricket to 50,000 children in the country's deprived black townships. Bacher, rather hopefully, appealed to international cricket to support his scheme on the grounds that it was helping to undermine the apartheid system. But the politics of South Africa went far beyond what any cricket administrator could influence, and on the very day when the Indian government sat down to decide its policy toward the England tour, the world watched in despair as South African police broke up a church service being held by Archbishop Desmond Tutu.

On 9 September, the Indian Foreign Ministry issued its statement: 'We must make abundantly clear that we would not permit entry into India, for the purposes of the tour, to any player having, or likely to have, sporting contact with South Africa.' Half of the England team would not be issued with the visas they required to enter India. There was no way the tour could go ahead. The TCCB realised at once there would be no point trying to fight the decision. 'I don't see much realistic hope of the tour taking place' A. C. Smith told the press. 'Decisions on the acceptability of players are ultimately not the ICC's to make. Visas are issued by governments.'

For some figures in English politics, the cancellation of the tour would be welcomed. Conservative MP Timothy Janman congratulated the TCCB for not giving in to Indian pressure to replace half the team and suggested that England might tour South Africa instead 'in order to show that, on purely sporting grounds, we play against whichever countries we like.' Such a move would, however, have risked isolating England within the ICC. Had the TCCB sought, unilaterally, to bring South African cricket back into the fold it could not rely upon the support of Australia or New Zealand for a measure of such dubious morality, while any reciprocal tour of the UK by South Africa itself would surely have provoked the highest possible levels of disruption from the anti-apartheid movement. There were implications too for the players themselves. Should any of the England players now seeking alternative engagement for the winter choose to head for Cape Town or Durban, the England selectors would inevitably need to consider the consequences of selecting them for any future tour.

The TCCB decided to head off this particular threat by asking the players to sign their winter contracts anyway. If no alternative tour could be arranged, this would mean that they would pocket their £12,000 touring fee for nothing, but at least it would preclude them from entering into any other contractual arrangement with South Africa. On 11 September, although the board had yet to officially announce the cancellation of the India tour, A. C. Smith did leave the door ajar for an alternative: 'we will explore all possibilities' he said. 'I can't see any way out of it, but we will be kicking it around for a few days.'

But if the England party as selected was not acceptable to India, to whom would it be acceptable? Not to Pakistan, surely, although six players with South African links had toured there with England the previous winter. Nor to the West Indies, who had taken the strongest possible line against South Africa and had cancelled a Test match in 1981 when Guyana would not admit Robin Jackman with the England team. The probability was that only the 'white' nations of Australia and New Zealand would not object to the composition of the squad, and Australia had already ruled out the possibility of hosting England, ACB chief executive David Richards saying 'it is fair comment to say we could not fit England in. We have so much cricket.' New Zealand too already had Pakistan booked in for a three-Test tour from January to March and it was rumoured that they themselves would be filling in the vacancy left by England in India.

Any hope the TCCB had of arranging a replacement tour would rely upon swift action, but no such action could take place until the tour of India was formally abandoned. By the final week of September, this was still yet to happen. Amid suggestions that the TCCB might seek financial compensation for cancellation of the tour, neither board had yet taken the step of calling the whole thing off. At last, on the evening of 26 September, a telegram arrived at Lord's from the BCCI, announcing that it supported the stance of the Indian government in objecting to the inclusion in the team of eight players with South African connections. The TCCB considered this the next day, but still decided not to call the tour off, instead asking the BCCI to resolve the situation one way or the other by midday the following Monday 3 October. An official statement declared that unless the BCCI were able to resolve the visa issue 'we must deem that they have withdrawn the invitation to tour.' If India were seen to have cancelled the tour themselves, then this might leave open the possibility of a claim for compensation by the TCCB. The board could not, at this stage, seriously have expected India to back down.

Not only were the Indians not going to back down, they were not going to fall into the TCCB trap quite so easily either. The 3 October deadline was conspicuously ignored by the BCCI. The next day, BCCI secretary Ranbir Singh stated that 'it is up to the TCCB to cancel the tour or not.' It was beginning to look as though the issue would not be resolved until the England party turned up at Heathrow and found themselves unable to board the plane.

At the end of that week, on Friday 7 October, common sense at last prevailed and the TCCB abandoned the tour themselves. Exactly two months later the New Zealand Cricket Council announced that it had agreed with the TCCB an itinerary for a two-Test tour from 20 February to 3 April, despite the opposition of the New Zealand government and the likelihood of disruption from the organisation HART (Halt all Racist Tours), which had similarly objected to the South African rugby tour of New Zealand in 1981. Their disruption plans involved hurling numerous cricket balls onto the pitch and distracting the batsmen with mirrors. HART's spokesman, Dick Cuthbert, suggested that the group would drop its objections if the blacklisted players each signed a declaration that they would not go back to South Africa, but this idea, which had also been mooted as a solution to the impasse with India, ran into the obstacle of the unanimous Cricketers' Association vote in April, which condemned any restriction on sporting links with South Africa as a restraint of trade.

The very idea of the tour had a mixed reception. For many cricket writers the relentless treadmill of international cricket – on which they too were trapped – had left all involved in much need of a few months' break, and memories were still too fresh of the three dull draws Mike Gatting's team had played out a year earlier. But it would not be the overloaded international cricket calendar that would put paid to England's hopes of arranging an alternative tour that winter. That duty would fall, once again, to politics.

Although the New Zealand government had no intention of taking such as strict line as India and barring blacklisted players from entering the country, it was acutely aware of the embarrassment it would suffer on the international stage if such a tour went ahead. Just as India had been sensitive to the implications for its bid to stage the 1994 Commonwealth Games, the New Zealand city of Christchurch was scheduled to host the 1990 Games. If admitting an England side with a blacklisted captain and seven other players had caused the Indians to fear losing African and Caribbean votes for its bid, New Zealand now considered the possibility of a boycott and the absence from the games of countries such as Jamaica, Kenya and India itself. With the 1986 Edinburgh Games having proved a financial disaster, anything less than a full complement of teams would threaten Christchurch with a similar bill. Accepting the England tour, said New Zealand's Minister of

Foreign Affairs, Russell Marshall, would not 'be viewed kindly by some other countries.'

This view was swiftly endorsed by the South African Non-Racial Olympic Committee, whose spokesman Sam Ramsamy declared that in accepting the tour, New Zealand was 'disregarding India's anti-apartheid stand.' More condemnation came the following day when twenty-six members of the Commonwealth Games Federation called on the New Zealand Cricket Council to 'reconsider its decision to invite the English team.' Worse followed one week later, when Pakistan, who were scheduled to take part in a three-way tournament of one-day internationals with New Zealand and England as part of the tour, officially withdrew. 'Playing against such a team is contrary to the Pakistani stand in various international forums' said Arif Abbasi, secretary of the BCCP. Such a statement left open the possibility that even touring teams visiting England would refuse to play against any team containing blacklisted players.

By now, even the TCCB was beginning to realise that their hopes of arranging a tour were going to fail. 'There must be some doubt about the tour,' conceded A. C. Smith. 'If it is not possible to stick to the original programme... then it simply may not be viable.' Discussions continued for the next week, but at last, three days before Christmas, the New Zealanders finally brought down the curtain on a disastrous year for English cricket. 'We were simply not prepared to take the financial risk of having a second tour without the novel element of the triangular tournament to maintain public enthusiasm through a greater than usual programme' said New Zealand Cricket Council chairman Barry Paterson.

None of the TCCB's officials would have felt much sorrow as they bade farewell to 1988 in the company of their families over Christmas and New Year. But if they looked forward with confidence to happier times ahead they were to be sorely disappointed. Several more years of chaos and failure lay in store, and 1989 would be among the very worst of them.

14

Like a Soldier to the Stage

If the prospect of a cricket-free winter was a disappointment for the TCCB, so it was also for the players. For many it was simply an unwelcome hiatus, but for Essex's John Childs it meant a premature end to an international career that had barely begun. Instead of utilising skills and experience developed over two decades in county cricket on the spin-friendly pitches of the subcontinent, Childs spent the winter selling advertising boards and marquees for one of Essex's sponsors. His colleagues too found a variety of ways to pass the empty months before the 1989 season. Derek Pringle worked for a survey company in Cambridge, Kim Barnett found a job in the commercial department of one of Derbyshire's sponsors, Jack Russell continued to develop his skills as an artist. David Lawrence, having turned down the offer of a season in Perth grade cricket to make himself available for the England tour, found himself unemployed. As individuals they all shared a missed opportunity to cement their places in the team and look forward to an Ashes series in 1989 as the men in possession; collectively they were denied a chance to forge themselves into a team that might begin to repair the damaged pride of English cricket and take on the Australians with some positive momentum behind it. Instead, the chance of a new beginning under Graham Gooch had been lost. The series of matches he had been appointed for would not now take place, so the England team found itself once again without a captain. The team, in truth, was not a team at all, since nobody knew whether any of those chosen for the abandoned tour would be picked to face Australia in six months' time. Would the experience of Gatting and Broad see them return to the ranks or would young talents like Maynard and Bailey get their chance again? It was impossible to predict, not least because by the end of 1988 it was no longer clear who would be picking the England team.

Let four captains bear Hamlet, like a soldier to the stage.

Where Fortinbras called for four captains to bear away the body of the tragic Prince of Denmark, no such grave duty fell to Mike Gatting, John Emburey, Chris Cowdrey and Graham Gooch. But England's summer of four captains left Peter May's credibility as Chairman of Selectors fatally undermined, and it came as no surprise when, after seven years in the job, May stepped down on 25 November. What was widely reported as his resignation was, he insisted in an interview with Christopher Martin-Jenkins for *The Cricketer* in February 1989, in fact a retirement, based on a desire to focus on his final year with City of London insurers Willis Wrightson. 'He has done the job conscientiously and steadfastly,' said A. C. Smith, 'but whoever is chairman is exposed to brickbats when things are not going well.' Things had gone so not well that England had won only six of its eighteen Test series under May's stewardship, not all of which had been against sides as powerful as the West Indies.

Throughout his life in cricket, May was known to loathe media attention more than most of his contemporaries. It was thought to have played a serious part in his premature retirement as a player, and the increasing focus on his own position during 1988 cannot have gone down well with this most private man. He revealed his sensitivity to criticism in his *Cricketer* interview with Christopher Martin-Jenkins; 'I told Bobby Robson over a game of golf the other day that he's lucky. He only gets stick for ninety minutes and for a day or two either side. We get it for five days, before and after, and Sundays as well for good measure!' What Robson said in retort was not recorded, what Graham Taylor might have said can surely be imagined.

May was a fundamentally decent and well-meaning man, but his lack of social skills, his inability to communicate with people outside his immediate circle, left him singularly ill-equipped to deal with the public relations aspect of any prominent position in cricket. Indeed, May found the requirement for constant dealings with the media a baffling and unnecessary part of the modern game. 'I think we give too many interviews,' he told *The Cricketer*. 'It's not fair on the captain to have to explain this and that every day. The writers see every ball so why can't they make their own minds up?' It was a view Mike Gatting had shared at the beginning of 1988. As well as leaving him a sitting target for the press, May's stiff manner also made him a difficult character for the players he selected to understand. 'I never got to know him very well,' recalled Graham Gooch in his autobiography, 'nor, I think, did most of the other players. We felt that he was a little remote, but that, I imagine, was the result of his shyness.' It might have been written by any of the four captains he selected that summer.

As Peter May left office, he could have been forgiven for ducking to avoid a final volley of brickbats heading his way. They ranged from the simply dismissive – *The Sun's* 'Mr Flop' – to the more analytical, such as Matthew Engel's look at his seven years in charge in *Wisden Cricket Monthly*. May had been, according to Engel, 'a very bad chairman, not merely unsuccessful, but bad.' The key to his failure had been the inconsistent thinking behind his choices, the multiple trains of thought identified by Mike Selvey: 'it was hard to discern what Peter May was actually for. Selectors can have all sorts of guiding principles: Pick the players in form! Ignore averages and back class! Go for the youngsters! You can't beat experience! Give the captain the team he wants! Perhaps the best principle of all is the simple, uncompromising one: That bloke can play – I want him in! Which of these theories did Peter May support? After seven years I have not got a clue and I rather fear that the man himself never discovered either.'

Pick the players in form? Richards and Athey at Headingley. Back class? Gower and Lamb at Trent Bridge. You can't beat experience? Pringle and Downton at Trent Bridge. Go for the youngsters? Bailey, Maynard, Russell and others. That bloke can play? Robin Smith. There were examples of May subscribing to each of these theories in 1988 alone. For Scyld Berry, this had not been a summer of applied theory, but of mismanagement of resources in which the selectors had 'stumbled from match to match.' John Emburey remembers one of May's methods: 'I turned up for my first selection meeting, and the *Daily Telegraph* was open at the cricket averages, and the Chairman of Selectors was going down the page with his finger looking at the batsmen and what their batting averages were. I just found that strange. We'd go through all this pre-amble of seeing what people's averages were, and talking about players who might have been doing well over the early part of the season, but their averages had come right down and now they were not in any sort of form.'

A better communicator than May might have developed more formal links with coaches, umpires or senior players around the county circuit. But that was not May's way. 'I have yet to meet a manager, coach or captain who has received so much as a single phone call from the wintery faced mandarin, Mr May,' wrote *The Guardian's* Frank Keating. Instead, May relied perhaps too heavily on his co-selectors Sharpe and Titmus, and on the newspapers.

Resignation or retirement, the departure of Peter May meant that at least one of the factors cited as having helped to cause England's shambolic summer could not be cited in future. While the TCCB was engaged in futile negotiations with India and New Zealand, the cricket press in the UK had been indulging in an equally frantic debate about what had gone wrong with English cricket and what could now be done about it. Peter May himself had called for an improvement in the state of pitches in the County Championship, for a programme of sixteen four-day matches and for just one overseas player to be registered per county. In September's edition of *The Cricketer*, Christopher Martin-Jenkins called for the TCCB to spend more time focusing on improving cricket and less on its marketing. He suggested the Cricket Committee, under Chairman Ossie Wheatley, should have genuine executive powers.

The Cricketer devoted much of its October issue to a debate on 'the way ahead' for English cricket. Much of the debate centred on pitches, with the weight of opinion being in favour of less 'sporty' surfaces that did not offer easy wickets to mediocre bowling or shatter the confidence of promising young batsmen. It was a point that had also been made in an editorial for *Wisden Cricket Monthly* in September. 'The root cause of the English anaemia is poor-quality pitches,' wrote David Frith, 'many counties deliberately prepare substandard pitches upon which there will be no draws, only results ... but this kind of cricket breeds only bowlers who rely on grass and cracks and uneven bounce, and batsmen who have uncertainty built into their systems.' In an interesting contribution to *The Cricketer*, Chris Cowdrey compared the game in 1988 with that he had first experienced in the 1970s, and warned that there was a trade-off between pitches that developed patience and technique, and the excitement offered to spectators by the unpredictable surfaces and balls with pronounced seams of the current day. While in his younger days long hours of spin with the old ball as spectators dozed off their lunches in the sun had been the norm, 'county cricket is great fun nowadays', he observed. The fun would continue through another seamer's summer in 1989, until in 1990 flatter pitches and less pronounced seams led to an orgy of run-scoring at both county and Test level.

There were other points too. The experiment with four-day cricket earlier that season had encouraged many to think it worth persevering with, but it was also suggested that there should be a regional competition to concentrate the best talent in just four top-class teams and whittle down the number of players from whom England would select their Test XI. The structure and organisation of the TCCB was also analysed, while the presence of overseas players, the effects of too much one-day cricket and the very nature of a selection committee had been topics for debate across the media all year. Perhaps the most concise opinion on selection methods came from Peter May himself: 'I don't think it honestly matters what system there is. If the players are good enough, they will pick themselves.' Perhaps England's problem in 1988 had simply been that there were too many players who were good enough.

Through the seventies, eighties and nineties, English cricket, riddled as it was by dodgy pitches, overseas players, too much one-day cricket and all its other manifold problems, continued to produce good players. England began the summer of 1988 with a batting order that included Gooch, Gower, Gatting, Lamb and Broad; subject to fitness it could have selected bowlers from Dilley, Foster, Jarvis, Agnew, Small, and Emburey. When Emburey's form dipped, John Childs came in and won universal praise for his skill with the ball. This was not an era devoid of talent, nor even, in an individual sense, of achievement. At the same time, in county cricket a new generation was beginning to emerge that would include the likes of Michael Atherton, Alec Stewart, Graham Thorpe, Robin Smith, Graeme Hick, Mark Ramprakash, John Crawley and Nasser Hussain. Angus Fraser began to make his mark in 1988, so too did Martin Bicknell and they would soon be followed by Darren Gough, Andy Caddick and Phil Tufnell. But despite continuing to produce talented players, England remained a nation whose cricket team added up to less than the sum of its parts. And the reason for its failure would remain the same too.

The end of season soul searching in the cricket press made for fascinating reading then, as it does now. But well conceived as many of the opinions were, the whole debate seemed to be missing an essential fact. England had begun the summer by avoiding defeat against the best team in the world. Their record of not winning any Tests for over a year had always indicated that their bowling would struggle to force victory against the West Indies, but the batting had shown itself to be strong enough to resist them, as it had against Pakistan, Australia and New Zealand in previous months. Even observers from the West Indies had thought at the outset that, in Gooch, Broad, Gatting, Gower and Lamb, England had a top five to rival any in the world. But, one by one, England had let them fall by the wayside until only the indefatigable Gooch remained. The England batsmen who took the field at Trent Bridge had a total of forty-three Test centuries between them, the ones who took the field at The Oval shared just eight. Remove Graham Gooch from the equation and they had none.

First Gatting had gone, fatally wounded by the Shakoor Rana affair and at last finished off by a tabloid scandal. Then Broad, rightly warned about his conduct after a winter of indiscretions, but then sidelined for expressing disappointment to himself when a camera happened to be pointing in his direction. In the six Test matches before he was dropped, Broad had averaged 46 runs per innings. The loss of Allan Lamb to injury was pure bad luck, but when Peter May first suggested that David Gower be dropped, after Old Trafford he had just made 34 of his team's second innings total of 93 – more than double the number of runs made by any of his colleagues. This followed decent knocks at Trent Bridge and Lord's. It has often been the way with England selectors that, faced with an embarrassing rout, they choose for their scapegoat the most talented of their batsmen. Those of whom expectation is the highest frequently cause the most bitter disenchantment when they fail to live up to it. To axe Gower for Headingley would have been rash; to axe him after Headingley, when injury had deprived England of their only other experienced middle order batsman, was an act of desperate folly. So it was that Graham Gooch stood on the burning deck, alone but for the most raw and untested of recruits.

Would it all have happened if the TCCB had not allowed itself to be browbeaten into declaring that selection would be based on behaviour as well as performance and thereby thrown a red rag to the red-top bulls? Would it have happened if they had either sacked Mike Gatting after the Shakoor Rana affair or, having once stuck with him, treated the tabloid controversy after Trent Bridge with the contempt it deserved? In the search for a catalyst for all the events of 1988, it is hard to see beyond these points. But that poor decisions, sometimes just too many decisions, continued to be made also cannot be denied. John Emburey recalls how, at the team dinner before each Test match Peter May would address the team, telling them that they were the best team, the best players in the country, the best suited to the job at hand. 'It was fine at Trent Bridge, but by the end of the summer we'd used so many players it didn't really lend any credence to the idea of us having the best eleven players. To me, the best eleven players were in that first Test match. Given that everyone was fit, they should have played the majority of games.'

The culpability of Peter May and his committee for the shambolic selections of 1988 cannot be ignored – its effect would be long lasting. In their defence, it should be remembered that May's committee was not alone in its continual search for the right combination of eleven players for that elusive magic formula that might allow England to compete with the West Indies on level terms. For most of the summer of 1988 the selectors were criticised more for the quality of their decisions than their quantity, only at the very end when the number of players chosen became a statistic of record did the focus switch. Had the responsibility for selecting the team lain not with May, Sharpe and Titmus but with Berry, Engel, Selvey, Deeley, Martin-Jenkins, Frindall or Frith, or even one of the many groups compiling their Test elevens in the dressing rooms of county cricket grounds, in the bar of the Red Lion or the dining rooms of the Oval, would the story have been any different? It probably comes down to whether, at the beginning of it all, they had been placed under the *force majeure* of the TCCB's stance on selection by behaviour. Remove the catalyst and the reaction must inevitably be changed.

Those who had argued that the composition of Peter May's selection committee was largely to blame for the fiasco of the previous summer were no doubt gladdened when the whole committee was disbanded after May's retirement. Ted Dexter had been one such, calling for the committee to go in his *Newsnight* interview, and it was Dexter – often called the England 'supremo' – who would be appointed to head a new 'England committee' together with Micky Stewart and the *ex-officio* input of A. C. Smith and Ossie Wheatley. Dexter's committee had greater control over preparation and development and during his time important innovations such as regular 'A' tours for developing players were introduced. But, despite the structural change, Dexter found the job of selecting a winning team no easier and the summer of 1989 proved to be just as chaotic and disappointing as the one that preceded it. Where twenty-eight players had been thrown in against West Indies and Sri Lanka, Dexter and his committee chose a total of twenty-nine as England surrendered the Ashes to Allan Border's touring Australians. Graham Gooch, who might have expected to begin the summer as incumbent Test captain, found himself the only one of three prominent candidates not to have been interviewed for the job. Having spoken to both David Gower and Mike Gatting, Dexter chose Gatting as his preferred candidate. He took his recommendation to the TCCB, only to find it vetoed by cricket committee chairman Ossie Wheatley, as Gatting remembers. 'Ted Dexter came back to me three days later and said "sorry, Gatt, it's a unanimous decision, David Gower's going to be captain." I said, "Ted, don't be stupid, don't talk to me about a unanimous decision, Ossie Wheatley's vetoed it, hasn't he?" Well, we all know what happened. By the end of the fourth Test match when we were four-nil down it all came out.'

None of England's three senior batsmen was to have a happy summer. Gower found his revolving-door team outclassed in all departments by Border's well-drilled unit, while Gooch endured a tortured series against the wicket-to-wicket seam and swing of Terry Alderman and Geoff Lawson. Gatting played only once in that series, without success. Having been selected for the first Test of the summer at Headingley, he withdrew with a broken thumb. Recalled for Lord's, he scored 0 and 22, then missed the third Test at Edgbaston due to a family bereavement. As another summer of desperation lurched towards its close he found himself embroiled in preparations for a rebel tour of South Africa. 'I didn't even know about it, John Emburey had organised it and Ali Bacher came to me in the middle of July after the Benson & Hedges final at Lord's and said they want you to go over there. I said "let me think about it."' Gatting immediately contacted Micky Stewart and warned him that several senior players were about to defect from the national team. 'He said "oh we know about it", and I said "what do you mean you know about it? It's half the England side!"'

Mike Gatting was at a turning point his career. He told Stewart that he had not yet agreed anything. It was even mooted that Gatting might take over from David Gower at the end of the summer and captain England once more on tour in the West Indies. For Gatting, this would have been the ultimate redemption. But, faced with the prospect of working once more for the people whom he felt had let him down so badly when he was captain, he walked away. Having been expected to return to the England side for the fourth Test at Old Trafford, he now publicly declared himself unavailable for the tour of the West Indies. On Wednesday 2 August 1989, the day after Australia had regained the Ashes at Old Trafford, he was revealed to the media as the official captain of an unofficial England side that would tour South Africa. The fact that the Apartheid regime began to collapse in the middle of their tour would not affect the fact that by signing up for the tour, each of the sixteen players had condemned himself to a four-year exile from international cricket. For some, this was no real sacrifice. The last fourteen months had left a string of senior English cricketers with a lingering sense of disenchantment against those in charge of the national game. For John Emburey, at the age of thirty-six and with all his international ambitions fulfilled, the prospect of a significant pay out in South African Rand to help fund his children's schooling made the choice a simple one.

For several other senior players, whose England careers were either finished, disrupted or had never begun, the punishment was no deterrent at all: David Graveney, aged thirty-six, was never going to play for England, although he later became one of its most successful selectors; Roland Butcher, also thirty-six, had played the last of his three Tests in 1981 and had lost his place in the Middlesex side in July – a financial calamity in his benefit year; Bill Athey's Test career had come to an end in 1988, with a batting average of 23 from the same number of Tests; Bruce French, first choice wicketkeeper less than two years earlier, had lost his place in the side through a string of unfortunate injuries and the emergence of Jack Russell meant he was unlikely to get it back – at the age of twenty-nine a South African payout was a sensible choice; Richard Ellison, the Kent swing bowler who had destroyed Australia in 1985 had never quite got back to his best following a serious back injury in 1987 – he was twenty-nine and had played the last of his eleven Tests in 1986; Tim Robinson had played against Sri Lanka and been selected for the abortive India tour in 1988 – omitted again at the start of 1989, he was recalled for the third Test at Old Trafford, but scored just 0 and

12; and Chris Cowdrey, whose international career had been ended by an Adrian Jones yorker twelve months earlier. Few of these players had any realistic hope of representing their country again, but many of their prospective teammates did.

The other eight members of the party had, together with John Emburey, been among the thirty players asked by the selectors to confirm their availability for the tour of the West Indies that winter. Mike Gatting himself was only thirty-two-years-old and at his peak as a batsman. Chris Broad, having missed out on selection for a second consecutive tour of India, found himself opening the batting for England again at the start of 1989, but after two Tests in which his highest score was 37 he found himself on the shelf once again. In a series of profiles of the prospective 'rebels' Matthew Engel described Broad as 'embittered', an adjective he applied equally to ex-skippers Gatting and Cowdrey. Less embittered, but equally frustrated was twenty-nine-year-old Kim Barnett, who had played in the first three Tests of the summer. After a lively 80 in the first match at Headingley, the Australians had cottoned on to his habit of flashing outside the off-stump and runs had been hard to come by. A potential future captain less than twelve months previously, he was now considered to have been found out at the highest level.

England's bowling was even more seriously hit. Not just Emburey, but the core of England's Test attack over the past three years had been tempted by the Rand. Graham Dilley, increasingly troubled by injury and having missed out on a lucrative benefit by moving from Kent to Worcestershire signed up, and so did Neil Foster, visibly upset when the news broke as he was playing on the final day of the Old Trafford Test. 'Neil was a brilliant cricketer,' remembers Graham Gooch, 'feisty, aggressive, argumentative, all the traits that go well with a fast bowler, but his body gave him problems right through his career.' It would only be a matter of time before injury ended Foster's Test career; here was a chance for him to bow out on his own terms. Not only had England's first choice new-ball pairing defected, so had two of their most likely understudies – Paul Jarvis, who had again bowled with little luck at Lord's and Edgbaston and Phillip DeFreitas, dropped after taking 3 for 216 at Headingley, both had likely international futures.

A few days after the announcement of the initial sixteen, its two black players, Butcher and DeFreitas, withdrew following heavy pressure from the anti-apartheid movement. Sprinter John Regis had declared that the two had 'betrayed all black sportsmen.' For Butcher, it was effectively the end of his career, he would play only two further first-class matches in 1990. Phillip DeFreitas, however, would finally begin to make the most of his talent and became a key bowler in Tests over the next five years, claiming thirty Test wickets in the summers of 1991 and 1994. They were replaced by Greg Thomas and Sussex batsman Alan Wells.

Perhaps the greatest loss to the Test team of the future was Matthew Maynard. Aged only twenty-three, the young Glamorgan batsman was ripe for development within a suitable team setting, but he had been disappointed at having been ignored by the selectors following his sole Test appearance in 1988. Ted Dexter and his committee had enquired about his availability for the West Indies tour, but having endured a disappointing summer following the glories of the previous year, he had looked about and seen little to encourage him as a young England hopeful. The prospect of a winter contract worth £80,000 seemed an altogether more concrete reality. Maynard would return to the Test side in 1993, but having lost four key years in his education for international cricket, his return to the side was brief and unrewarding.

There were other fine players coming through, but they too would suffer from the inconsistent selection policies that dominated this period in English cricket, never entirely sure of their places in the side, and always one bad match away from rejection. What chance was there for them? Denied not only the chance to settle in to the side and stake a claim for a long-term place over the course of a whole tour or series, but also the guidance of a core of senior players whose experience and wisdom would be of benefit to their development. 'If you had a bad day or a bad match you were always looking over your shoulder,' remembers John Emburey. 'The selectors didn't give you any confidence. You were in and out of the side and it was very difficult to get on top of your game all the time because you were playing under pressure.' 'It's easy to stick with players if your team is going well,' says Graham Gooch:

If you're losing, the pressure from the selectors and the people behind the scenes is to change. But how can you be successful if you keep chopping and changing? You've got to build an environment, you've got to build trust, you've got to build relationships. I look back on my time as captain and we probably changed, in retrospect, too much. That was the norm through that period, and before.

For Mike Gatting this was a source of particular regret:

> We had some wonderful players coming in, we had Michael Atherton,
> we had Gough and Caddick just coming in to replace the old guys and
> if we'd kept the bulk of it [the senior core of the team] coming though
> we would have had a very good side, we would have been number two
> in the world, I'm sure. But what do we find ourselves with? Years later,
> second from bottom, because the side was ravaged.

With Gower embattled and Gatting embittered, England would turn
once again to Graham Gooch as captain for the West Indies tour in
early 1990. His renewed partnership with Micky Stewart and a posse
of young guns, some of whom, like Rob Bailey, had their international
baptism under Gooch in 1988, took England to a first Test win in
Jamaica for many years. But while there were many flickers of hope
during Gooch's tenure, there were as many disappointments. Within
a few short years, much of the prescription for the regeneration of
English cricket offered by the players, officials and cricket writers of
1988 was delivered. Regulations limiting the size of the seam on the
cricket ball were in place by 1990 and pitches too became more reliable
for batsmen. Three-day cricket was ditched and a full programme of
four-day Championship matches introduced instead. Restrictions on
the number of overseas players were brought in.

Yet, as the 1990s progressed, English cricket continued to stagnate
at international level. Regaining the Ashes became an ever more
distant hope and selection remained inconsistent and disruptive to the
development of talent. By the end of the decade England had reached
a nadir. Eliminated from the World Cup they were hosting even before
the team's official song had been released, they then subsided to a Test
series defeat at home to New Zealand that left them bottom of the
world rankings. English cricket no longer had confidence in its ability
to compete on the world stage; it no longer seemed even to know who
its finest cricketers were. The events of 1988 left a barren decade of
disappointment in store for England fans and players alike.

Bibliography

Bird, 'Dickie', *80 Not Out: My Favourite Cricket Memories* (London: Hodder & Stoughton, 1994)

Botham, Ian, *My Autobiography* (London: Headline, 1994)

Blofeld, Henry, *A Thirst for Life: With the Accent on Cricket* (London: Hodder & Stoughton, 2000)

Chalke, Stephen, *Micky Stewart and the Changing Face of Cricket* (Bath: Fairfield, 2012)

Edwards, Peter (ed.), *Essex County Cricket Club 1989 Yearbook* (Chelmsford: Essex County Cricket Club, 1989)

Frindall, William, *10 Tests for England: Scorebook and Journal for 1988* (London: Columbus, 1989)

Gooch, Graham, *Captaincy* (London: Stanley Paul, 1995)

Gooch, Graham, *Gooch: My Autobiography* (London: Stanley Paul, 1995)

Gower, David, *On the Rack: A Testing Year* (London: Stanley Paul, 1990)

Lee, Alan, *Lord Ted: The Dexter Enigma* (London: Gollancz/Witherby, 1995)

Lee, Alan, *Raising the Stakes: The Modern Cricket Revolution* (London: Victor Gollancz, 1996)

Miandad, Jared, The Cutting Edge: *My Autobiography* (Oxford: OUP, 2004)

Ross, Alan & Eagar, Patrick; *West Indian Summer: The Test Series of 1988 (*London: Hodder & Stoughton, 1988)

Steen, Rob, *David Gower: A Man out of Time* (London: Victor Gollancz, 1995)

Synge, Allen, *Sins of Omission: The Story of the Test Selectors 1899–*

1990 (London: Pelham/Stephen Greene, 1990)
Wright, Graeme (ed.), *Wisden Cricketers' Almanack 1989* (London: John Wisden & Co.)

Periodicals:

Daily Express
Daily Mail
Daily Mirror
Evening Standard
News of the World
The Cricketer
The Daily Telegraph
The Guardian
The Independent
The Mail on Sunday
The Observer
The Sunday Times
The Sun
The Times
Today
Wisden Cricket Monthly

Archive Material:

Christopher Martin-Jenkins Notebooks 1976–2012. Held in the MCC Archive, Lord's.
Bill Frindall Collection 1965–2009. Held in the MCC Archive, Lord's.

Also available from Amberley Publishing

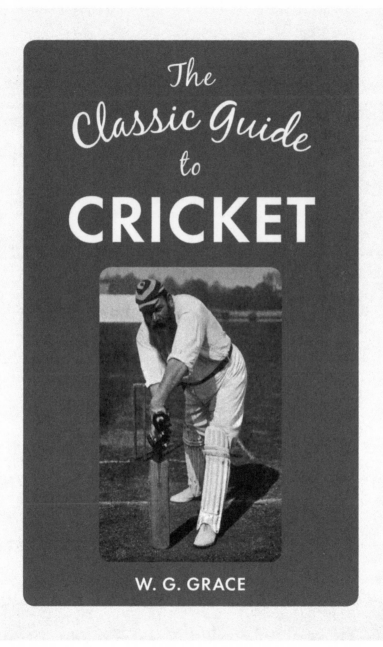